W9-DDH-775

INVENTIONS OF TEACHING

A Genealogy

INVENTIONS
OF TEACHING

A Genealogy

BRENT DAVIS
University of Alberta

LAWRENCE ERLBAUM ASSOCIATES, PUBLISHERS
2004   Mahwah, New Jersey   London

 # 52962908

Lawrence Erlbaum Associates, Inc., Publishers
10 Industrial Avenue
Mahwah, NJ 07430

 Camera-ready copy provided by the author.

 Cover design by Kathryn Houghtaling Lacey

Library of Congress Cataloging-in-Publication Data

Davis, Brent
Inventions of teaching : a genealogy / Brent Davis.
    p. cm.
    Includes bibliographical references and index.
    ISBN 0-8058-5038-4 (cloth : alk. paper) — ISBN 0-8058-5039-2 (pbk : alk. paper)
    1. Teaching—Philosophy. 2. Education—History.   I. Title.

LB14.7.D38 2004
371.102'01—dc22   2003061552

Books published by Lawrence Erlbaum Associates are printed on acid-free paper,
and their bindings are chosen for strength and durability.

Printed in the United States of America
10 9 8 7 6 5 4 3 2 1

CONTENTS

1

Inventions of Teaching:
STRUCTURES OF THINKING

The conviction persists, though history shows it to be a hallucination, that all the questions that the human mind has asked are questions that can be answered in terms of the alternatives that the questions themselves present. But, in fact, intellectual progress usually occurs through sheer abandonment of questions together with both of the alternatives they assume, an abandonment that results from their decreasing vitalism and a change of urgent interest. We do not solve them, we get over them.

— John Dewey[1]

Ten years ago, in a preservice education course, I decided to test out a colleague's suggestion that a surefire way to prompt students to engage with questions of the nature of pedagogy is to have them choose and discuss personally compelling synonyms for the word *teaching.* Using a thesaurus, I prepared a list that included *caring, conditioning, disciplining, educating, emancipating, empowering, enlightening, facilitating, guiding, indoctrinating, inducting, instructing, lecturing, managing, mentoring, modeling, nurturing, pointing, structuring, telling,* and *training,* among others.

True to my colleague's assurance, class members did participate enthusiastically. But the activity didn't go where I had naively expected it would. There were no critical interrogations of gaps and contradictions. Rather, everyone seemed to converge on the same, commonsensical conclusion: Teaching is multifaceted. The teacher wears many hats.

I had hoped that the discussion would gravitate more toward the suggestion that teaching can't possibly be about all these things—that what teaching *is* only makes sense when the issue is considered alongside prevailing assumptions about identity, learning, schooling, and so on. Unfortunately, as the activity demonstrated, the task of uncovering these sorts of conceptual commitments involves more than examining synonyms and metaphors. In particular, and in terms of the three main strands of discussion in this book, the task entails interrogations of commonsense beliefs about the nature of the universe, the sources of our knowledge, and the means by which we come to know.

Such beliefs have been subject to continuous refinements and occasional reformulations through the emergence of modern civilization. Although the assumptions that frame teaching have changed radically, vocabularies have tended to linger. As a result, as I seek to demonstrate, contemporary discussions of teaching rest on sedimented layers of vocabulary that have never been completely dissociated from the sensibilities that gave rise to them. It is not unusual, for example, to encounter references to teaching as *instructing* and *facilitating* in the same sentence despite that these terms actually point to conflicting, even contradictory, assumptions about learning. The concern that frames this book is thus how we speakers of English *invented*—that is, in the original sense of the word, "came upon"[2]—our current vocabularies for teaching.

In other words, this book represents an attempt to make sense of the knots of belief and commonsense that have underpinned efforts at teaching over the past few millennia. In it I trace out some of the conceptual commitments that are implicit (and sometimes explicit) in the terms we use to talk about teaching. In particular, I try to highlight historical moments in which vibrant new figurative understandings of teaching emerged and moments at which they froze into literalness. I do so by combining examinations of important trends in Western thought with etymological traces that foreground the sorts of assumptions and assertions that were in play when various terms for teaching were coined, co-opted, or redefined.[3]

LINEAR HISTORIES *versus* NONLINEAR GENEALOGIES

At first I thought this book would be a history of conceptions of teaching. However, when I began to sort through the historical, philosophical, theoretical, and etymological information that I had gathered, I realized that the material might be better organized around key conceptual divergences rather than any sort of chronology. In other words, this text is not a history, but several histories. More appropriately, it is a genealogy.

Most commonly, a *history* is understood to be an account of how something has come to pass. For instance, the history of a war or species is a systematic narrative, usually chronological, of the happenings that are taken as prequels to the given event or form. *Genealogy* has a similar sense, in that a genealogy is also a record of emergence. However, unlike a standard history, a genealogy is usually used to trace out several strands of simultaneous happenings. Whereas histories most often obey the image of a timeline, the image that is most commonly associated with a genealogy is a tree. Consequently, this book is not structured linearly as a narrative, but nonlinearly, around important breaks in belief or philosophy.

When the notion of genealogy is applied to the emergence of a concept—as opposed to, say, the lineage of a family—certain accommodations are required. For example, unlike families, concepts do not emerge through successive generations. Critical moments in the evolution of an idea can occur at any time as branches flourish, atrophy, or fuse. Hence, the emergence of a cluster of ideas, such as contemporary conceptions of teaching, cannot usefully be interpreted or represented in terms of any sort of chronology. As I hope is demonstrated in the discussions that follow, it makes much more sense to organize such a genealogy around key philosophical and theoretical developments, those moments at which thinking changed dramatically—not according to dates or people, but according to shifts in the ways that people talked and acted.

It is for this reason that this genealogy begins in the middle of the 19th century with Darwin, not in the first millennium BCE with the beginnings of formal Western philosophy. As detailed in chapter 2, Darwin offered a new way of thinking about the universe. He proposed a dramatic break from the model of the cosmos that had prevailed at least since the time of Plato. The influence of Darwin's ideas on contemporary thinking about learning and teaching has been nothing short of revolutionary.

In subsequent chapters, I address other key theoretical developments. In chapters 3 through 9, discussions are focused on the models of teaching and learning that have emerged from within mystical, religious, analytic philosophical, and analytic scientific traditions. Chapters 10 through 16 deal with the theories of teaching and learning that have emerged since Darwin's time, as oriented by structuralist, poststructuralist, complexity scientific, and ecological discourses.

Because the book is organized around branches that keep branching into branches, rather than an orderly linear argument, I have included an overview of the structure—a map—in Appendix A. In the hope that it might help you keep track of where the discussion is and where it's going, I've also attached a partial image of that map on each odd-numbered page. (It turns out that this mnemonic also works as a flip-book. You can watch the tree grow by riffling the pages.) I have also included a brief introduction to the area of study that prompted me to organize the book in the manner presented—namely, fractal geometry—in Appendix B.

I feel it important to emphasize here that the notion of a genealogical tree is offered as a useful tool for organizing a great deal of information, not as a model for the way things really are. As a model, it fails on several counts, not the least of which is the fact that divergent strands of thought don't always remain separate. They are often wound together to generate new interpretive hybrids. (In the realm of real trees, as well as in medical surgery, this process is known as anastomosis, "the joining of strands".) A better model to illustrate the crossings and recrossings of sensibilities would be something more weblike. Closely related is the fact that this manner of representation has required that I ignore the finer branches of thought, focusing more on broad movements than specific interpretations. Oddly enough, this particular issue was brought home to me not while writing, but while preparing the tree image. It comes from a photograph of a real tree, but I had to trim (i.e., erase) most of the limbs and shoots out of the original picture to get to the final image.[4] I did a similar sort of conceptual pruning to create this text. However, the intention here is neither to represent the full diversity of ideas nor to sketch out all of the entanglements of knowledge. It is, rather, to unravel some of the conceptual commitments that are spun into a few strands of thought while underscoring that even the most disparate ideas are usually connected to one another.

The chapters in this book are deliberately brief. I did not want in any way to give the impression that this writing is an attempt at a comprehensive overview of conceptions of teaching. It isn't. The book is offered as an introduction to the diversities of opinion and assumption that are asserted when teaching is referred to as, for example, nurturing, enlightening, modeling, or empowering. (To keep the discussions brief, I've deferred many of the details to endnotes and Appendix C, a glossary.)

My intention in this project of making sense of the varied meanings of a set of words is not to generate a classification scheme of conceptions of teaching. Rather, consistent with a shift in thinking prompted by Darwin, the aim is as much about understanding the interconnections as the divergences among notions. In the following sections, I discuss this attitude and its implications for the structure of this text. Those elaborations are not essential to the discussions that follow, so you may choose to move directly to chapter 2.

DICHOTOMIES *versus* BIFURCATIONS

Living beings discern. Even those creatures that consist of a single cell must have the capacity to make distinctions so that they, for example, might reorient themselves in directions that offer a greater promise of nourishment.

We humans tend to identify ourselves as the most adept distinction-makers on the planet. This self-bestowed title is implicit in the frequent suggestion that, among all species, ours is the most *intelligent*—a term derived from the Latin *inter-+legere*, "to choose among, to discern".

The capacity to cut up the world is biologically rooted and culturally elaborated. Biologically speaking, recent neurological research into the brain's "binary operator" has demonstrated the presence of a distributed capacity that prompts humans to frame the world in terms of polar opposites.[5] Closely related, our perceptual systems are predisposed not only to make distinctions, but to amplify them—and, on occasion, to impose some that just aren't there in any objective or measurable sense. Two brief exercises in visual perception can help to demonstrate this point.[6] In the following figure, for example, where the gray blocks meet one another, it appears that the lighter one gets lighter and the darker one gets darker.

In fact, in terms of ink density, each block is uniformly shaded. What's more is that the difference in tone between adjacent cells is not actually as great at it might appear. If you lay a pencil across one of the borders, you'll see the neighboring blocks are close to the same shade.

A second example that I find even more compelling is the next image. Most people see a completed circle here, and one that might seem brighter than (and perhaps even floating above) the background.

The point? To reiterate, our perceptual systems sometimes impose borders that aren't there and often overemphasize edges that are. In survival terms, these tendencies actually make sense. Boundaries are the most useful information in the environment. We might expect sight, hearing, smell, taste, touch, and our other senses to be oriented toward fishing out details about edges and exaggerating them.

Humans have extended this perceptual tendency into conceptual habit. We are constantly making conceptual distinctions—and often amplifying them. The habit is vital for our processes of self-definition and collective identification—to our having a reality. One tool that has greatly enabled our abilities to discern—our intelligence—is language. We use this flexible and powerful technology to weave possible worlds through naming, contrasting, likening, and other acts of association and dissociation.

There are different ways to think about the distinctions we use to organize our worlds. For example, through the past few millennia in the Western world, the prevailing belief has been that the distinctions drawn are accurate descriptions of the universe. In scientific terms, this belief has supported what might be called an attitude of *dichotomization*. Derived from the Greek, *dikha+tomie*, "two parts", to dichotomize is to generate two mutually exclusive categories by imposing a sharp distinction. As discussed in more detail in chapter 7, almost all of modern mathematics and much of modern science has been framed by the assumption that the forms and phenomena that we encounter in this universe can be organized into unambiguous categories through processes of dichotomization.

Carving the world into nonoverlapping categories is not the only means of making discernments. Another method that has risen to prominence over the past few centuries is *bifurcation*. Derived from the Latin *bi-+furca*, "two-pronged or forked", a bifurcation is a branching into two parts, rather than a breaking into two pieces. The purpose behind the branching image is to underscore and preserve the rationale for any distinction that is made—in effect, to foreground the fact that *someone* is making a distinction for *some reason*.

An example would probably be useful here. Consider that most fundamental of distinctions between BLACK and WHITE. As a dichotomy, BLACK/WHITE (note the slash to indicate a severing) might be interpreted in terms of the following Venn diagram:

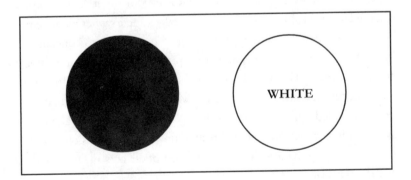

There is no overlap. Objects and issues that are seen as appropriate to this particular sort of classification are understood to fall into one circle or the other, never both. By contrast, in terms of a bifurcation, BLACK and WHITE might be illustrated as a branching:

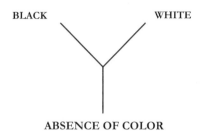

This sort of image prompts me to wonder about the concerns that underpin the distinction. For example, one reason to separate BLACK from WHITE is to classify phenomena that lack color.

A consequence of this manner of representation is that it always generates a new term—which, in turn, might be further examined as half of another bifurcation. The phrase "ABSENCE OF COLOR", for instance, prompts my attention to the "PRESENCE OF COLOR", a bifurcation that might have arisen in an analysis of the visible spectrum. In turn, the phrase "PRESENCE OF COLOR" leads me to wonder about how I might begin to classify phenomena that fit in this previously unconsidered category. One possible distinction is "WARM COLORS versus COOL COLORS". In terms of diagram, the emerging picture is the following:

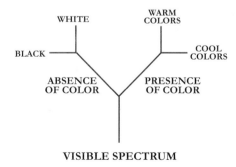

This process of bifurcating is fractal (see Appendix B). It does not get simpler as I zoom in on a particular term, it does not get simpler if I try to zoom out for a broader view. The phrase "VISIBLE SPECTRUM", for instance, triggers a thought about the "INVISIBLE SPECTRUM", and the phrase "COOL COLORS" could serve as the stem of several different layers of bifurcation depending on whatever purpose I might have in mind. (On this count, for the sake of argument, I deliberately skirted issues around the social and cultural relevance of the distinction between black and white. I do address such topics later in chaps. 10 through 13.)

This constant foregrounding of "whatever purpose I might have in mind" is vital for understanding the differences between dichotomization and bifurcation. Dichotomization, because it is rooted in the assumption that it is a process of labeling parts of the universe as they really are—that is, as if the observations were independent of the observer—has tended to be cast as an ethically neutral, objective process. Moreover, the terms of a dichotomy can sometimes seem totalizing, as if they span the full range of interpretive possibility. Consider: UP/DOWN, DEAD/ALIVE, MALE/FEMALE, TRUE/FALSE, TEACHER-CENTERED/LEARNER-CENTERED, SELF/OTHER, INDIVIDUAL/COLLECTIVE, and so on.

Bifurcation, by contrast, is attentive to the partialities associated with any distinction. Here *partiality* is understood to refer both to the distinction-maker's prejudices and the incompleteness of a distinction. That is, a bifurcation foregrounds both the biases that prompt a distinction and the biases instilled by a distinction. As illustrated in the BLACK-versus-WHITE example, a bifurcation also points beyond itself to a broader web of interpretation. One might say that the underlying attitude here is hermeneutic, oriented to and by the intertwining questions, What is it that we believe? and How is it that we came to think this way?

The branching image is useful to highlight some important qualities in the evolution of ideas. In addition to foregrounding the rationales for distinctions that are made, the bifurcation image also underscores that the terms in such dyads as BLACK-versus-WHITE, TEACHER-versus-LEARNER, and EMPOWERED-versus-DISENFRAN-CHISED have more in common than first appearances might suggest. The bifurcation attitude is concerned with samenesses and shared assumptions, in contrast to the dichotomization attitude that is attentive principally to differences.

The branching image is also useful as a visual metaphor to talk about the sometimes-rapid proliferation of new forms. With each new level of this sort of diagram, the number of possibilities doubles. That is, at every moment, at every site of distinction, there is a potential for the exponential growth of new possibilities. The numbers of these possibilities can vastly exceed the number of branching points—as seems to be the case for the current range of beliefs about the nature of teaching. As I try to develop in this book, most of the tremendous diversity among contemporary conceptions of teaching can be traced to a handful of distinctions that have been made over the last few thousand years.

As you might have already noticed, in this text, I use an upper case V to signal a bifurcation, in contrast to the slash that is commonly used to flag a dichotomy. My principal reason for this choice is that a V is intended to call to mind the branching image and, hence, the notion of bifurcation. A secondary reason is that, along with vs., V is often used as an abbreviation for *versus*, a Latin word currently used to refer to contrasts and conflicts, but that originally had to do with turning, bending, or winding, not fragmenting. (These meanings are better preserved in the cognates *converse* and *diverse*.) In its ancient senses, versus is well fitted to what I have in mind.[7]

THE CHAPTERS AHEAD

Because the discussions that comprise this book aren't (and can't be) arranged in a linear sequence, I'll comment briefly on contents and order of the chapters that follow. I'll start with a modified version of the genealogical tree image presented in Appendix A. In the following figure, I have identified key bifurcations and indexed them to chapters (in the black circles). The numbers that appear at the tips of the branches correspond to the chapters in which I examine conceptions of teaching that emerge from particular sensibilities.

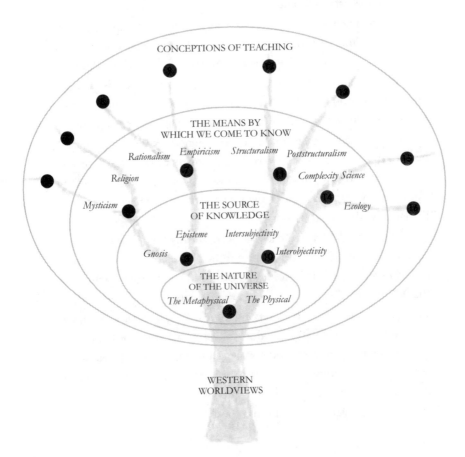

In chapter 2, I contrast two major Western attitudes toward the nature of the universe. The first and more established frames its interpretations and explanations in terms of other-worldly forms and entities. The second makes sense of the cosmos in terms of this-worldly happenings. For reasons detailed in the pages that follow, I refer to this bifurcation as *The Metaphysical* V *The Physical.*

In chapter 3, I look more closely at divergent sensibilities within *The Metaphysical.* The discussion is framed by an ancient distinction between spiritual knowledge and practical know-how. Because English lacks terms that distinguish these categories, I use the ancient Greek words to name this bifurcation: *Gnosis* V *Episteme.*

Chapter 4 deals with the two main categories of cultural traditions that are associated with *Gnosis* (spiritual knowledge)—namely, *Mysticism* V *Religion.* Following up on this discussion, in chapters 5 and 6 I turn to examinations of the synonyms for teaching that arose, respectively, among Western mystical and religious traditions.

In chapter 7, I turn to *Episteme* (practical know-how). As it turns out, modern analytic philosophy and modern analytic science sprang from this once-modest category of knowledge. In presenting some of the history of this emergence, I speak to the bifurcation *Rationalism* V *Empiricism.* This discussion is followed by examinations of conceptions of teaching that are associated with rationalist analytic philosophy (chap. 8) and with empiricist analytic science (chap. 9).

The second half of the book is concerned with branches that appear on the other side of the tree—that is, those associated with conceptions of the universe that are framed in terms of *The Physical.* In chapter 10, I address two related, but divergent, strands of thought—*Intersubjectivity* V *Interobjectivity*—in which metaphysical assumptions are rejected. In the first of these strands, knowledge and truth are understood in terms of social accord; in the second, knowledge and truth are framed in terms of possibilities that arise and lock into place as the universe evolves.

In chapter 11, I elaborate some of the discourses that embrace notions of *Intersubjectivity.* I organize these discourses around a *Structuralism* V *Poststructuralism* bifurcation. These terms are, in turn, used to frame discussions of teaching that are associated with constructivist and social constructivist discourses (chap. 12) and cultural and critical theories (chap. 13).

In chapter 14, I explore two branches of *Interobjective* discourses through the bifurcation of *Complexity Science* V *Ecology*. These discussions set the stage for chapters 15 and 16, the final examinations of diverse and divergent conceptions of teaching.

A FEW MORE COMMENTS

I must underscore that, like any piece of writing, this text is grounded in a particular way of making sense of the world. Specifically, my thinking is informed by complexity and ecological discourses (see chaps. 14–16). A key theme in these academic movements, embraced in this writing, is a critique of the notion of objectivity (see chap. 10). While I aim to provide a reasonably balanced account of divergent sensibilities, I don't pretend that my reportings and interpretations are unbiased.

I have attempted to foreground my prejudices in the actual structure of the book. As will be developed, the nonlinear branching motif is rooted in a complexivist and ecological sensibility. A consequence of this structure is that the chapters can be read in different sequences to the one presented—and, in fact, the parts were written in a completely different order. Alternative sequences for reading, where appropriate, are suggested at the end of each chapter. As well, a number of cross-references are incorporated into the writing.

2

Western Worldviews:

THE METAPHYSICAL
V
THE PHYSICAL

Almost no one is indifferent to Darwin, and no one should be. The Darwinian theory is a scientific theory, and a great one, but that is not all it is. The creationists who oppose it so bitterly are right about one thing: Darwin's dangerous idea cuts much deeper into the fabric of our most fundamental beliefs than many of its most sophisticated apologists have yet admitted, even to themselves.

— Daniel C. Dennett[1]

Charles Darwin's *The Origin of Species* met with intense reaction the moment it was published in 1859. By all accounts, this was to be expected. The book represented an unveiled challenge to the ideals and sensibilities of organized religion at the time. It continues to do so as evidenced by the fact that some school jurisdictions are still mired in debates around whether creationism should be taught alongside evolution—and, in some cases, whether evolution should be taught at all.

The fury sparked by *The Origin of Species* within popular arenas has actually served to eclipse the conceptual revolution prompted by

Darwin's theories. As Darwin anticipated, the major consequences of his proposals had to do with science, not with religion or the relationship between science and religion. Darwin did much more than challenge the belief that the species we observe are divinely wrought. In proposing mechanisms by which forms might transform and diversify through time, he disputed a deeply engrained orthodoxy about scientific reality. His theories challenged prevailing beliefs of the nature of the universe—and, in the process, they did nothing less than trigger a transdisciplinary upheaval. Issues of knowledge, learning, and teaching were not left untouched in this intellectual convulsion. Indeed you would be hard pressed to find any area of academic inquiry—or, for that matter, popular discourse—that has not been influenced by evolutionary thought.

The purpose of this chapter is to examine two contrasting worldviews: the one framed by metaphysical assumptions and the other framed by the conviction that explanations rooted in the physical are adequate to make sense of how the universe works. I discuss each of these sensibilities in turn. The final section of the chapter is a discussion of their common origins and current divergences.

THE METAPHYSICAL: THE UNIVERSE AS DETERMINED

The term *metaphysics* was used in the 4th century BCE by Aristotle in his project to separate and organize the "theoretical sciences".[2] The word is derived from the Greek *meta+ta+phusikos*—literally, "the things after (or beyond) the physical (or natural)". The study of metaphysics, for Aristotle, had to do with the identification of unchanging laws and principles that governed forms and phenomena that exist in the realm of the physical.

Since Aristotle's time, metaphysics has been taken up and applied in ways that depart from the original meaning. In fact contemporary usages vary dramatically. For example, alongside mentions of logic and rationality in current dictionary definitions of metaphysics, there are references to religion, mysticism, and the supernatural as sources of truth and knowledge. The seeming incompatibility of sensibilities is resolvable, however. Mystical, religious, and logico-rational attitudes alike are rooted in the conviction that Truth is an ideal and incorporeal form—something that is out there, beyond the physical.

Aristotle was profoundly influenced by his teacher, Plato, on this matter. Within Plato's theory of Ideas, physical objects are seen as reflections or flawed copies of perfect, timeless forms that exist in an Ideal (or Platonic) realm. Obviously, such a realm would not be directly accessible to imperfect and changing beings, such as ourselves. However, Plato argued that aspects of the ideal realm could be deduced through careful use of logical argument.[3] A classic illustration of this mode of thought is the notion of the circle. No perfect circles exist in this physical universe, yet a perfect circle is easily imagined and readily defined. Moreover, there are many, many physical forms that might be seen as not simply circular, but as striving toward the ideal of a perfect circle—the sun, the moon, an orange, and so on.

Plato applied this contrast between the ideal and the actual to all Earthly things. For him, the cat on my lap (and there is, in fact, a cat on my lap as I write this) manifests catness. She is a reflection of the ideal of Cat, even though she will never achieve perfection. Aristotle helped make Plato's ideas a bit more accessible by adding the notion of *essences*. He taught that all Earthly things have two kinds of properties: essential (from the Greek for "to be") and accidental (from the Latin for "to happen"). Essential traits are the ones that he took to be reflective of the other-worldly ideal; accidental traits are the variations that one encounters among members of the same families of forms. Siamese cats and Balinese cats both demonstrate essential catness, for instance, but vary according to the accidental trait of hair length. Siamese cats and Doberman pinschers share the same accidental trait of short hair, but one does not conform to the essential traits of catness.

Underlying the notion of essence is a particular attitude toward change—which, of course, was seen as a phenomenon that occurs only in the physical realm. Plato and Aristotle identified two categories of transformations. The first included any change to an essentail trait, which might currently be called *development*. All living forms were seen as striving toward their ideal forms, and hence natural developmental changes were understood in terms of progress toward perfection.[4] Put differently, the universe was understood in teleological terms—that is, as progressing purposefully according to an ultimate design. The second category of transformations included all other manners of physical change, and pertained mainly to accidental traits. Those that seemed random or to depart from or violate a natural developmental trajectory were understood in terms of defect and corruption.

Given this backdrop, it followed that science would be seen as mainly concerned with the classification of forms—that is, with parsing up the universe through the identification of essential distinctions and using those distinctions to construct taxonomies.[5] (Significantly, *science* derives from the same Indo-European root as *scissors*, *incisor*, and *schism*.) Like the development of an organism, the scientific project of tracing out the fault lines of the universe was understood in terms of a steady progress toward an ideal: Truth.

It is not difficult to understand how Aristotle's use of the term *metaphysics* has come to be conflated with religious and mystical traditions. The Platonic realm of ideas is not too conceptually distant from a heaven ruled by a perfect God. Further, a physical universe that is an imperfect reflection of an Ideal realm is easily fitted with the belief that humanity has fallen from grace.[6]

In summary, the key markers of the metaphysical attitude are: a conceptual commitment to an Ideal realm that is seen to transcend and, in some ways, direct physical existence; a belief that access to that realm can only be achieved by some sort of mental effort (either through logical deduction or spiritual discipline); a loathing of all change that is not seen to be oriented toward perfection; and an attitude toward knowledge that involves the dichotomization of forms.

THE PHYSICAL: THE WORLD AS EMERGENT

In general, in current translations of Plato's work, the Greek word *eidos* is rendered *idea*. At the time that Darwin wrote, in the mid-1800s, it tended to be translated as *species*. The terms are all etymologically related. Idea and *eidos* come from the Greek *idein*, "to see", and species from the Latin *specere*, "to look"—as echoed in the words *spectator* and *spectacle*.[7] (As developed in chap. 3, one of the hallmarks of a metaphysical discourse is the prominent usage of vision- and light-based metaphors.)

Darwin's proposal of an "origin of species", then, was radical. As mentioned, to that point, species-ideas were understood in terms of fixed forms that did not have beginnings. They simply were. Darwin did nothing less than strip species of the permanence and perfection. In the process, he reduced established classification systems to little more than temporary and flawed conveniences for making sense of differences among organisms.

For Darwin, change was the norm, the definer of creation and creative possibility, much in contrast to the metaphysician's attitude. With this move, he disposed of the Ideal realm of Platonic forms. In Darwin's frame, cats are not striving toward catness. Rather, they're caught up with other living forms in a grand evolutionary dance—a continuous tinkering with their own shapes and with the organizations of their contexts. Darwin described *physical* mechanisms by which one species-idea could transform over time into another—without the supervision of an intelligent designer.[8] Nature, he suggested, could be seen to pull itself up by its own bootstraps through a sort of quasirandom self-assemblage. He went further to suggest that nature is always in the process of becoming something else, constantly (but not deliberately—evolution does not plan ahead) testing new species-ideas, forever pushing out the borders of possibility and filling in the spaces that it creates.[9]

This theory did more than interrupt an entrenched assumption. It challenged what it meant to do science, particularly the biology and geology of the time. The dichotomizing attitude championed by the ancient Greeks did not suit phenomena whose forms could change, in particular because the kinds of transformations foregrounded by Darwin were more about interrelationships than differences. To re-emphasize, evolutionary theory highlights relationships, not differences. Distinctions between housecats and tigers or between foot-hills and mountains are still seen as important concerns of science, but with the prompt of evolutionary theories the main interests of researchers have turned to the origins of differences. In the terms I'm using in this text, the quest for dichotomies has given way to examinations of bifurcations—a shift from taxonomies to genealo-gies and webs.

Despite this difference, there has been a tendency to impose meta-physical principles on Darwinian thought from the beginning. Per-haps the most persistent example of this habit is captured in the phrase "survival of the fittest", which is often coupled with the no-tion that evolution is slowly but steadily nudging lifeforms toward perfection. In fact, Darwin's suggestion was more toward the sur-vival of the *fit* than the *fittest*. He argued that forms persisted because they were adequate in their immediate contexts, not because they were closer than others to some sort of optimality.[10]

It bears mention that Darwin cannot be properly identified as the sole author of evolutionary thought. Like Aristotle's articulation of essences, Darwin's writings can be construed as elaborations of emergent cultural sensibilities. For instance, nearly 30 years before the publication of *The Origin of Species*, Charles Lyell published *Prin-ciples of Geology*, in which he argued that natural landscapes were shaped and continuously reshaped by geological forces, not by the hand of God. By the mid-1800s, linguists had developed branching tree dia-grams to illustrate the bifurcations of European languages from a common protolanguage. With regard to biological evolution, Denis Diderot, Jean-Baptiste Lamarck, and Erasmus Darwin were among those who had already speculated on the common origins of differ-ent forms more than a half century before *The Origin of Species* appeared. These sorts of developments helped set the stage and prepare the audience for Darwin's treatise on the emergence of life itself.[11]

Once published, Darwin's theories spread rapidly to other branches of the sciences, including botany, zoology, and astronomy. In an essay to mark the 50th anniversary of the publication of *The Origin of Species*, John Dewey commented that Darwin had already trumped Aristotle within the sciences. Within philosophy and the humanities, however, his influence at the time of Dewey's writing was "as yet, uncertain and inchoate".[12] In the near century that has passed since Dewey's analysis, the situation has changed dramatically. In a more recent survey of Darwin's influences on contemporary thought, Daniel Dennett shows how evolutionary theories have supplanted metaphysical assumptions as the commonsense backdrop of almost all academic and most popular discourses[13]—a matter that is more thoroughly addressed in chapter 10. (He also discusses some of the applications and misapplications of Darwin's ideas, by both friend and foe. See endnote 10.)

A major contributor to this broad acceptance appears to be the emergence and proliferation of computer technologies. As Dennett points out, more complicated models of evolution coincide in time with the development of computers sufficiently powerful to test out those models through simulations. As well the contributions of electronic technologies to the accelerated evolution of other technologies, to general knowledge, and to culture have provided theorists with many instances of evolution that occur in accessible time frames of months and years rather than millennia and eons. The proliferation of dot.coms and other e-businesses in the late 1990s is one good example.

The main reason for the broad embrace of evolutionary theory, however, is the actual accumulation of evidence—in more than the fossil record. For instance, DNA research has helped underscore the relationships of diverse lifeforms. There are even living examples of speciation—that is, of the gradual transition from one species into another distinct species.[14]

COMMON ROOTS, DIFFERENT BRANCHES

There's a certain irony in the fact that Darwin's theories have over-taken Platonic and Aristotelian perspectives. Although Darwin did break with some deeply engrained beliefs about the nature of reality, he did so within the structures of Western academic discourse that were championed by the ancient Greeks. His theories had to conform to rigorous standards of rational thought and empirical evidence—standards that sprang from and that at the time were anchored in metaphysical assumption (see chaps. 3 and 7). Evolutionary theory, then, is simultaneously an affirmation of scientific inquiry and a challenge to the sensibilities out of which science arose. Plato and Darwin are rooted in the same soils.

Because my main purpose in this writing is to make sense of the current ranges of theories of learning and models of teaching, I will end this chapter by underscoring some of the ways that the conceptual break between metaphysics and evolution have played out in discussions of learning and teaching.

As far as matters of formal education are concerned, perhaps the most important issue that arises in the separation of metaphysically oriented theories from physically oriented theories is the contrast in attitudes toward development and change. The metaphysical atttitude—that the changes associated with growth are oriented toward attainment of an ideal form—has been formally represented in developmental models and curriculum structures that cast learning as an orderly and linear progression from incomplete child to completed adult.

In evolutionary frames, change is understood more in terms of biological unfolding than linear trajectories. On the matter of personal development, growth is not understood as closing in on a predetermined goal. There is no ideal person waiting to be actualized sometime in the future, merely an ever-emergent identity that arises in the confluence of biology and culturally mediated experience. Perhaps the most significant contrast of evolutionary perspectives with metaphysical perspectives, then, is that evolution is understood to operate not according to a specific goal in the distant future, but according to the range of possibilities that is immediately present.

As developed in the second half of this book, an important upshot of the shift in thought away from the metaphysical is that learning is seen less in terms of developmental progressions and more in terms of ongoing adjustments that are needed to maintain coherence. There is no separation of knower from known world in this frame. Learner and context are understood in terms of co-implication, not separation. Further, the process of learning is cast more in terms of tranforming than collecting—that is, of committing to or opting for particular possibilities and paths that eclipse (most) other possibilities and paths. Learning is further understood as a recursively elaborative process rather than an accumulative process. Each new event of learning entails a transformation of what has already been learned as it opens up new vistas of possibility.

It is much more difficult to talk about teaching within an evolutionary frame, in large part because the commonsense assumption that teaching causes learning is rejected. Learning is understood to be dependent on teaching, but not determined by it. Hence, a new vocabulary has begun to emerge around teaching over the past several decades, moving away from notions of direct causality and toward notions of necessary participation—for example, facilitating, enabling, modeling, empowering, and occasioning.

These issues around learning and teaching are among the recurrent themes of subsequent chapters. I'll close this chapter by reiterating some of the main conceptual breaks that arise in the split between metaphysical and physical accounts of existence. Once again, the former relies on and develops a logic of dichotomization (cutting up) focused on how forms are different. The latter relies on a logic of bifurcation (branching) concerned with how phenomena are related. Within metaphysical discourses, the universe is seen as finished and/or preplanned, and hence is understood in terms of ideals and essences. Within emergent perspectives, in which explanations are framed in terms of the physical, the universe is understood as un-folding—and hence in terms of transformations and diversifications. Metaphysical traditions tend to draw on ocular metaphors (e.g., in-sight, clarity, enlightenment) and images from Euclidean geometry (e.g., lines, distinct regions), whereas emergent interpretations tend more toward auditory metaphors (e.g., voice, discourse, resonance) and fractal images (e.g., trees, webs). Closely related, within meta-physical traditions, change is often framed in terms of the upward (e.g., toward a higher realm), the forward (e.g., progress to a goal), and the future. Within explanations framed by the physical, transfor-mation is understood more in terms of the outward, multidirectional, and the present (e.g., diffusion into the current space of possibility).

Finally, a key aspect that distinguishes metaphysical from evolu-tionary sensibilities is their respective attitudes toward perception. Within the former, perception is seen as a flawed and fallible conduit for information—and hence the site at which the person is separated from the world. In the latter, perception is understood as that aspect of an agent that orients her or him to the world. Perception, that is, is not understood as a conduit, but as an interface—not something that disconnects, but that connects as a sort of common boundary be-tween bodies. I return to this point in later chapters.

WHERE TO NOW?

I've left a great many details hanging in this introduction to the two principal strands of Western belief around the nature of the uni-verse. Most of these details are picked up in chapters 3 and 10, in which I address prevailing beliefs about the nature of knowledge. Chapter 3 moves into a more thorough discussion of some of the variations within metaphysical worldviews; chapter 10 does the same for mindsets that are oriented more by evolutionary principles. In terms of the coherence of the discussion, I've attempted to struc-ture the text so that readers can move to either of those chapters.

3

The Metaphysical:
GNOSIS V EPISTEME

May God us keep
From single vision and Newton's sleep!

— William Blake[1]

These lines, from Blake's 1802 verse letter to Thomas Butts, are often used to point to a tension that accompanied the rise of science in Western societies—a tension that is frequently expressed in such terms as God versus Newton, religion versus science, the transcendent versus the reductive, and enchantment versus explanation.

By the time Blake wrote, science had established a strong hold on the collective imagination. It had displaced religious texts and traditions as the principal arbiters of truth. In the light cast by science, ancient accounts of the origins of life and the nature of reality were beginning to appear more and more as trite and naive efforts to make simple sense of complex happenings. For Blake, belief and reason, once comfortably coexistent in matters of knowledge, had fallen out of balance.

Perhaps more accurately, two different categories of knowing had been collapsed. This is actually a fairly difficult point to make in English because, whereas other languages have two or more terms to refer to distinct categories, we seem content to collect all forms of awareness under the term *knowledge*. For instance, the French words *connaisance* and *savoir* are both translated into English as knowledge, but they mean different things—and the distinction is not an easy one for most Anglophones. Connaisance is used in personally meaningful situations. The sentence "Je le connais" ("I know him") indicates familiarity, even intimacy. Savoir, by contrast, is used when talking about awareness of details and facts. The sentence "Je le sais" (roughly, "I know that") is an acknowledgment that some bit of information hasn't escaped my attention.

Despite the fact that this sort of distinction between categories of knowledge is not so explicitly made in English,[2] it has played an important role in the history of Western thought. In fact a similar distinction was at center stage during one of the most important shifts in philosophy in the past few millennia.

It appears that, prior to the Enlightenment era, people had little difficulty meshing their mystico-religious beliefs with their logico-rational modes of thought. Historically, both modes were seen as essential and complementary rather than redundant and oppositional. The key to their comfortable coexistence was a tidy distinction—a dichotomy—that assigned each its proper area of competence. The ancient Greeks flagged the distinction with the dyad *gnosis* and *episteme*. Gnosis—a reference to mystico-religious belief and the word from which the French *connaissance* is derived—had to do with matters of existence and questions of meaning. It was associated with *poiesis*, the creation of forms and artifacts that were intended to sponsor creative interpretation. Episteme—that is, everyday know-how that is based in a logical-rational mode of thought—was focused on practical matters around how the world works. It was associated with a mode of production known as *tekhne*, craft knowledge or skill, the original sense of which is well preserved in the current words *technique* and *technology*.[3]

Gnosis and episteme were not originally seen as oppositional. They were understood to serve different and nonoverlapping purposes, and hence both were regarded as necessary. That changed dramatically in the 1600s. A new movement in philosophy arose that pitted them against one another—and episteme, the one associated with rational thought, won the day. Nevertheless, as evidenced in contemporary mystical and religious movements, the interest in spiritual truths to which gnosis refers has hardly disappeared.

The main aims of this chapter are to explore this distinction and examine the transition from the once complementary relationship of gnosis and episteme to their current antagonistic relationship.

GNOSIS: KNOWLEDGE AND MEANING

A first point to be made is that, historically, different modes of representation were associated with gnosis and episteme. Gnosis, with its focus on the meanings of existence, tended toward more poetic genres and made use of such figurative devices as myth, parable, fable, allegory, personification, and metaphor—devices that went along with an acknowledgment that some things exceed human capacity to understand in explicit and direct terms. Episteme, more oriented toward practical, everyday matters, was more suited to linear chains of reasoning and literal expressions.

Figurative devices such as myths and parables are not intended to be taken as factual. Historically they have been used to peer back at the sources of the universe, life, humanity, and civilization. Joseph Campbell suggests that myths help to keep us in contact with the ground of our existences.[4] In effect, myths tell us how to be human, and their powers lie in the fact that metaphors, symbols, and other figurative tools can be used to address matters of meaning in ways that logic and reason cannot. As Karen Armstrong develops further, the myths of a society provide citizens with means to situate the events of their day-to-day lives against a backdrop of the eternal and universal.[5] In the process of providing a map of the conceivable universe, myths serve ethical, pedagogical, sociological, and psychological purposes. For example, they sketch out the contours of right and wrong—and, through promises of punishments and reward, provide means to encourage people to adhere to guidelines for action and interaction. Closely related, by codifying and legitimizing structures of interaction within a society, myths teach people how to conform and advance in society. These rules, often tacit in myths just as they are in life, help foster social cohesion and collective efficacy. At the same time, they provide individuals with the tools not just to interpret, but to transform their worlds.

In brief, then, gnosis has to do with the big questions that are addressed through narratives that provide contexts, ascribe purposes, and provide meanings. Such forms as fairy tales, folklore, and other popular accounts can serve as repositories of deep insight, cultural memory, and biological history.[6] Closely related, the personification and deification of natural forces that cannot be easily predicted (much like a person) are useful figurative devices to explain and reconcile oneself with events that surpass efforts at control. More broadly, various forms of visual and performing arts can serve the same sorts of purposes.

Art has a curious status in today's world, and particularly in the episteme-focused academic world. It often seems—in fact, in my own experience, it almost always seems—that when a painting, play, piece of music, or another work of art is presented, the first question to come up is around the artist's intention. What was the painter, author, or composer trying to say?

Such a question is rooted in the assumption that the artist is fully aware and in full control of the elements that are woven together into a finished piece. When gnosis was more balanced with episteme, expressive forms like paintings, music, poetry, fables, and sculpture would not likely have been interpreted so narrowly. The notion of an artist's singular intent, in fact, probably made little sense. At other times and in other places, such forms were associated with efforts to establish collective meaning, not to express personal opinion. Like myth, art is not a literal expression, but an effort to point beyond itself to prompt attentions to possibilities that exceed us at the moment and to events that surpass rational explanation.[7] Philosopher Hans-Georg Gadamer makes this point by suggesting that art, to be art, must fulfill a twofold function. First, it must *represent*—that is, it must remind the experiencer of something familiar. Second, it must *present*—that is, it must offer new interpretive possibilities, ones that are not necessarily accessible to even the artist.[8]

This point is further demonstrated in the attitude toward history that prevailed in more ancient times, as embodied in the texts that have survived the past few millennia. As is evident in the first written records of oral histories, chronicles of the past were not originally seen in terms of sequences of events that are linked causally, but as manifestations of timeless realities that were expressed as repetitions and themes. Historical narratives were structured to foreground this eternal dimension.[9] Herodotus' *The Histories* is a good example. To the modern reader, this text would probably seem like a nonchronological jumble of fact and fiction, including gossip, hearsay, and fantasy. Such a (mis)reading, of course, rests on a modern assumption that a proper history is a sequential gisting of events that is undertaken for practical purposes. As will be developed in the next chapter, the contemporary tendency toward literal readings of ancient texts—this eclipsing of gnosis by episteme—underlies the emergence of social and religious movements that are profoundly unaware of their own histories.

To reiterate, then, gnosis might be understood as a mode of thinking—one that makes use of various figurative devices in the effort to make sense of existence. As such, the elements of gnosis, such as myths and allegories—along with related expressive forms like painting, sculpture, music, and ritual performance—were never intended to be taken literally or to be read analytically. Hence, to insist that historical and scientific evidence is needed to prove that there was a Great Flood or a pantheon atop Mount Olympus is to mistake the natures and purposes of these stories. It is to confuse gnosis and episteme.

Worse, actually, it is to subject the creative spirit implicit in gnosis with the rigorous (from the Latin for "stiffness") standards of episteme. Myths needn't be taken literally to be taken seriously.

EPISTEME: EVERYDAY KNOW-HOW

Whereas gnosis points toward wisdom and ethical action, episteme points to the rational and pragmatic competencies that enable us to function well in the physical world. In one sense, as a category of knowledge, episteme refers only to mundane information, facts, know-how, and so on. In another sense, episteme is the core of knowing. After all, to be effective, one must have some basic awarenesses of how things work. Gnosis looks to the mysteries and depths of the transcendent and intuitive; episteme is focused on the immediate and conscious aspects of experience. Its truths are seen to be literal ones that are almost always phrased in a linear, cause–effect or assumption–implication manner: When you release the spoon, it falls to the floor; if A is taller than B, who is taller than C, then A is taller than C.

Gnosis relies on figurative devices and the arts, whereas episteme is more given to logical modes of thought and practical undertakings. Gnosis tends to look backward in time to ask big questions about the way things are, whereas episteme is forward looking, reaching into the future with questions about possibility.

Armstrong suggests that both gnosis and episteme were regarded as indispensable in the ancient world.

> *Each would be impoverished without the other. Yet the two were essentially distinct, and it was held to be dangerous to confuse mythical and rational discourses. They had separate jobs to do.*[10]

The narrative structures and analogical bases of gnosis complemented the causal structures and logical bases of episteme. The category of epistemic knowledge was of tremendous use in practical matters, but useless to make sense of tragedies, morals, and values. In the 1600s and 1700s, however, the limitations on episteme were removed.

The break was perhaps most clearly articulated in the work of mathematician and philosopher René Descartes (1596–1650), who is often cited as *the* key figure in the rise of modern philosophy. Descartes was actually one of many who helped initiate a broad transformation in sensibility popularly referred to as the *epistemological turn*, wherein episteme not only shifted out of balance with gnosis, but came to be seen as sufficient in and of itself. In the light of reason, it was argued, there was no need to fall back on uncritical folklore for interpretive assistance. This view was shared by such luminaries as Francis Bacon, George Berkeley, Thomas Hobbes, David Hume, and John Locke in England; Immanuel Kant and Gottfried Wilhelm von Leibniz in Germany; Hugo Grotius in Holland; and Galileo Galilei in Italy, to mention only a few.

Descartes' great insight, developed in his 1637 *Discourse on Method*,[11] was his recognition of the power of formal logic. This mode of argumentation could not only ensure unimpeachable conclusions (assuming one's starting assumptions were valid), but could be used to separate muddled mysticism from genuine scholarship. Descartes regarded the science of the time as a befuddled mix of rational assertion, inherited assumption, and mystical realism. His project was to pry truth from mistruth, and he believed that an approach to argumentation that was modeled on Euclid's geometry was the tool for the job.

Descartes' work, then, was thoroughly rooted in the work of the ancient Greeks. Although he rejected the figurative and artistic as a basis for scientific insight, he did not reject gnosis as a category of knowledge. Further, it appears that Descartes did not even think to question the culturally entrenched metaphysical assumption that knowledge had some sort of pre-existent, incorporeal form that was independent of knowing agents. Like Plato and Aristotle, he accepted that only the disciplined mind could have access to that which is certain and eternal. The key was the *analytic method*. Derived for the Greek *analusis*, "dissolving", the analytic method aims to reduce all claims to truth to their root assumptions in order to reassemble an unshakeable edifice of knowledge. It is a method in search of universal laws, fundamental particles—basics.

Descartes wrote in the early 1600s. By the early 1800s, confidence in the analytic method had reached an extreme, as is evident in mathematician Pierre Simon de Laplace's bold assertion:

> *Given for one instant an intelligence which could comprehend all forces which nature is animated and the respective situations of the beings which compose it—an intelligence sufficiently vast to submit these data to analyses—it would embrace in the same formula the movements of the greatest bodies and those of the lightest atom; for it, nothing would be uncertain and the future, as the past, would be present to its eyes.*[12]

This passage is often cited as the quintessential statement of determinism—that is, the idea that there are no accidents. Everything that is going to happen is absolutely determined by what has already happened.

In terms of the relationship between gnosis and episteme, the real significance of Laplace's statement is that he not only cast the future as determined, but also the past—the traditional domain of gnosis. The passage might seem to leave a place of a higher being—an "intelligence sufficiently vast"—but it is clear that such an entity is seen to be constrained by the laws of the universe. There are no decisions to be made. All that was and all that will be is seen to be folded into what currently is. Logical thought was deemed sufficient to untangle it all and derive meaning for life.

Descartes' analytic method was not the only new approach to knowledge and truth that was articulated at the time. Francis Bacon (1561–1626), in his 1620 *Novum Organum*,[13] presented a view that was diametrically opposed in terms of method, although lodged in the same metaphysical traditions. Bacon argued for careful, controlled, and replicable experimentation as the only reliable route to certainty. This matter, popularly known in terms of the tension between rationalism and empiricism, will be the focus of chapter 7, but I mention it now to highlight that Descartes' rationalism and Bacon's empiricism are really two shoots off the same epistemic branch. Both eschewed the mystical, both were rooted in the metaphysics of the ancient Greeks, and both aimed to uncover the fundamental principles that were seen to define the workings of the universe.

COMMON ROOTS, DIFFERENT BRANCHES

The notions of gnosis and episteme were first articulated against the backdrop of a universe assumed to be complete, perhaps even preplanned. Even when the two categories of knowledge started to be seen less as complements and more as contradictions, that overarching metaphysical assumption continued to hold sway.

Some traces of their common conceptual origins are still manifest in a few of their shared metaphors. For example, light- and vision-based notions are prominently used to describe both gnosis and episteme: truth as light, understanding as insight, teaching as illuminating, learning as coming to see, intelligence as brightness, genius as brilliance, opinions as perspectives, and so on. Perhaps not surprisingly, narratives about light are central to both as well. The myths that support gnosis are rife with stories of the separation of light from darkness and gifts of fire, for instance. Correspondingly, few treatments of the history of science fail to give heed to Newton's studies of the properties of light, to the seemingly paradoxical realization that light can be considered either a wave or particle, or to Einstein's use of the speed of light (c) to relate mass and energy in his $e = mc^2$.

Gnosis and episteme split around core metaphors, particularly around the notions used to describe dynamics. Gnosis, with its concerns for the transcendent and complex, tends toward more organic metaphors or personifications to talk about growth, intertwinings, intentions, and so on. Episteme, with its original concern for everyday know-how, tends toward more mechanical metaphors. Descartes maintained this habit by ignoring organic notions as he likened the universe and the healthy human to a well-made clock—one of the most advanced mechanical technologies of the time. The trend continues today, with computers being the most prominently used metaphor—one that is often taken literally—for the universe and for human thought.[14]

Gnosis and episteme are also split on their attitudes toward language. Episteme, concerned with literal truths, might be described as oriented by a technical attitude toward words. As evidenced by such common phrases as "putting thoughts into words" and "finding the right words", within an epistemic mindset there is a sense that the world and one's thoughts about the world are independent of and uninfluenced by the vocabulary used to represent them. Such beliefs are indicative of what has come to be called a "correspondence theory" of language. Words are understood as labels—in effect, containers or small parcels of meaning that are shunted about among communicators. It is a notion that fits well with the assumption that the truth is out there waiting to be snared in a net of appropriate vocabulary.

As developed, more poetic attitudes toward language are associated with gnosis. The point of a myth or an allegory is not to label the world, but to weave a meaningful backdrop for a labeled world. Word-making for this purpose was often deemed to have a sort of mystical power,[15] as suggested by the histories of such terms as *spelling* and *grammar*. The two meanings of spell—magical incantation and the ordering of letters in a word—have the same ancient root, hinting at a sense that words were believed to have a certain power. The case of grammar is similar, although the Middle English term *grammarye*, "spell-casting power", has slipped out of common usage. Such examples point to a belief in the constitutive and transformative powers of language—a sense that likely underlies the frequent

caution to be careful about what one says. This admonition is prominent in almost all Western religious traditions, and it underlies the
taboos around swearing and cursing. As different as this attitude might
seem from the one associated with episteme, it too relies on a correspondence theory of language. (See chap. 11 for a discussion of an
alternative theory of language.)

Another way to foreground the difference between the two sorts
of knowledge is to point to the contrast to the sorts of questions
posed within gnosis-artistic and episteme-scientific traditions. In the
case of the former, a good question is one that has to do with meaning and wisdom. Although it might not be directly answerable, it is
oriented toward appropriate action, toward living well within particular circumstances. The latter is less concerned with matters of wisdom and more focused on issues of capability. A good question here
is one that can be answered with certainty and whose answer promises the knower a greater control over circumstances. Morris Berman
describes the shift in collective sensibility that began in the 1600s in
terms of a transition from one fundamental question to another:
"How?"—the concern of episteme—grew in importance; "Why?"—
the concern of gnosis—became irrelevant.[16] Berman further suggests
that in the 20th century, "How?" became our "Why?" Alternatively,
gnosis-artistic might be associated with the question, "Should we?"
and episteme-scientific with the question, "Can I?"

The subjects of these questions—the *we* of gnosis and the *I* of
episteme—point to one more category of common assumption and
divergent conclusion. In metaphysical traditions, mythical and rational alike, the individual human is seen as the fundamental unit of
agency and existence. Indeed the word *individual* means, literally, "indivisible" or "irreducible". It's a notion that was first articulated in
mathematical terms, tied to the ancient realization that all nonprime
numbers can be expressed as products of primes, whereas primes are
indivisible.[17] In a cosmology in which numbers are seen as woven
into the fabric of the universe—or, in some variations, in which the
universe is seen to be spun from number—the notion of indi-

visibility is tied to the notion of essence. When applied to humans, indivisibility-individuality projects not just a sense of irreducibility of identity, but of ideality and permanence.[18]

The tendency to think of humans in individualistic terms continues to be pervasive. In fact the assumption of individuality is foundational to Descartes' philosophy (see chap. 7). That being said, the status of the individual is slightly different between gnosis and episteme. Gnosis, with its focus on meaning, casts the individual as a participant in a universe permeated by the divine. The individual is not the focus, but one of many actors in a cosmic drama. The emphasis in gnosis is thus not on *I*, but on *we*. A central role of the myth, cultural narratives, and other tools of gnosis is to frame actions within social, cultural, and environmental circumstances. By contrast, for episteme, the individual tends to be construed in much more dichotomous terms—insulated from the world, isolated from fellow knowers. Even when considered as part of a collective in discourses oriented by episteme, the individual is treated as a fundamental particle, as demonstrated by much of the sociological and economic research through the 19th and 20th centuries. In fact, and consistent with the underlying use of mechanical metaphors, researchers in sociology and economics often use the same or similar sorts of probabilistic and statistical tools to describe interactions among people that physicists and chemists use to describe the interactions of atoms and molecules. Until recently, under the rule of episteme, the social collective has been seen mainly in terms of the sum of *I*s rather than a coherent *we*. (See chap. 10 for a discussion of a shift in sensibility around this particular issue.)

In many ways, the complementarities and differences that I've listed are moot points. In modern English at least, the preference for episteme over gnosis, as prompted by Descartes and his contemporaries, is pronounced. Not only has episteme eclipsed gnosis as the privileged means by which we come to know, it has hijacked the term. The word *knowledge*, derived from gnosis, is now mainly used to refer to the sorts of knowings that the Greeks associated with episteme.

In fact as phrases such as "knowledge industry" and "knowledge engineer" demonstrate, the term is often considered synonymous with information—with *data* rather than *doing*.

Further to this point, consider the word *cognition*, another derivative of gnosis. Gnosis points to the fabric of the universe—to the manners in which we are woven into a grander tapestry with all other things. In rather extreme contrast, cognition is now most often understood in terms of mechanical processes that are trapped in the head—cut off from the real world, subjective.

Even so, although gnosis might have fallen into the shadow of episteme in this modern era, it has certainly not been erased from the collective psyche. This point becomes quite evident as one examines the contemporary mystical and religious beliefs, as well as the pedagogical imperatives, that arise from the transcendent interests of gnosis and the pragmatic concerns of episteme. Such are the topics of the next six chapters.

WHERE TO NOW?

This chapter was concerned with divergent conceptions of knowledge within metaphysical traditions. It parallels chapter 10, in which I look at divergent conceptions of knowledge prompted by more emergent or evolutionary sensibilities. It also precedes discussions of beliefs around how we come to know—learning and knowledge production—that are associated with gnosis (chap. 4) and episteme (chap. 7). Each of those chapters serves as an introduction to discussions of divergent beliefs about teaching that are rooted in various conceptions of learning.

More broadly, worldviews that are not framed by a separation of gnosis from episteme are taken up toward the end of the book, particularly in chapters 14 and 16.

4

Gnosis:

MYSTICISM V RELIGION

*There is a basic mythological motif that originally all was
one, and then there was a separation .... So now the eternal
is somehow away from us, and we have to find some way to
get back in touch with it.*

— Joseph Campbell[1]

At first blush, it might seem odd to discuss the branch of
thought associated with spirituality before addressing the branch
that supported the rise of modern science. As a survey of the contents of almost any professional or research journal would demonstrate, the mystical and the religious have not just been eclipsed, but
rendered irrelevant in the current academic literature around matters
of knowledge, learning, and teaching.

The fact of the matter is, however, that mystical beliefs are alive
and well, as are the attitudes toward learning and teaching that are
rooted in ancient beliefs about the natures of the universe and knowledge. For instance, a recent poll of religious beliefs indicated that about
90% of Americans believe in a personal God who can perform miracles
and who answers prayers, and close to 30% of them completely reject
the suggestion that humans evolved.[2] On the more mystical
side of things, in a 1975 study, more than 35% of Americans

answered "Yes" to the question, "Have you ever felt as though you were very close to a spiritual force that seemed to lift you out of yourself?"[3] Although not quite so rigorous as a source of data, the current popularity of Harry Potter, *Lord of the Rings*, fantasy games, and various New Age trends might also be taken as strong indications that mysticism has hardly faded into our distant past.

The resiliency of religious belief in this age of science almost certainly harkens back to the original gnosis V episteme distinction. Despite its original promise, science has not provided *meaningful* answers to such questions as "Why is there something rather than nothing?", "Why am I here?", and "What are beauty, love, and honor?" By contrast, a god-concept does. What's more is that its answers are more readily understood than current scientific accounts of the slow and somewhat accidental emergence of order in a self-organizing universe.[4]

The main purpose of this chapter is to review the historical and contemporary spectrums of mystical and religious belief around the matter of how we come to know, with a view toward unraveling some of the attitudes toward learning and teaching that have risen out of the gnosis category of knowledge. The bifurcation that I use to structure this chapter is between mysticism and religion, presented here as two complementary but distinguishable attitudes toward spiritual truths. Mysticism is associated more with a belief that metaphysical truths are immanent or inherent within all forms and phenomena. The task of the knower is to divine—through intuitive, supernatural, or other means—these truths. By contrast, religion is more associated with knowledge that is meted out by an omnipotent, all-knowing entity. The knower in this case is charged with obedience to revealed laws and insights.

MYSTICISM: KNOWLEDGE THROUGH DIVINATION

The notion of divination—of peering into the realm of the transcendent—bespeaks a particular attitude toward one's moment-to-moment perceptions of reality. Such perception must be fallible and unreliable, readily deceived if not deceptive. This is the attitude of *mysticism*, which is an umbrella term that refers to a broad range of perspectives clustered around the belief in a reality that exceeds normal human experience and perceptual capacities.

The word *mysticism* is subject to quite a wide range of interpretations. It is, for example, the object of scorn in many established religions (where it is often seen as occultism) and of ridicule within the sciences (where it is often seen as confused thinking and obscure belief). Evelyn Underhill, in a major work on the topic, writes against such judgments. She argues that mysticism

> *is not an opinion: It is not a philosophy. It has nothing in common with the pursuit of occult knowledge.... It is the name of an organic process which involves the perfect consummation of the Love of God .... [It] is the art of establishing ... conscious relation with the Absolute.*[5]

This notion of union with an absolute is common to virtually all Western mystical traditions. (For that matter, it's a common notion in most non-Western traditions, as is further developed later.) As will be discussed in the next chapter, many of these traditions also have well-developed systems and regimes designed to support the achievement of this transcendent goal—systems and regimes that in turn have influenced contemporary beliefs around knowledge, learning, and teaching.

Western mysticisms do not necessarily posit a God, at least not a God conceived in personified terms of an independent, conscious agent. However, most mysticisms do posit a grand Unity, an Absolute, a One, or oneness of some sort, albeit in more pantheistic frames. In mystical traditions, the Unity tends to be understood in terms of nature, rather than something apart from or above nature. Humans and the material universe are seen as manifestations of the divine, but not as intentional products.

The origins of Western mysticism are most commonly traced to Pythagoras (c. 569 BCE–c. 475 BCE). He founded a major school of philosophy-and-mysticism (the contemporary distinction between these terms didn't really apply) that was focused on the mystical intertwinings of nature, number, and souls. However, the honor of the "most important figure" in Western mysticism usually goes to Plato who lived some 150 years after Pythagoras. In fact most of Western mystical traditions are identified as *neoplatonist*. Neoplatonism is a movement that began in the 3rd century CE, about 600 years after Plato's death. It started as an effort to articulate, synthesize, and elaborate Plato's metaphysics. Although essentially Greek in character, this work was undertaken in Alexandria, Egypt, a meeting place of many cultures. It is thus that Roman, Judaic, Eastern, and other sensibilities came to be represented in neoplatonist doctrine. Much later, in the 15th century, this work gained greater acceptance within Roman Catholicism and thus came to influence and be influenced by Christianity.

In brief, within neoplatonism, the ultimate or ideal reality is conceived in terms of an unknowable, infinite, and perfect One. Departing from Plato's philosophy, human souls are not seen as mere reflections or images of the Ideal, but as part of a single vast order that contains different levels and sorts of existence. Aspects of Plato's separation of Idea and Matter are maintained, however, specifically around the issue of human perception. For the neoplatonist, sensory perception is deceptive, fitted only to the pursuit of carnal pleasures. Other—mystical—means of perception are needed to divine the One. Hence, as conscious, self-determining beings, humans might pursue either a path of ignorance or a path of enlightenment. *Ignorance* (a word that originally meant, literally, "not gnosis") is seen to arise from a false sense of independence from the One and is associated with the pursuit of depraved sensual desires of the flesh. Enlightenment, along with the all-pervading ecstasy of salvation, might be attained by choosing the opposite course of abstention. In brief, then, among the key tenets of neoplatonism are the dichotomization of spirit and

flesh based on Plato's dichotomization of Idea and Matter; a profound suspicion of human sense perception; and a conviction that
one might free oneself from a base, sensory-rooted existence through
a life of rigorous self-denial of worldly comforts and pleasures. (This
last point was formally articulated as a doctrine of asceticism and has
since been widely represented in Western mystical and religious movements.)

Although the subject matter of neoplatonism is mystical, its roots
and methods were originally quite rational, in keeping with the logical traditions of ancient Greece. The logic, however, was secondary
to the belief structures, as described in the preceding paragraph. As
well, over the centuries, the core logic of neoplatonism underwent
steady erosion—a process that actually began early on as other mystical traditions from many different cultures began to be grafted onto
the belief structures. These other traditions included demonology,
astrology, numerology, and divination. To make a long story short,
the original emphasis on rational method morphed into a focus on
the mental and an abjuration of the physical. It is this radical separation of mind and body that most distinguishes neoplatonism from
other prominent movements in Western mysticism.

One of these movements—hermeticism—also arose in Alexandria early in the Common Era. (The term *hermeticism* is derived from
the name of an ancient Egyptian thinker, Hermes Trismegistus, who
is thought to have lived sometime between 1400 and 1000 BCE.) Like
neoplatonism, hermeticism was influenced by the diverse cultures
that flowed through the city. Unlike neoplatonism, hermeticism did
not centrally embrace the rational method. Rather, it opted for a spiritual eclecticism, openly exploring and assimilating aspects of other
traditions. It is thus that some key tenets and assumptions are shared
by neoplatonism and hermeticism, including the central principle of
an ultimate divine unity that is both immanent and transcendent. Similar to neoplatonism, hermeticism holds that the great work of humans and humankind is to return to a state of unity with the
divine—a project that is understood to require considerable

effort. There the similarities end. In its mystical eclecticism, hermeticism urges those on the quest of reunification with the divine to seek balance by embracing all things—a principle that prompts a poetic rather than an ascetic worldview. For the hermeticist, access to the realm of the transcendent is not earned by labor and self-denial, but through creative and transformative engagement.

For citizens of the modern, Western world, perhaps the most familiar expression of hermeticism is alchemy—which most people know as the medieval project to transmute base metals into higher ones (e.g., tin into silver and lead into gold). However, *alchemy* is more appropriately defined as a mystical art intent on the transformation of the human spirit into a higher form of being. As a variety of hermeticism, alchemy also arose in Alexandria in the confluence of Eastern mysticism, Taoist philosophy, Aristotelian theory of the composition of matter,[6] and middle Eastern astrology, among other traditions. Alchemists emphasized one principle of hermeticism in particular—that the universe is intrinsically and intricately interconnected. To understand the cosmos, then, one must understand the deep intertwinings of all things.

The shared principles of neoplatonism and hermeticism are worth underscoring, partly because they continue to be represented in much of the broad array of current mystical practices, but more important because they explicitly announce some notions that have come to serve as a transparent backdrop of current discussions of knowledge, learning, and personal identity. There is a good reason that the mysticism section in most large bookstores is larger than the science section. Some deeply engrained and commonsensical—but ultimately scientifically untenable—principles underpin current popular interests in channeling, extrasensory perception, parapsychology, and so on. The convictions that knowledge is some sort of substance that is out there waiting to be divined, that it dwells in minds and can be read, that minds do not require bodies, and so on were all expressed within ancient mystical traditions.

RELIGION: KNOWLEDGE THROUGH REVELATION

Academically speaking, the main difference between mysticisms and religions is that, for the latter, knowledge of higher things is not a matter of introspection, but of enforcing a body of knowledge that is imposed from the outside (or, perhaps more commonly, from above). For religion, truth is not about divination of immanent truth, but about revelation of sacred truth. In the most extreme versions of some religions, so-called *fundamentalisms*, followers are expected to accept such revelations without question as literal truths.

Not surprisingly, then, established religious traditions have tended to be strongly opposed to mystical movements. Roman Catholicism has dismissed Christian Gnosticism and those aspects of neoplatonism that press toward divination, Orthodox Judaism rejects the Kabbalah, and mainstream Islam tends not to embrace Sufism.[7] The list goes on.

Prominent Western religions are theistic—that is, they share the feature of being developed around the concept of a God who is understood to have created the universe and who can and does intervene in the daily lives of individuals. The Western God of Judaism, Christianity, and Islam communicates to the world through scriptures. He is seen to have moods and other human qualities. Such notions represent a dramatic departure from Western mystical traditions—which, across faiths, see the ultimate Unity as far beyond the reach of human comprehension. (The unknowableness of God is also a common feature of Eastern worldviews.) There are extensive and ongoing debates over the nature of such god-concepts—specifically over whether a god-concept is a figurative device used to point to something that exceeds human understanding or a literal reference to an empirically real entity. Nevertheless, the god-concept operates as an all-encompassing explanatory system within religions. Knowledge claims, ethical codes, and legal systems are imposed and legitimated by ascribing them to this extra-human being.

Of course religions do not begin as religions. As Karen Armstrong[8] details, they typically grow out of cults that have achieved a gradual acceptance by persons and cultures outside the original circles. As they grow, they compete with other belief systems, they institutionalize, they splinter into denominations and sects, they absorb other interpretive systems, and they transform themselves to fit with emergent cultural sensibilities. In contrast with mystical traditions, religions are focused more on collectives than individuals, giving rise to the speculation that they serve some important social purposes. In providing a shared set of narratives, a common religion can offer a basis for laws and moral codes—in effect, systems that make it possible to knit collectives out of individuals who might otherwise tend toward selfishness and idiosyncratic interpretations.

Much has been written about the common features of Western religions. Current work is largely influenced by the prolific writings of Carl Jung (1875–1961) and those who picked up on his work, including Mircea Eliade and Joseph Campbell. Among the religious archetypes[9] that are identified in their work are a creation story, a trickster character, an event of separation of the mortal from the divine, a redemption myth, and an apocalyptic finale. These stories of how the world came to be and how it will end, how evil arose and how it will be defeated, and so on, are almost always framed as pairs of irreconcilable opposites or dichotomies—in contrast to mystical accounts that tend more toward notions of continuum. The device of the myth provides a means of reconciling these opposites. For example, the story of Jesus is framed by an impassable gap between a pure God and a fallen humanity. Jesus offers a resolution by virtue of his simultaneous human and divine parentage, which make him both condemned to human suffering (and death) and destined for eternal life (through resurrection).

Such themes echo through Western religions. In fact they are also pervasive in Eastern mindfulness traditions and ancient Western mystical systems. Buddha, for example, offers a salvation of sorts by showing how practices of mindfulness awareness and compassion can interrupt the grasping tendencies that underpin human suffering. By engaging in these practices, one might move closer to a proper state of sublime oneness with the universe.[10] Other heroes and gods in narratives of human reconciliation with a grander order include the Greek Dionysius, the Egyptian Osiris, and the Syrian Adonis.

The major monotheistic religions of the West and Near East—Judaism, Christianity, and Islam—share some more profound aspects. Most prominent, perhaps, all are focused on the revelation of a Supreme Being who is supernatural and separate from the physical world. Even so, across these religions, God is personified. In fact, somewhat ironically, he tends to be described (and is often pictorially represented) in ways that suggest an actual, physical being. Theological discussions of this issue have been diverse, with the weight of scholarly opinion favoring the interpretation that the ultimate essence of God is well beyond human comprehension.

The conception of a God that surpasses human efforts of representation, however, is much less common outside academic discussions of theology. In the popular realm, God and God's Word are more often treated in much more literal terms for reasons that Armstrong and others link to a collapse of gnosis and episteme.[11]

As developed in the previous chapter, the tidy separation of gnosis (or spiritual knowledge) and episteme (or everyday know-how) has ceased to apply, owing in large part to the rise of rationalist methods in a culture oriented by and toward science. Over the past few centuries in particular, Western religious texts have been increasingly subject to the same sort of treatment as Western scientific texts—logical analyses and literal readings. In a detailed discussion of this conflation of sensibilities, Armstrong offers a compelling account of the rise of fundamentalist sects within Judaism, Christianity, and Islam.[12] At the moment, fundamentalisms are prominent religious and political forces in many regions of the world. For example, the largest Christian denomination devoted to literal readings of the Bible, Southern Baptists in the United States, currently has about 15 million members. Several Arab states are ruled by fundamentalist Islamic sects. In Israel, fundamentalist sects are disproportionately represented in the country's government.

Against this backdrop, it's interesting to note that the term *fundamentalism* is a recent one. According to Armstrong, it only came into
common use in the 1920s. The word is also an interesting one, because it is derived not from religious tradition, but from philosophy.
As will be developed in chapter 7, notions of foundations and funda-
mentals owe much more to Plato and Descartes than to Moses, Jesus,
or Mohammed. Perhaps more than any other domain of human activity, contemporary fundamentalisms demonstrate the inadequacy
of the tree image that I'm using to organize this text. A more appropriate image in this case might be the formation of rigid bones as
many, many simultaneously bifurcating strands of fibers overlap, knit,
and interlock.

COMMON ROOTS, DIFFERENT BRANCHES

Both mysticism (divined knowledge) and religion (revelation) posit a
transcendent unity. Mystical traditions generally discuss this unity in
terms of a divinity that is pervasive, manifest in everything—or, in
some versions, everything manifest in it. Religions, by contrast, more
commonly frame transcendent unity in terms of binary dualisms.
Hence, religious myths consist in the main of tales of division and
reconciliation. In formal terms, that is, mysticisms tend toward pantheism, religion toward theism. For the mystic, the focus is on deep
intertwinings, knowledge of which must be carefully sought out. For
the religious adherent, knowledge is given, not discovered.

Not surprisingly, historically and currently, religions have tended
to be afforded greater cultural privilege than mysticisms—no doubt
because religions are oriented toward social and cultural order, whereas
mysticisms tend to value more independent thought. (Notably, the
word *heresy* originally meant "free thinking".)

The tensions between religions and mysticisms are actually more
matters of common assumption than of incompatibility. For the most
part, mystic and religious zealot alike regard truth as a fixed and un-

changing thing. They part company on the issue of who is allowed to go in search of divine truths. The mystic tends to regard the matter in terms of personal right and obligation, the religious adherent as a matter of God's priority and discretion. As such there is profound mutual suspicion of the validity of one another's knowledge. The current blanket condemnation among fundamentalist Christian sects of anything mystical provides a good illustration of this point. From their perspectives, any claim to spiritual truth that is not already stated in the Bible (and often in the phrasing of the oldest translation in the language of debate[13]) is deemed to be of Satanic or demonic sources. The mystic counters that literal readings of the Bible are, in fact, profound misreadings.

Such differences, of course, are irreconcilable within the belief systems. However, to an outside observer, the disagreements might seem superficial. Mystic and religious adherent alike work from an uninterrogated assumption that spiritual truths arrive from a different and higher place, realm, or domain. Consistent with Plato's metaphysics, this other realm is cast in terms of perfection, oneness, and transcendent unity, in which the spiritual is almost always distinguished from and given priority over the physical. The branching point of mysticism and religion is neither on the nature of the universe nor the nature of knowledge, but on whether or not truths should be actively mined or passively awaited. This bifurcation is especially obvious around mystical and religious attitudes toward dreams. Historically, both traditions have seen dreams in terms of portals to a higher realm. In mysticism, they are seen as allegories that must be interpreted—sites for divination. In the case of established religions, dreams are more often occasions of outright revelation, as in the case of the angel Gabriel's visit to the Virgin Mary.[14] Even in Biblical cases in which interpretation is required, as in Daniel's interactions with the recalcitrant Nebuchanezzar,[15] the readings are matters of revelation, not divination.

One further matter merits discussion: identity. Western mysticisms and religions alike tend to regard personal identity as pregiven, unchanging, and eternal. There are many variations on this theme. For example, the human soul is sometimes seen as an entity that cycles through physical forms on the route to perfection. In other traditions, the soul is seen as a breath of life, direct from the Almighty and fated either to eternal bliss or eternal damnation depending on such factors as birthright, lifestyle, and opting into or out of a particular set of doctrines. Across the range of beliefs, however, the common theme is that the soul is a kernel of pure being that is independent of, but imprisoned within, a physical form.

This assumption is so prevalent that it has a certain plausibility outside of mystical and religious circles. A popular theme in stories and movies, for instance, is the transport of personal identity from one body into another (child to adult, human to animal, animate to machine, etc.). The fact that such storylines seem sensible at all reveals the deep cultural commitment to Platonic assumptions.[16] This commitment has significant ramifications for matters of learning and teaching, but the implications vary dramatically depending on whether one assumes a mystical or religious attitude.

WHERE TO NOW?

This chapter dealt with divergent perspectives on gnosis (spiritual knowledge)—or, more specifically, with the *sources* of knowledge. As ot turns out, the *nature* ofknowledge is not much debated within mystical and religious traditions. Chapter 7, which deals with divergent perspectives on the complement of gnosis—episteme—is a parallel discussion.

In chapters 5 and 6, I look at the conceptions of learning and teaching that have arisen, respectively, in mystical and religious traditions. Those two chapters are terminal, in that I don't carry the bifurcation structure any further. Because my goal is to trace out a genealogy of contemporary conceptions of teaching, I see the discussions in those chapters more in terms of foliage than branches.

5

Mysticism:

TEACHING AS DRAWING OUT

Even a stone can be a teacher.

— Buddhist saying[1]

The word *teach* is derived from the Old English *tacn*, which meant something like "sign"—and by which any object or event could potentially serve as a teacher. The act of teaching, that is, was originally understood strictly in terms of its effects on the learner, *not* at all in terms of any deliberate effort to affect learners. To teach was to perturbate; a teaching was, to borrow from Gregory Bateson, any difference that makes a difference.[2]

Conceived in such terms, and as will be developed in all of the chapters that appear at the tips of branches in this text, it is not difficult to appreciate how such a broad range of philosophical traditions can so readily absorb the word *teaching* into their particular modes of interpretation. However, those traditions that are aligned with gnosis— with questions of deep meaning—are the ones that seem best fitted to the broad senses that were originally suggested by the word *teaching*.

Within mystical traditions, the core problematic in matters of learning and teaching arises in the assumption that knowers are always and already part of the wholeness of creation, but that they have somehow lost or forgotten their place within this grand unity. One's life (or the sequence of one's lives, by some accounts) comes to be seen in terms of a difficult return to oneness—a slow progression punctuated by frequent lapses and occasional manifestations of deep and meaningful insight or epiphanies.[3]

Epiphanies, as framed by mysticism, are hinged to a particular attitude toward intuition. In the most general sense of the term, *intuition* refers to events of knowing (or suspecting) something without any direct knowledge of the source or the means of that knowledge. In Middle English, intuition originally meant "insight"—that is, a looking inward—and was derived from the Late Latin for "looking at". Various traditions place their own spins on the natures and origins of intuitions, and these spins are useful for uncovering differences in beliefs about learning and teaching represented in contemporary discussions. For example, in mystical traditions, where the notion first arose, intuition tends to be seen as a mode of knowing that exceeds purely rational analysis. An intuition is a moment of direct connection with the cosmos, an event in which one finds within oneself a knowledge that surpasses oneself. Again, such events were understood in terms of recovered knowledge, not new insight, reflecting the underlying assumption of an initial separation from perfection.

It is thus that, in virtually all mystical traditions, intuition is something that demands one's attention. (Intuitions are regarded as suspect in most other traditions.) Yet the situation is not quite so simple as embracing one's inklings. Within almost all mystical traditions, there are rigorous systems of discipline (from the Latin *discere*, "to learn") that are intended to enable devotees to cultivate their intuitions and, in the process, reachieve some measure of unity with the universe. In most cases, these systems involve some means to loosen the grip of the conscious mind. Many examples could be given from Western and Eastern mysticisms. For essentially the same reason, for instance, Kabbalistic Jews engage in intricate mental manipulations of images and numbers, Christian ascetics take part in various sorts of self-mortification and intense prayer, and Zen practitioners concentrate on nonsensical koans. The goal is to diminish the din of moment-to-moment thought, to allow oneself to attend to thoughts that are not anchored in immediate, Earthly concerns. Despite the variety of disciplinary practices, they are all rooted in the common belief that to attain mystical union one must free the spirit from the limiting passions of the ego and the delusions of physical perception. In this frame, learning is all about a suspicion of—and, hence, a suspension of—things of this world.

It is out of this manner of thinking that the word *educate* originally arose, derived from the Latin *educare*, "to drag out or pull out". To educate was to draw out, by whatever means, what was assumed to be already there, woven into one's being from the beginning. Hence, educating was originally and fully focused on matters of gnosis. The mundane details of everyday life, of episteme, were expected to take care of themselves.

The sense of personal knowledge—as inherent but largely unrealized—may sound implausible, but it is still very much at work in contemporary thinking about formal education. The literature is rife with references to personal potential (i.e., the assumption of inborn possibilities toward which one must strive), ideal careers (i.e., the assumption of innate personalities that are perfectly suited to particular sorts of social roles), and pregiven identities (e.g., often represented in such phrases as "the person you're meant to be"). These beliefs in prespecified possibilities and unchanging identities—that is, in fate and/or predetermination—have long been coupled to the mysticist premise of gradual recovery of original union. Such beliefs have had strong influences on assumptions about what schools should do and how teachers should intervene in learners' lives.

Aspects of how teaching is conceived within mystical traditions might best be introduced by pointing to clusters of terms that are thought to serve as synonyms for learning and teaching. As already mentioned, learning is seen mainly as a process of actualization of one's true self—that is, of realization of potential, of meeting one's fate, of mastering one's destiny, of discovering one's innate nature and proper place. For the most part, success in such learnings is seen as a matter of self-discipline, which is often associated with striving to move beyond the superficial concerns of everyday life and of conscious thought.

This last point is one that tends to be diminished and forgotten in contemporary discussions of teaching, although notions of self-actualization and personal potential continue in force. In fact much in contrast to the intents of mystical traditions, notions of personal potential tend today to be attached to what might be described as ego-grasping. Popularly, that is, mystically rooted notions of finding and discovering oneself have detached from their original commitments to locating oneself within the web of existence. Today the goal is not to let go of the ego, but to bolster it, to make it stand out, to distinguish oneself.

Much of the vocabulary originally fitted to mystical sensibilities about teaching has undergone similar sorts of redefinition. Nevertheless, *educating* has tended to retain much of the original sense of developing the innate capacities of learners. Among its synonyms, clustered around the assumption of innateness, are *nurturing* (from the Latin for "suckle"), *fostering* (from the Old English for "food" or "nourishing"), and *tutoring* (from the Old French for "to protect"). All these terms were used to refer to teaching before the middle of the 15th century,[4] which, significantly, is prior to both the invention of the modern school and the works of Descartes and Bacon.

Each term foregrounds the teacher's role in protecting and actualizing the assumed-to-be predetermined possibilities of the learner. Significantly, each hints at an avoidance of efforts to be overly directive. As such it makes sense that this manner of teaching is not conceived in terms of preset curriculum objectives, but in terms of un-realized possibilities. A further quality of these attitudes toward teaching is that they project a sense of universal responsibility—in two senses of the phrase. First, because teaching is understood in terms of the effect on the learner and not the intentions of the teacher, anyone, anywhere, anytime might be a teacher. Everyone, everywhere, at all times is thus seen to have a certain ethical responsibility to behave well. Second, this responsibility is not so much oriented toward other individuals as it is realized in one's actions toward others. It is actually oriented to and by the universe.

Aspects of the thinking that underlies these notions remain prominent in contemporary discussions of teaching, including in some of the theoretical literature. An example that is currently quite popular is *learning styles* or *learning modalities*. These theories are based on the assumption that each person is imbued with specific traits and abilities that determine interests, modes of engagement, and social roles. Not surprisingly, notions of teaching as nurturing and fostering fit well with and tend to be represented alongside these sorts of populist theories.

So too does the model of teaching known as the Socratic method. Preserved for us in the writings of Plato, one of Socrates' students, the Socratic method might be described as a questioning technique that is oriented by a belief that the teacher's task is to draw out of the learner what is already there. The teacher in this case does not give information directly. Instead, she or he poses questions that are based on the learner's answers—questions intended to prompt learners to realize their own misconceptions or bolster their existing understandings. The underlying idea is that knowledge is innate. Although the learner sometimes needs assistance with pulling together the threads of understanding into a coherent conclusion, all that is needed to knit a reliable knowledge of the universe is already present in one's psyche.

The Socratic method remains popular—a fact that underscores just how deeply mystical assumptions are inscribed in contemporary thinking. Indeed some assumptions—like the notion that all of the raw materials of knowing are present in the hermetically sealed knower—reappear in conceptions of learning and teaching that are far removed from mystical traditions.

WHERE TO NOW?

This chapter was concerned with the origins and conceptual implications of synonyms for teaching that are associated with mystical traditions—specifically, the terms *educating, nurturing, fostering,* and *tutoring*. In chapter 6, I undertake a similar examination of conceptions of and metaphors for teaching that are associated with religious traditions.

6

Religion:

TEACHING AS DRAWING IN

Train up a child in the way of the Lord; and when he is old,
he will not depart from it.

— Proverbs 22:6[1]

Discussions of learning and teaching, at least since the time of the ancient Greeks, have tended to gravitate toward the dichotomy of self versus society. Which should the teacher privilege, the individual or the collective?

This ancient tension is certainly present in the contrast between mystical and religious attitudes toward learning and teaching. Despite their shared conviction that teaching must first and foremost be concerned with matters of the spirit, their divergent assumptions about the origins of gnosis give rise to very different, even incompatible recommendations for the teaching of children. This point can be illustrated by contrasting the usages of such terms as *mastery* and *discipline*. In mystical traditions, concerned with the nurturance of individuals, such terms were used to describe the work of the learner or the means by which the learner might come to a deeper appreciation of her or his place in the cosmos. Mastery and discipline—or at least the roots of these terms—were used in reference to one's relationship to one's personal existence.

In Western religious traditions, discipline and mastery are not seen as responsibilities of the learner, but as duties of the teacher. Consider, for example, the double meaning of the phrase "someone who is disciplined". To the mystical ear, this would almost certainly be heard as a description of someone on the path to heightened awareness. To the religious ear, concerned more with drawing persons into established systems of thought than drawing thought out of persons, the phrase would likely be heard to refer to someone who has been punished by someone else—or at least to someone who has surrendered his or her own authority to someone else's, as suggested by current definitions of the word *disciple*. Much the same could be said about mastery. In mystical traditions, mastery is something toward which the individual strives; in religious contexts, the word *master* came to be used as a synonym for teacher, the one responsible for disciplining.

This shift in sensibilities is also evident in the diminished status of intuition among formal religions. As developed in chapter 5, the word *intuition* is derived from a Latin root that means "to look inward", and the notion is key to mystical attitudes toward knowledge. From the religious perspective, the implied self-reliance is inappropriate because truth is understood to come from the outside. Further, among all major Western religions, the inward self is seen as easily corrupted. It should perhaps not be surprising, then, that the word *tuition*—literally, "watching over", in contrast to the "looking inward" of intuition—should emerge as a synonym for teaching.

The learner's surrender of authority is rendered possible in the assumption that knowledge has an existence that is independent of knowers—which, in turn, is tied to the conviction that the source of all knowledge (gnosis) is a godhead or other supernatural source—which, in turn, is hinged to the belief that the mental-spiritual realm is distinct from and even opposed to the physical-fleshly world. What's more is that the surrender of personal authority is not just deemed possible, but necessary within most Western religious traditions. Religions tend to frame the overarching theme of gnosis—that is, the recovery of a lost perfection—in terms of *earning* one's way back to a promised land, as opposed to the mystical emphasis that is more toward *learning* one's way back. Hence, within religions, one often encounters narratives of atonement through sacrifice, hard work, piety, modesty, silence, or other means of self-denial.

Self-denial, of course, would be expected as a core theme among organized religions because their projects are explicitly framed in terms of a collective corpus. This point is underscored by the vocabulary for teaching that one encounters in religious contexts. As just mentioned, for example, teaching is often understood as synonymous with *mastering* and *disciplining*. It is also seen to be a matter of *indoctrinating* (literally, "bringing someone into a body of doctrine"), *inducting* or *introducing* (both from the Latin for "pulling or drawing in"), *training* (from the Latin *tragere*, "to pull or drag"), and *guiding* (which is from Old French and has to do with "showing the way").[2] At the moment, most of these terms have fallen into disrepute, in large part because discourses that are focused on indoctrinating and disciplining youth into a specific system of belief are popularly seen as problematic at the moment—except, of course, by adherents.

A few synonyms for the teacher are also worth noting—specifically, as already mentioned, *master/mistress* (from the Latin for "one with authority", and which has become the title bestowed on those who earn a higher university degree) and *doctor* (related to doctrine and indoctrinate, and the title bestowed on those who earn the highest university degree). Accompanying the senses of specialization that are now implicit in the terms was the idea that teaching is a vocation—literally, a divine calling. This idea represents a significant break from mystical conceptions, in which anyone or anything could be a teacher because teaching was understood in terms of the learner's response not the teacher's intention. In religious traditions, it's all about the teacher's aims. As such, although terms like *master* and *doctor* have come to be attached to a broad range of cultural activities, one point that has been retained is that authority is invested in the master, doctor, or teacher rather than in the disciple, patient, or pupil.

That being said, there are at least two divergent conceptions of the teacher's role at play here, each of which arises from different conceptions of sacred texts and inherited rituals. As developed in chapter 4, religions and religious sects are often divided on the matter of the status of sacred books and practices. Some regard an artifact like the Bible as a compendium of era-specific, somewhat inconsistent narratives that require careful analysrs and continuous interpretation to uncover the meanings and relevancies of the stories for today's world. Within other, more fundamentalist approaches, texts like the Bible are taken as wholly and literally true. In the case of the former, the teacher is usually one who has been trained in the techniques of interpretation, and her or his preparation would include studies in history, literary tropes, and so on. Such is the case for most major religions, at least historically speaking. Examples include Jewish rabbinical traditions (*rabbi* is the Hebrew and Aramaic word for teacher) and many Christian denominations, as flagged by the notions of *ministering* (from the Latin for "serving") and *pastoring* (for the Latin for "shepherd"). These more reflective attitudes stand in stark contrast to the somewhat forceful and divisive emphases that are often manifest in North American fundamentalist movements. All major religions have spawned literalist splinter groups in which teaching is not understood as a service to others but as a righteous imperative to impose authority on others.[3] For them, phrases like "the teachings of Christ" or "the word of God" are more often taken as divine dictates than spiritual allegories. Teaching becomes a matter of telling rather than interpreting, ministering, or shepherding.

It would be tempting to dismiss this point as reflective of small and isolated portions of the population. However, as terms such as *master* and *doctor* filtered their way from religious traditions into the secular educational establishment, they brought with them senses of teacher as *professor* (from the Latin *profitieri*, "to lay claim to, to declare openly") and teacher as *lecturer* (from Middle Latin, *lectura*, "a reading, lecture"). Both these terms date back at least to the 1300s, and both came to be applied to teaching in nonreligious contexts in the 1700s—

during the rise of the modern school. The idea that teaching is a matter of imparting knowledge might have sprouted in the soils of religion, but it blossomed in the sunshine of Enlightenment thought (see chaps. 8 and 9).

Of course, the suggestion that teaching is a matter of transmitting information only makes sense if knowledge is conceived in terms of something tangible that can in fact be conveyed. As developed in chapter 2, the underlying knowledge-as-object metaphor is deeply inscribed in Western traditions. Such terms and phrases as "grasping concepts", "acquiring knowledge", "exchanging ideas", "passing along information", "food for thought", "cold, hard facts", "drowning in details", and "thirsting for knowledge" represent only the tip of the iceberg on this issue.[4] In English, at least, knowledge is overwhelmingly framed in terms of physical forms despite ancient religious and philosophical convictions that physical forms are little more than poor reflections of divine, incorporeal truths.

However, with the senses of permanence, firmness, and substantiveness that accompany notions of divinely wrought truth, it is perhaps not surprising that a knowledge-as-object metaphor would take root. Given this metaphor's seductiveness and hold within religion-framed worldviews, it is also not surprising that learning came to be popularly understood in terms of taking things in, grasping, and acquiring. Corresponding to such notions is the idea that the learner is a repository of knowledge—a vessel to be filled. These figurative framings are so resilient that even those who are most critical of the underlying metaphors do not always catch themselves using such phrases as "cramming for exams", "empty headed", and "taking it all in", or, for that matter, using the word *matter* to refer to matters of knowledge.

Arguably, these sorts of literalized metaphors continue to have the most profound shaping influences on contemporary efforts at teaching. The influence of religion and its institutionalized sensibilities are further represented in, for example, current understandings of ability (in terms of "gifts from above"). Yet perhaps the most significant and enduring contribution of religious thought is the notion of soul—that immaterial essence that is credited with the faculty of thought and that is seen to animate the fleshly prison that contains it. Long ago, the soul—the individual—was carved out as the fundamental particle of knowing, a form oriented to but separated from the ideal realm and akin to but isolated from other souls. The implications of this framing continue to be manifest. As is discussed in subsequent chapters, even among those theories that have managed to move beyond the knowledge-as-object metaphor, there continues to be a strong tendency to maintain the idea that the individual is a monad—a fundamental singular autononous metaphysical entity.

WHERE TO NOW?

This chapter was concerned with the origins and conceptual implications of synonyms for teaching and teachers that are associated with religion traditions—specifically, the terms *tuition, disciplining, indoctrinating, inducting, introducing, training, guiding, master,* and *doctor.* It completes the gnosis branch of the discussion.

In chapter 7, I discuss episteme, the complement of gnosis. In particular, I examine the strands of thinking that gave rise to the scientific revolution and to dramatically different ways of thinking about knowledge, learning, and teaching.

7

Episteme:

RATIONALISM V EMPIRICISM

Nature and Nature's laws lay hid in night:
God said, "Let Newton be!" and all was light.

— Alexander Pope[1]

The Enlightenment is generally seen to have begun in the early 1600s, as England and continental Europe turned a rather remarkable corner in the history of knowledge. By many accounts, the turn was so rapid and dramatic that the image of switching on a light seems strangely appropriate.

As with most social movements, however, this one had been on a slow simmer for centuries, helped along by such thinkers as Copernicus and Galileo. The simmer turned to a boil in the 1600s, with a revolution in Western science that began with a few key treatises on how the scientific might be cleaved from the unscientific. Two of the major figures in this movement, as mentioned in chapter 2, were Francis Bacon (1561–1626) in England and René Descartes (1596–1650) in France. Bacon and Descartes are the two persons most often credited with the rise of the modernism—or at least with providing the first formal statements on the structures and attitudes that would characterize the modern era.

Historically, this period is defined by such co-implicated cultural events as the emergence of mass communication through print media, the rise of capitalism, the industrial revolution, urbanization, democratization, and European imperialism. Philosophically, the modern era might be succinctly defined as the triumph of episteme over gnosis. The intertwining historical developments just mentioned, coupled with the embrace of logico-rational thought among the educated elite, supported (and were supported by) the rapid expansion of formal science. Scientific knowledge quickly exceeded its modest roots in the everyday know-how of episteme. It made incursions into many aspects of the cosmos that had previously been seen as the purview of gnosis, such as the relationship of Earth to the rest of the universe. In effect, the comfortable co-existence of gnosis and episteme collapsed as prevailing cultural sensibilities began to shift from theism (the belief that God, the creator, intervenes in everyday life) to deism (the belief that God, the creator, set the self-determining universe in motion and no longer intervenes), agnosticism,[2] and even atheism.

Two major branches of thought emerged within the epistemological turn: rationalism, most often associated with Descartes' philosophy, and empiricism, commonly associated with Bacon's writings. In this chapter, I highlight the conceptual similarities and differences of these perspectives as I move toward a discussion of the perspectives on knowledge, learning, and teaching that have come to be associated with rationalist and empiricist approaches to inquiry.

RATIONALISM:
KNOWLEDGE BY DEDUCTIVE REASONING

Descartes, whose contributions to mathematics and physics compare with his contributions to philosophy, is the person most often associated with the rise of modernism.[3] Philosophically, Descartes both drew on and broke from the traditions inherited from the ancient

Greeks. His major break was with scholasticism, a conceptual blend of Aristotelian philosophy, neoplatonist mysticism, and medieval Christian theology. Descartes rejected scholasticism as an uncritical mix of episteme and gnosis. He argued that the two needed to be separated once again—and that the sole route to unimpeachable truth was deductive logic. His model in this project was Euclid's geometry of the plane. Euclid had distilled all of the geometry of ancient Greece into a formal system that sat on a foundation of five fundamental axioms[4] which, via logico-rational methods,[5] could be knitted together to generate all other geometric truths.

Although Descartes was critical of scholasticism, his work was still oriented by the Platonic metaphysical assumptions that truth exists in an ideal realm and one can only gain access to it through careful, deductive thought. One must begin, Descartes argued, as Euclid began—with self-evident, irrefutable truths. From there, he assumed, one could rationally derive all other truths. Descartes' starting place was his infamous *cogito*, "I think". Clearly this was a truth that could not be disputed. In his 1637 *Discourse on Method,* Descartes reported on how he had applied his "method of doubt", as he called it, to arrive at this premise. For him, whatever could be doubted must be rejected—simply because a claim to truth must be beyond question. As he labored to cut away layers of unsupported belief and uninterrogated assumption, he found himself left with one simple fact: that something existed that was capable of doubt—himself. The deduction of that epistemic fact represented a violent incursion of the traditional territory of gnosis—specifically, into questions of being and existence, albeit that the answer was presented as naked fact, stripped of meaning and of bases for action. Even so, it was sufficient to displace gnosis from the space of proper academic (read: rational) debate.

Like his reliance on deductive logic, Descartes' method of doubt was also drawn from the philosophy of the ancient Greeks—in this case, the doctrine of skepticism. Cohering in the 4th century BCE, skepticism arose as a reaction to a fairly sudden proliferation of divergent belief systems. The skeptics undercut the emergent tensions by questioning the possibility of knowledge of an objective reality. It is an attitude toward knowledge that has threaded its way through the history of Western thought ever since, and Descartes was a key figure in breathing new life into it for the current era.

Following the model of Euclid's geometry, Descartes' next step after having established an unshakeable premise was to apply logic to reassemble knowledge piece by piece. Among his deduced truths was that he, as a knowing agent, was an incorporeal thinking thing—that is, a mind that was distinct from a body. In fact he developed an argument to demonstrate that the mind had no need of a body. He also argued that his mind must be individual in the sense handed down from the Pythagoreans as a fundamental and irreducible form independent of other similar forms. Descartes also published logical arguments on the existence of a God, the existences of other minds, and the existence of an external world.

This list of conclusions bears a striking resemblance to the assumptions of Platonic and Aristotelian thought, although it is admittedly much more rigorously assembled. What Descartes offered, then, was a rationale for embracing many of the dichotomies that had been assumed or posited thousands of years earlier, but never formally argued.

Descartes is often called the "father of modern (or analytic) philosophy" for his contributions to contemporary thought. Combined, his method of doubt and the exclusive reliance of logic are the two components of the analytic philosophical method—means by which all claims to truth can, in theory, be reduced to primary assumptions and then rebuilt. However, he is not usually identified as the "father of modern (analytic) science". That title most often goes to his contemporary, Francis Bacon.

EMPIRICISM:
KNOWLEDGE BY INDUCTIVE REASONING

I'll begin this section by laying out some of the important associations within and contrasts between rationalism and empiricism. Before doing that, however, I'll emphasize that these ideas are rarely, if ever, separated in practice. Although some thinkers might cast the differences in terms of "one or the other"—and despite that I might appear to be doing precisely that—it's important to bear in mind that, in practice, rationalist and empiricist sensibilities have a comfortable and complementary co-existence.

Rationalism moves, via logical deduction (i.e., through *a priori* reasoning), from first principles to conclusions about the universe. Empiricism begins with the study of phenomena, seeking via inductive logic (i.e., through *a posteriori* reasoning) to distill essential truths. Deduction is a method of inference that draws conclusions on the basis of already established premises. It eschews experience as a basis for claims to truth. Induction begins with observed facts and aims to derive principles that underlie or are manifest in those observations. Because rationalism is focused on deriving the world through reasoned thought, it is associated with analytic philosophy. Empiricism, with its emphasis on experiment and demonstration, is associated more strongly with analytic science. To reiterate, using one of the more popular formats associated with the analytic attitude, I might chart these difference in a summary table:

rationalism	empiricism
analytic philosophy	analytic science
deductive logic	inductive[6] logic
a priori reasoning	*a posteriori* reasoning
truth via mental construct	truth via physical demonstration

The common ground of rationalism and empiricism is evident in the adjective *analytic*. Both analytic philosophy and analytic science are concerned with reducing the universe to its natural constituents, true to the metaphysical heritage of Plato and Aristotle. In fact the idea of reducing the universe into its constituent parts dates back even further, at least to Democritus (460–370 BCE). As well, both domains of activity are oriented by a suspicion of human perception. The point of divergence is the question of how one might overcome the fallibility of the senses in the project of assembling an internal model of an external world.

Descartes, the rationalist, argued that one should build upward on a firm ground of premises that have been stripped of their dross through the method of doubt. Bacon, the empiricist, suggested that knowledge is "like some magnificent structure without any foundation".[7] Thus one is limited to making inferences about the truth on the basis of gross experiences. Bacon concluded that science should proceed by searching for patterns amid facts gathered through repeated testing—or, in a telling turn of phrase, to compel "the secrets of nature to reveal themselves ... [through] vexation".[8] Commonsensical as it may seem today, this move toward induction and engagement with the world marked a dramatic shift from the deductive reasoning of classical texts.

Bacon did not invent inductive logic. Scholars had long been devoted to the project of matching observations to theories, as demonstrated in the examples of Copernicus and Galileo. Bacon's major contribution was to prompt scientific research to move beyond the inherited and prevailing emphases on description and classification into the realms of theorizing, hypothesis testing, and creative exploration. To this end, and of great significance, Bacon did not propose a dry, mechanical scientific method like the sort perpetuated in grade-school curricula. In fact, he recommended the use of such figurative devices as aphorisms, illustrations, fables, and analogies, which to that point had been the tools of gnosis, not episteme. Bacon felt that such devices might help to interrupt entrenched beliefs by opening up imaginative possibilities. In other words, it would be inappropriate to reduce Bacon's contribution to popular, but mistaken opinions of empiricism as a rigidly objective, slavishly technical attitude toward the generation of new knowledge. On the contrary, it was an attempt at a disciplined, but imaginative departure from the constraints of tradition—a departure that, like rationalism, laid claim to some of the territory of gnosis.

Nevertheless, the title of Bacon's major work on the topic, *Novum Organum*, published in 1620, reflects a firm rooting in classical assumption. The title is borrowed from Aristotle's *Organum*. Although *novum* ("new") flags a departure from ancient Greek cosmology, the *organum* ("logical works" or "logic") betrays a conception of the universe as inherently mechanical and mathematical. As with Descartes, the ultimate desire was to uncover the fundaments of the cosmos. What Bacon helped set in motion, then, was more a new attitude toward gathering and verifying knowledge than a new attitude toward knowledge. That attitude might succinctly be described in terms of testability of claims. In setting out the structures for inductive inquiry, Bacon prescribed that all claims to truth must be verifiable through demonstration—which is to say, measurable.

Measurability has emerged as a useful tool to distinguish between the scientific and the quasiscientific. It separates physics from mysticism, biology from creation science, and astronomy from astrology. Measurability is also a central notion in the rise of one of the most radical expressions of empiricism—the much maligned positivist movement. First introduced to the vocabulary of science in the early 1800s, positivism saw analytic science and the scientific method as the only legitimate routes to knowledge. This sort of assertion represents a tremendous break with tradition because, although the roots of positivism extend into metaphysics, the movement involved an explicit denial of the possibility of access to metaphysical truths. (Note that positivists did not deny the existence of transcendent, eternal truths, merely the possibility of human access.) The term *positivism* is derived from the commitment of an influential body of scientists at the time that science must be focused on the generation of positive knowledge—that is, insights that affirm truths and that are testable, as opposed to claims to truth that are based on denials and negations. If positivism had a motto, it would be "Facts are measurable". Such an attitude does not deny the existence of immeasurable events (e.g., imagination), but a positivist scientist is compelled to ignore such phenomena as outside the purview of science.

However, not content to allow such human traits as intelligence and creativity to be excluded from scientific study, throughout the 1800s various positivist researchers began to construct instruments to measure these sorts of elusive human qualities. Up until then, the tremendous variation among humans had kept empiricism at bay within studies of humans. New interpretive tools—namely, probabilistic models and statistical methods—had begun to appear that made it possible to compress huge quantities of data into mathematical averages, measures of deviations from those averages, and linear relationships among different traits. (These tools were originally developed for business purposes. Specifically, statistical methods were first used to make predictions on life-span and related phenomena so that insurance companies could ensure reasonable profit margins.)

The one artifact of statistical analysis that figured most prominently in psychologically and sociologically oriented studies of learning and schooling was the normal (or bell) curve. The normal curve was easily aligned with the deeply entrenched assumption from metaphysics that there were ideals toward which all forms strived. This conception of ideals mapped tidily onto new statistical constructs such as population means (averages), which were then deployed to define the "normal man" in terms of typical height, ideal weight, and so on—even though no such human exists. By the end of the 1800s, psychologists had set their sights on more elusive targets, such as memory capacity, intelligence, aptitude, and the relationship between age and reasoning capacities. Tests were developed, averages were determined, and a fuller picture of normality began to be painted. In brief, through the application of statistical methods, positivist science had found a means to quantify ideality. More precisely, the word *nor-mal*, which was newly reframed as a mathematical construct, replaced *ideal*.[9] In fact normal also started to be taken as a synonym for *natural*.

Educationally speaking, positivist science has had some tremendous influences on the curriculum structures and classroom practices, some of which are discussed in chapter 9.

COMMON ROOTS, DIFFERENT BRANCHES

On close inspection of the projects of rationalism and empiricism, it becomes apparent that the only way to construe them as opposites is to ignore their explicit worldviews and focus on the technical differences of their extreme versions. This point is amplified in the fact that few researchers seem to have any trouble locating their work in both traditions. For example, Isaac Newton is commonly identified as one of the great rationalists (in particular, for his invention of calculus) *and* one of the great empiricists (especially for his studies of light, gravity, and motion). Perhaps an even more dramatic example of the synthesis of rationalist and empiricist sensibilities is what has come to be called "experimental mathematics"—an approach to research that involves computer-based experimentation that has emerged in the last few decades as an important movement in formal mathematics.[10]

Newton's work and experimental mathematics stand out as two examples of the power of analytic thought. They also serve as a reminder that analytic philosophers and analytic scientists alike do not see their work strictly as breaking things down to their basic units, but as using analytic methods as a means to better understand the phenomenon that was originally of interest. The driving idea is that a better understanding of the parts will contribute to a better understanding of the whole, which should in turn contribute to deepened appreciations of the parts and so on in a spiral toward total understanding.[11]

This prospect of totalized understanding had some rather severe entailments when it came to matters of gnosis—and, in particular, to matters of God. The rises of rationalism and empiricism were thus accompanied by a shift from theism to deism that culminated in Fredrich Nietzsche's 1885 proclamation that God was dead. As an explanatory principle, that is, science found that God was a construct that it did not need, and thinkers such as Nietzsche saw god-concepts as crutches that humanity had outgrown.

The perspective—or rather the perspectives—that arose around the assumed self-sufficiency of humans came to be called, appropriately enough, *humanism*. The term is currently used to refer to any system of thought that places human beings, as opposed to a god-concept or nature, at the center of the discussion. The humanist movement reached its peak during the Enlightenment, but it actually emerged at the end of the Middle Ages with a new (or perhaps renewed) confidence that humans had the wherewithal to distinguish for themselves between truth and untruth. Its early expressions were often interpreted within the religious establishment as direct challenges to theism—as demonstrated, for example, in the persecution of Galileo for his efforts to popularize Copernicus's theory that Earth was not the center of the cosmos.

The roots and immediate precursors of rationalism and empiricism thus highlight the deeply intertwined assumptions of the two attitudes toward the generation of knowledge. Despite these deep similarities, and the fact that they are generally seen as complementary within science, it turns out that the minor differences between rationalism and empiricism contribute to some major divergences when it comes to matters of learning and teaching. I'll begin by highlighting some of the common ground—namely, the conceptions of learning and individual knowers that work across rationalist and empiricist traditions.

I've already developed both points, but I'll reiterate and elaborate a few important details here to set up the discussions of teaching in the chapters that follow. On the matter of individual knowers, the epistemic traditions have tended to posit individuals in much the same terms as the mystical and religious traditions, as fundamental and irreducible units of knowing. Thought and knowledge were seen as uniquely human capabilities. (In fact there are still debates on the question of whether any nonhuman animals can think.[12]) Further, thought was seen as a strictly internal phenomenon. More specifically, personal understanding was conceived in what has come to be called *representationist* terms, as inner representations or models of the outer world. Such representations were seen to be based on deduction (rational), input from the senses (empirical), or a combination of the two.

I've used the past tense in the preceding few sentences to flag that these ideas are ancient. It would perhaps have been more appropriate to write in the present tense, however. Most popular and many current academic theories about cognition uncritically accept the premise that learning is a matter of constructing an inner subjective representation of an outer objective reality. *Truth*, in this conception, is defined in terms of the level of match between inner model and outer world. As far as personal knowing goes, the roles of philosophy and science are generally construed in terms of diagnosing and correcting any misalignments.

Both Descartes and Bacon, rationalist and empiricist, agreed that one's inner representation is doomed to be flawed. However, they offered contrasting proposals for overcoming the fallibility of personal convictions. Descartes prescribed systematic doubt and logical argument as the first and second principles of learning; Bacon insisted on extensive experience to provide a broad basis from which one might confirm or disprove interpretations.

From the seeds sown by Descartes grew a branch of psychology that focused on the mental operations of the individual learner—and that laid claim to the word *cognition* to refer to the assumed-to-be strictly brain-based mental operations of the individual learner. From the seeds sewn by Bacon and nurtured by positivists grew an opposed branch of psychology—behaviorism—that sought to understand learning strictly by focusing on what is observable and measurable.

WHERE TO NOW?

In chapters 8 and 9, respectively, I examine some of the implications for teaching of rationalist and empiricist perspectives on learning and knowing. I suspect that much of what is presented in these chapters will have a familiar ring to anyone who has moved through a preservice teaching program sometime during the past half century. Overwhelmingly, rationalist and empiricist sensibilities are used to frame teacher education and public school practices.

Chapters 8 and 9 complete the discussion of conceptions of teaching that are rooted in metaphysical traditions. In chapter 10, I turn to discussions of the nature of knowledge that arise from the conceptual break from metaphysics that was wrought by Darwin and his contemporaries.

8

Rationalism:

TEACHING AS INSTRUCTING

*The grand book of the universe ... is written in the language
of mathematics, and its characters are triangles, circles, and
other geometric figures ... ; without these one wanders about
in a dark labyrinth.*

— Galileo Galilei[1]

One of the legacies of the combined influences of ancient Greek
philosophy and Judeo-Christian belief is the use of light as a
basis of various figurative devices within discussions of learning and
thought. In fact with its prominent uses in such texts as the first
chapter of the Book of Genesis (e.g., "Let there be light ...") and
throughout Plato's *Republic* (in particular in his cave allegory), by
Descartes' time it had become the metaphor of choice around matters of knowledge and knowing.

However, Descartes introduced a new twist. Within mystical and
religious traditions, the universe was usually seen as rather dimly lit.
Humans thus had to strain in the relative darkness to make out whatever could be discerned in the available illumination—as in the case
of St. Paul, who lamented that, in this life, one could only
"see through a glass darkly".[2] Descartes thought differently
and argued that humans, "by the light of reason",[3] could

take the initiative to discern truths hidden in the shadows. We could shed light on things by ourselves. With this conceptual move, he pulled knowledge away from gnosis and toward episteme. He also prompted redefinitions of old metaphors for teaching. Words such as *enlightening* and *illuminating*, which were rooted in mystical and religious notions, were stripped of their spiritual connotations. Enlightening others came to be understood in terms of logical procedures through discrete concepts rather than in terms of imaginative engagements with the cosmos.

This particular shift contributed to yet another redefinition of the word *discipline*. As noted in chapter 5, within mystical traditions, discipline is a quality of the learner. And as noted in chapter 6, within religious traditions, discipline is taken up as a task of the teacher. Within rationalist traditions, the word *discipline* loses all sense of moral and ethical import as it is used to refer to a subject matter (as in "the discipline of physics").

It is of tremendous significance that Descartes took the discipline of mathematics as his model of valid truth, because it reveals that his work represented more an instantiation of prevailing sensibilities than a problematizing of entrenched assumptions. For example, mathematics is readily seen in terms of absolute, unshakeable, ideal, and benign truth—that is, in metaphysical terms as knowledge that is independent of knowers. (This should not be surprising given that etymologically the word *mathematics* is derived from an Indo-European term that meant "to learn" or "to think". As a model for all learning, a bias toward mathematics was already knit into European languages. Other domains of human knowledge, such as language and history, cannot so easily be considered quite so absolute, benign, and knower-independent.) Because Descartes was working from the assumption that personal knowing is a strictly mental construct, the presumed-to-be disembodied nature of mathematical knowledge was precisely what he needed to construe a rationalist model of learning.

Theories of learning that have descended from Cartesian thought are known as *mentalisms* because they are concerned only with internal, mental constructs. Historically, these theories have tended to be developed around metaphors of prominent cultural activities such as painting or writing. A popular notion in Descartes' era, for example, was that memory was an internal diary. There have also been pronounced tendencies toward describing cognition in terms of prevailing technologies. Descartes made frequent references to various mechanical devices to illustrate the manner in which logical inferences might be chained together to churn out reliable conclusions. Early in the 20th century, movie technologies became popular among mentalist theorists: Eyes were seen as cameras, memory as film-recording images, imagination as inner projection, and so on.[4] More recently, electronic technologies have been taken up. These metaphors have been so broadly embraced that the phrase "brain as computer" is often taken literally. An entire branch of psychology, known as *cognitivism*, has also emerged around this particular metaphor. (Some of the shortcomings of cognitivism are discussed in later chapters.)

Another metaphor that is common across mentalist accounts is learning-as-building. In fact this particular notion has risen to some prominence within current discussions of schooling and teaching— to the point that one of the mantras of formal education is that "Individuals construct their own understandings". This notion is sometimes deployed as if it represented some sort of critique of the rationalist assumptions that underlie such teaching emphases as direct instruction and linear movement through topics. Ironically, however, Descartes' point was precisely that individuals construct their own understandings as they go about assembling inner representations of outer reality. Hence, the current popularity of the notion is more an indication of a collective commitment of rationalism than anything else. (Ernst von Glaserseld[5] coined the phrase "trivial constructivism" to distinguish such commonsensical notions from more radical uses of the metaphor of construction. See chap. 12.)

In any case, in the 1600s, Descartes' new suggestion that valid knowledge must be logically constructed—that knowledge was an edifice that must be made to rest on firm foundations—gave rise to a new wave of metaphors for teaching. These notions all pointed to the role of the teacher in helping learners construct a logically coherent world. In particular, the word *instructing* (understood literally in terms of helping learners to structure inner knowledge) quickly became synonymous with teaching. Closely related, two important aspects of teaching were understood to be *explaining* (from the Latin for "to lay flat") and *telling* (from an Indo-European root for "number, count" and, by extension, "recount, relate"). The purposes of explaining and telling were to lay out information in clear, unambiguous, straightforward ways. Other words that were co-opted and redefined included *informing* (i.e., helping learners with the formation of inner knowledge), *edifying* (i.e., helping learners to construct the edifice of knowledge), and *directing* or *direct instruction* (from the Latin for "straight", helping learners to set straight their understandings).[6]

Implicit in all these terms is a conception of teaching that is most concerned with logical, carefully planned movements through topics. This attitude is embodied in the phenomenon of the linear lesson plan, a structure that is developed more around a topic than around a group of learners. (Indeed in my home university, preservice teachers are commonly required to plan lessons and units in absence of any connection to any particular group of learners. Apparently, *what* is taught is thought to be independent of *who* is taught.) This attachment of teachers to a specific subject matter, and the consequent detachment of teachers from learners, is the hallmark of a rationalist model of teaching. It is also the reason behind the co-opting and redefining of such religion-rooted terms as *professor* and *lecturer* to refer to the teacher.

As for the subject matters that came to be represented in the curricula of the modern school, the most significant influence turned out to be tradition. From the ancient Greeks, rationalists inherited the belief that to be truly free in life one must develop the abilities to uncover faulty assumptions and expose flawed arguments. This particular educational emphasis traces back to the ancient Greek notion of the examined life—or, more famously, to Socrates' assertion that "the unexamined life is not worth living".[7] Socrates argued that we must engage in an unremitting assault on our own ignorance. Through the lineage of his students, which included Plato and Aristotle, a curriculum of liberal arts was gradually defined and put into place. (*Liberal arts* means, literally, "arts that are liberating".) From the beginning, the emphasis was on fine arts, literature, and mathematical topics. By medieval times, the liberal arts had evolved into two clusters: the quadrivium of geometry, astronomy, arithmetic, and music; and the trivium of grammar, logic, and rhetoric.

Significantly, all of these topics were drawn from the gnosis category of knowledge. These—the arts—were the domains that the ancient Greeks felt demanded the interventions of teachers. The more practical, everyday know-how issues that constituted episteme were not considered appropriate for formal schooling. Everyday know-how, it was assumed, would be developed as necessary by engaging in the world. No special or formal instruction was required.

That attitude prevailed in the schools for the wealthy and well-positioned, but not for everyone. During the first stages of the Scientific and Industrial Revolutions, with the prospect of mass education, there were extensive debates over the wisdom of allowing working-class children to learn to read or do any mathematics beyond simple arithmetic.[8] (The wealthier classes had vested interests in ensuring that the lower classes continued to live unexamined lives—a situation that continues in various guises today.[9]) As a result, in curricula that were intended for working-class children, a key consideration was practicality—episteme. Topics had to be justified according to their utility in the work-a-day world. The tension between the liberal arts and practical skills continues, as evidenced in seemingly endless debates over basics, teaching for understanding, and so on. (I return to this issue in chaps. 12 and 13.)

Mathematics was well positioned within this tension. It was seen both as a core element of rationalist thought and a source of eminently practical knowledge. The subject was thus assigned a privileged core status in the curriculum of the modern school. With regard to the design of curriculum, mathematics leant itself to a highly systematic structure that began with basic, elementary competencies that were logically combined into more sophisticated concepts through the years of schooling. Soon all modern standardized curricula began to be patterned after the model of the geometric proof. Correspondingly, teaching strategies moved toward logical linear lesson plans as teachers abandoned practices of organizing learning tasks around practical or philosophical problems. Following the new model, the teacher and curriculum planner first determined the desired outcomes (i.e., what one sought achieve), then identified the foundations that would enable the eventual attainment of those outcomes, and finally laid out a sequence of incremental steps that led from start to end. The results were lessons and programs of study that, like prevailing beliefs about knowledge, were assumed to be independent of time and place and, hence, suitable for everyone, everywhere.

Perhaps the most extreme articulation of this particular attitude was the North American "New Math" of the 1960s. This movement was prompted in large part by a perceived scientific superiority of the Soviet Union—explicitly around their more advanced space program at the time, but implicitly around matters of military technologies. Politicians and scientists succeeded in laying blame for the slower pace of American technological progress at the feet of grade-school teachers. The principal response was the development of mathematics curricula that were focused on the "structure of the discipline".

Structure was understood in terms of a rigid and logical organization of ideas, much in keeping with Descartes' philosophy. School mathematics was reconceptualized strictly as a formal system of propositions, and programs of study were redesigned around key theorems and laws. Problem solving was de-emphasized and formal proofs were stressed. Alongside these redefinitions of curricula, efforts were made to teacher-proof the new programs of study by imposing texts and other resources that reduced teaching to the sequential presentation of prescribed lessons, administration of standardized tests, and so on.

For reasons discussed in subsequent chapters, the New Math movement failed. One of the main problems was the Cartesian assumption that personal learning is a linear and logical process. This same assumption underpins contemporary debates over the basics in education—or, rather, around the manner in which the basics should be taught. Popularly, hardly anyone seems to dispute notions that "the basics", as currently defined, are indeed fundamental to human knowledge—much less the appropriateness of basing the notion of basics on the model of the geometric proof. It is thus that we have found ourselves with sometimes anachronistic curricula. Through centuries of schooling, many notions and competencies that were indeed basic to life in a newly industrialized society some 300 or 400 years ago have become locked into current thinking as necessary knowledge—even if that knowledge is necessary only for success in school. Not without irony, school mathematics seems to be the best example. For instance, despite technologies that mean we will never have to perform long division outside of the classroom, the suggestion that the months spent on this skill could be given over to other topics is rarely entertained, let alone the dozens of other concepts jammed between the covers of contemporary textbooks. Further, despite that most of current mathematical knowledge has been developed in the past century, there are few topics in a contemporary mathematics curriculum that weren't already specified some 400 years ago.

Another important aspect of rationalist teaching is the continuous need to examine learners' understandings. This particular emphasis follows quite logically from the dichotomization of the learner's world and the real world. With this sort of assumption in place, it only makes sense that the teacher must engage in ongoing comparisons of subjective sense-making and objective knowledge. This particular emphasis has supported the rationalist tendencies toward teachers who are more attached to subject matters than to learners, examinations that are often constructed and administered by persons and agencies other than the actual teacher, and test results that follow individual learners but rarely inform teaching decisions.

In summary, for the past several centuries, most schooling practices and much of educational research have rested on rationalist assumptions about learning. The consequences of this focus are evident in the tremendous similarities among curriculum structures and teaching methods across tremendous diversities of subject matters, learners, and contexts.

WHERE TO NOW?

This chapter was concerned with the origins and conceptual implications of synonyms for teaching that are associated with rationalist philosophy—specifically, the terms *instructing, explaining, telling, informing, edifying, directing, lecturing,* and *professing.* In chapter 9, I undertake a similar discussion of terms associated with empiricist science. In chapter 9, I also go into more detail on the origins of some of the structures and practices that define the modern school, such as the graded organization and choices of subject matters.

9

Empiricism:

TEACHING AS TRAINING

Good and evil, reward and punishment, are the only motives to a rational creature: these are the spur and reins whereby all mankind are set on work, and guided, and therefore they are to be made use of to children too.

— John Locke[1]

There is an interesting parallel between the sorts of educational commitments and obsessions that arose in the traditions of gnosis and those that emerged in the traditions of episteme. In both cases, one of the major strands of thinking focused mainly on the individual and the other more on collective matters. Rationalists, like those oriented by mystical beliefs, tended to emphasize personal sense-making, whereas empiricists focused more on the generation of structures and principles that would render formal education a more mechanically efficient process.

Many of the social attitudes and cultural beliefs that contributed to the scientific and industrial revolutions, European imperialism, and the emergences of capitalism and urbanization also underpinned the development of the first modern public schools—as might be expected. It was this cluster of co-implicated events that made the modern school necessary in the 16th and 17th centuries. Although the phenomenon of "education for all" was still a few centuries to the future, suddenly there were needs for a modestly literate workforce, a means to keep children out of the labor market and off the streets, and a way to maintain stratification of social classes. Schools were a good response—and a relatively easy one. Administrative and curriculum structures had already been developed by religious institutions, which had in turn borrowed from ancient Greek models of education.

Hints of the characters of the first modern schools can be distilled from the emergence of a few new terms in 17th-century England. Near the start of that century, the word *school* was used for the first time, signaling the institutionalization of mass education. Departing from many of the practices and structures of its precursors, the modern school moved relatively quickly toward linearized curricula, stratification of learners by age, and simultaneous mass instruction. Indeed the word *schooling* quickly came to refer to scripted movement through topics and tests in a manner highly reminiscent of an industrial assembly line. Incomplete children were seen as progressing toward completed adults, able to fit into their appropriate social and corporate roles.

The task of the teacher within these structures, again paralleling life on the assembly line, came to be framed in terms that reflect the empiricist concern with control of processes and predictability of outcomes. A cogent illustration of this movement is the use of the word *tutelage* in the early 1600s. Derived from the Latin term for "watching over", the tutor was a supervisor overseeing the processes of schooling. Indeed, as Michel Foucault[2] details, the school building was constructed in a manner that would facilitate tutelage by placing the students under the watchful gaze of the teacher at all times. The emphasis on surveillance continues and is currently manifested in the rhetoric of classroom control, classroom management, and similar obsessions of beginning teachers.

Perhaps the most distinguishing characteristic of the modern school is the phenomenon of the classroom. The term *class* was borrowed by educators in the 17th century from the broader cultural reference to social stratifications that were based mainly on financial status, pedigree, and political positioning—qualities that were assumed at the time to be part of the natural order.[3] The principal means of grouping pupils into classes—or *grades*, or *ranks*—in the modern school were gender and age. (Classing by social class was unnecessary, because members of different classes attended different schools.) The shift toward classed groupings was coupled with shifts in teaching practices. These differences are illustrated by the two images below, both from the 17th century. The first, the 1662 "The School Master" by Adriaen Jansz van Ostade, shows the teacher among a group of learners of different ages who are engaged in a range of activities. In the second (artist unknown), students are all male, all the same age, all focused on the same topic, all doing the same thing, and all facing the same direction. The shift in positioning of the teacher is also significant—away from the center of the action to the edge of the room, where surveillance of everyone is made possible.[4]

In terms of the preferred method of teaching, another word that came into use at about the same time was *inculcation*. Derived from the Latin for "force upon" or "stamp in", this teaching emphasis focused on rote repetition of routinized processes. The emphasis was likely as much the product as the source of the standardized and linearized—that is, rationalist—curriculum structures that had begun to appear.

In terms of curriculum content, as developed in chapter 8, the modern school differed in two significant ways from the medieval academies after which the school was modeled. First, several new subjects were added to the core of the liberal arts. In particular, mathematics was reworked and given more prominence. There was also an increased emphasis on practical skills associated with the sciences. Second, all subject matters—including the fine arts—were parsed and linearized. Such parsing was prompted by the rationalist impulse to impose a logical order on all areas of knowledge—a practice that was spurred along in the 1800s with the statistics-based psychologistic construction of "normal development". With the emergence of developmental psychology, concepts and teaching methods began to be organized according to such notions as "developmental readiness" and "age appropriateness".

The idea that humans move along a steady and stable developmental trajectory from birth through adulthood is, as already mentioned, an ancient one that was originally associated with the mystical assumption that humans must engage in a continuous project of regaining a lost perfection. The notion of a predictable, measurable pattern of development presented a site for a newly scientized field of psychology to focus its attentions in its efforts to better understand the processes of education. In fact, by the beginning of the 20th century, the field of psychology had started to refer to itself as "the science of education".

Through positivistic, statistics-based constructs of normality and normal development (see chap. 7), during the late 1800s and early 1900s, the graded and ranking structures already in place in the modern school became even more rigid. Teaching came to be more and more oriented by the notion of the normal child—a construct that, of course, is immediately suggestive of all sorts of abnormality. Oriented by the assumption that individuals should not stray too far from average on any measure, educational research began to examine such newly invented categories as hypo- and hyperactivity, retarded and advanced intelligence, introversion and extroversion, and other forms of deviation. Schooling practices followed suit with programs to respond to new categories of "special needs". In these efforts, a new set of metaphors for teaching was borrowed from medicine. For learners with specific traits or abilities that were deemed to wander too far from the mean, teaching was understood in terms of *diagnosing* and *remediating*.

Closely related, another branch of thought that has had significant impacts on educational policies and practices is nativism. The word *nativism* is derived from the Latin *nasci*, "to be born", also the root of innate, nascent, and nature. Nativists assert that each brain has unique, inborn structures that do not change through experience—an idea that is little more than a modernized restatement of the mystico-religious belief that souls are pregiven and unchanging. As it turns out, recent neurological research has demonstrated that brains aren't fixed. They're actually tremendously plastic. The physical structure of the brain is always changing and is utterly dependent on experience.[5] Even so, assumptions about static brains are so deeply entrenched that an array of nativist discourses has captured the contemporary educational imagination. These include theories of personality types, learning styles, and multiple intelligences—all of which are anchored in grains of truth (e.g., certain differences among people have a lot to do with the structures of their brains), but all of which are fundamentally flawed in the assumptions of inflexible brains, specialized modules, and hard-wired cortical areas.[6]

As the constructs of normality and nativism came to be defined in greater detail, psychology-oriented educational researchers grew more and more confident on matters of *what* to teach and *when* to teach it. However, through the 1800s, empiricist methods were proving to be ineffective on issues of *how* to teach. A concerted effort to address this lack arose in the early 1900s in the form of the behaviorist movement in psychology.

Behaviorism, true to its empiricist origins and its positivist commitments, began with the premise that teachers and researchers should not be focusing on mental functions for the simple reason that thinking is unobservable and, hence, unmeasurable. The proper places to focus scientific attentions, it was argued, were behaviors, contexts, and other quantifiable variables. Delimited in this way, learning came to be defined in empiricist terms as changes in behavior that are due to changes in the environment. Teaching, concerned as it is with effecting such changes, was thus recast as a matter of *conditioning* or *training*—that is, of doing what must be done to increase the probability of a desired response to a set of conditions.[7]

The early champions of behaviorism, such as John B. Watson, Edward Thorndike, and B.F. Skinner, were more than assured that this approach to the study of learning was appropriate, as might be interpreted from Watson's confident claim:

> *Give me a dozen healthy infants, well-formed, and my own special world to bring them up in and I'll guarantee to take any one at random and train him to be any type of specialist I might select—doctor, lawyer, artist, merchant-chief, yes, even beggar-man and thief, regardless of his talents, penchants, tendencies, abilities, vocations, and race of his ancestors.*[8]

Of course the conditions specified by Watson (i.e., normal children and a "special world") render the claim an empty one, especially relative to schools where lone teachers must keep track of many actual children who are coping with the contingencies of the day-to-day world. Nevertheless, by the mid-1900s, behaviorism had become the dominant discourse in educational research, policy making, and curriculum development. Although the influence has waned, one still encounters insistences for clearly stated and measurable behavioral learning objectives, unambiguous learning outcomes, well-defined reward structures, and so on. In fact, in my home university, the sole course in the undergraduate education program devoted to theories of learning is almost entirely focused on behaviorist principles.

It's worth mentioning here that Watson's assertion is indicative of immense shifts in thought around matters of personal identity and one's place in the universe. In mystical and religious traditions, identity was seen to be pregiven, and one's role in life was either a matter of predestination (in the case of mysticism) or divine calling (in the case of religion). Within empiricist traditions, such notions are erased. One's personality and role in life were suddenly and completely understood as matters of one's experiences. A similar shift in thinking also occurred around the phenomenon of intuition. Rejecting suggestions of access to a transcendent domain of knowledge, empiricists redefined intuition in terms of skilled pattern recognition that was entirely rooted in experience, although not necessarily conscious experience. It was further argued that those events of intuition that cannot be explained in such terms were merely the result of coincidences that, by the laws of probability, might be expected to occur on occasion.[9]

Actually, the shift probably wasn't all that sudden. One early and prominent empiricist in England, John Locke (1632–1704), argued that all personal understanding is based in experience. In effect Locke ruled out the possibility of spiritual or divine knowledge (gnosis) by asserting that "No man's knowledge can go beyond his experience".[10] He is most famous for his description of a newborn as a *tabula rasa*,[11] Latin for "soft tablet", a blank slate ready to be inscribed and imprinted by encounters with the world. As is evident in the quote from Watson, this belief was incorporated into behaviorist psychology. Locke's emphasis on personal experience, a reflection of the prevailing empiricist sensibility, also underpins the contemporary prominence of "discovery learning"—a construct that only makes sense if the truth is imagined in metaphysical terms as something out there waiting to be uncovered.

Lest I've seemed to suggest that behaviorism has little or nothing to offer education, let me backtrack a little. Principles of behaviorism have been applied to great success in many situations, especially in cases that involve desires to overcome phobias and inhibitions. Behaviorism has also helped foreground some of the largely unconscious dimensions of human learning.

Much of what we know and do never passes through conscious-ness—and, hence, could never be subject to rational analysis. Yet our knowing and doing are clearly triggered and affected by unnoticed environmental circumstances. This realization was an important re-sponse to the rationalist insistence that individuals must consciously assemble an internal reality. As such, a major contribution of behav-iorism to discussions of teaching has been its acknowledgment of the roles of context and experience in learning. These themes have come to figure prominently in virtually all contemporary discussions of teaching and schooling, as is underscored and elaborated in sub-sequent chapters.

But behaviorism is less and less useful as learnings become more and more complex. Whereas the implicit cause–effect logic of be-haviorism is effective for, say, training children to sit still in uncom-fortable chairs for long periods, it is of limited use from making sense of children's early mastery of language, much less for making sense of the complex webs of association and meaning that arise as chil-dren begin to experiment with words and stories.

To get to such matters, researchers have found that they have to question some of the core assumptions of not just behaviorism, nor merely empiricism, but the metaphysical notions that underpinned the emergence of modern science.

WHERE TO NOW?

This chapter was concerned with the origins and conceptual implica-tions of synonyms for teaching that are associated with empiricist science—specifically, the terms *schooling, inculcating, conditioning, train-ing, diagnosing,* and *remediating.* This chapter ends both the discussion of teaching emphases that arise from the epistemological turn in Western thought and the discussion of educational attitudes that are rooted in metaphysics. In chapter 10, I move to accounts of the cos-mos that are rooted in the physical rather than the metaphysical.

10

The Physical:

INTERSUBJECTIVITY
V
INTEROBJECTIVITY

*Everyone knows that in 1859 Darwin demonstrated the oc-
currence of evolution with such overwhelming documentation
that it was soon almost universally accepted. What not everyone knows, however, is that on that occasion Darwin introduced a number of other scientific and philosophical concepts
that have been of far-reaching importance ever since. These
concepts, population thinking and selection, owing to their
total originality, had to overcome enormous resistance. One
might think that among the many hundreds of philosophers
who had developed ideas about change, beginning with the
Ionians, Plato and Aristotle, the scholastics, the philosophers
of the Enlightenment, Descartes, Locke, Hume, Leibniz,
Kant, and the numerous philosophers of the first half of the
nineteenth century, that there would have been at least one or
two to have seen the enormous heuristic power of that combination of variation and selection. But the answer is no. To a
modern, who sees the manifestations of variation and selection wherever he looks, this seems quite unbelievable, but it is
a historical fact.*

— Ernst Mayr[1]

As mentioned in chapter 2, Darwinian theory had already had a revolutionary impact on scientific inquiry a century ago.[2] The suggestions that physical forms are historical rather than pregiven and that the differences among them were natural elaborations of once-small variations rather than reflections of supernatural states prompted the realization that the project of accumulating a complete knowledge of the universe, once deemed possible, could never be achieved. The target was moving. Since Darwin's time, science has been steadily shifting away from efforts to name, classify, and measure things toward emphases that are more tentative, historically attentive, and theory-generating.

In contrast, in the social sciences at the turn of the 20th century, theorists and researchers were only starting to make sense of the significance of a new worldview in which matters of knowledge and identity were beginning to be construed in terms of contextual contingency and historical effect rather than the ideals and absolutes of metaphysics. Now, 100 years later, we can say that much was actually happening at the time in this regard. The late 19th and early 20th centuries saw the emergence of psychoanalysis, phenomenology, pragmatism, structuralism, and other academic movements that embraced the logic of evolution and would contribute to fundamental redefinitions of research in the social sciences and humanities. Even more recently, particularly over the last few decades, rapid developments in information technologies, the neurosciences, and other areas have contributed to provocative new ways of thinking about knowledge, learning, and teaching.

A survey of the discourses and fields that rose to prominence over the past century reveals an ever-growing gap between research oriented by empiricist (especially positivist) attitudes and research that is informed by more Darwinian sensibilities. The most extreme example of divergent opinions might be in the field of psychology, where positivistic behaviorism became influential at the same time that psychoanalytic theory was capturing the popular imagination. The former allowed itself to look only at objects that could be unambiguously measured; the latter was interested in the invisible and unmeasurable mesh of experience and interpretation of human subjects. Both claimed to be scientific, indicating that these two movements sprang from very different conceptions of what science was all about.

More appropriately, perhaps, the chasm that exists between such strands of inquiry as behaviorism and psychoanalysis arose in the recognition by major researchers in the late 1800s that the universe-as-machine metaphors that had been assumed within both rationalist and empiricist traditions didn't work. This point was made in various ways through the early 1900s. In particular, two main critiques of modern science arose, the first from outside of science and the second from inside.

From outside, many theorists based in the arts and humanities—including, in particular, philosophy, anthropology, and sociology—began to interrogate the assumptions that were implicit in modern science as it had been conceived by Descartes, Bacon, and their contemporaries. In effect, Darwin's theories were applied to the history of science, and it became clear that its truths were constantly evolving. In fact at times entire species of ideas[3] went extinct by competition from new, more robust species. Thomas Kuhn coined the phrase "paradigm shift"[4] to refer to these events of conceptual upheaval. The challenge to the assumption that rationalism and empiricism were about *creating* truth—rather than *discovering* truth—was so effective that analytic science came to be seen by many within certain areas of the arts and humanities as a hindrance to insight rather than a means to it.

Within science, a few thinkers offered a different sort of response to the fragmenting and reductionist emphases of empiricist science. This contribution revolves around the recognition that there are different categories of phenomenon—and that different interpretive tools are needed to make sense of each. In 1948, information scientist Warren Weaver described one way to distinguish among the objects of interest to science. He identified three general sorts of systems: simple, complicated, and complex.[5]

In Weaver's terms, *simple systems* tend to involve only a few interacting agents or variables. Examples include trajectories, orbits, and collisions—in effect, the sorts of events that were studied by Galileo, Descartes, Newton, and other Enlightenment thinkers. The laws and equations that they developed, in particular Newtonian mechanics, were applied so successfully that they continue to be used to examine, predict, and manipulate simple systems.

As Newton recognized, however, the tools used to study simple systems can give rise to intractable calculations when the number of interacting parts increases only slightly. For these *complicated systems*, science responded by taking up probabilistic models and statistical methods—which, as mentioned in chapter 7, actually began outside of the sciences. Significantly, the driving assumption of science didn't much change. The embrace of statistics represented more a resignation than a shift in thinking. Most scientists still felt that Newtonian mechanics described how the universe worked. The problem, it was believed, was that they lacked the abilities to measure and the power to compute the actions and interactions of parts when more than a few were involved.

Weaver noted that these two categories—simple systems and complicated systems—do not cover the full range of possibility. In both cases, the systems are mechanical. That is, they arise in the interactions of inert components. However, many systems and events emerge in the interactions of agents that are themselves dynamic and adaptive. Examples include microorganisms, cells, organs, animals, animal packs, cities, societies, species, and the biosphere. Such phenomena are not entirely predictable, because members of the same class of phenomenon have the capacity to respond differently to the same sorts of influences. Such is not the case for simple and complicated systems. Just as significantly, complex systems can learn new responses. This means that, unlike simple and complicated systems, complex systems embody their histories. The conditions under which they came to form are woven into and enacted through their physical structures. Analytic methods such as Newtonian mechanics and statistical regression are not useful for making sense of such phenomena. These methods were never intended for forms that can transform themselves. (In fact, and somewhat telling, the word *statistics* is related to *state*, *stasis*, and *static*. They are all derived from the Greek *stare*, "to stand", underscoring the point that statistics might be useful for generating a snapshot of a complex system, but not for tracing the dynamics of such a system.)

Although Weaver was speaking from within the sciences (and about the sciences), the point has relevance across academic domains. In fact the discourses mentioned a few pages ago—psychoanalysis, pragmatism, structuralism, and so on—might be characterized as efforts to make sense of certain complex phenomenon or sets of phenomena, such as personal identity, knowledge, or language. Well before Weaver offered his analysis, that is, many researchers of such phenomena had already rejected mathematical and statistical models and methods. This resistance to analytic methods was underscored by shifts in figurative devices—away from linear narratives, causal logic, and Euclidean images that are appropriate for simple and complicated events, and toward webs of signification, co-dependent arisings, and fractal forms that are better fitted to complex phenomena.[6]

Put differently, over the past 150 years, a topic of inquiry across discourses has been the way that phenomena emerge by their own accords. The accounts that have arisen are consistent with the ancient origins of the word *physical*—from the Greek *physis*, "growth, nature", a cognate of *phyein*, "to bring forth". (*Phyein* is also the root of the English infinitive, *to be*.) In this ancient sense, the discourses considered in chapters 10 through 16 are properly described as concerned with the physical—that is, with making sense of the ways in which forms and events are brought forth.

This chapter is an overview of the last half of the book. As such it touches on a wide range of topics, most of which are addressed in more detail in subsequent chapters.

INTERSUBJECTIVITY: HUMAN INTERPRETATION

There is an important distinction to be drawn between those movements that arose in the arts and humanities and those that arose in the sciences during the 20th century, one that might be interpreted as a sort of echo of a break between the social sciences and the natural sciences that occurred in the 1800s. Those movements that emerged within the social sciences, such as psychoanalysis and pragmatism, have tended to delimit their discussions to matters of immediate human concern. Prominent issues include personal identity, human learning, and cultural evolution—and a popular mantra across the movements has been that "all knowledge is socially constructed".

This idea that all knowledge is a matter of social interaction and accord—of intersubjectivity—is of course a response to the metaphysical assertion that "knowledge is out there". Given that this belief served as the original and originating assumption of scientific inquiry, the assertion that all knowledge is socially constructed has appeared in various guises over that last century as a critique of modern science. However, it is more appropriately understood as a critique of metaphysics, given that the scientific project has been redefining itself as much as any other area of cultural activity.

In some of the more extreme cases, the assertion that knowledge is strictly intersubjective has been articulated as a sort of biophobia—a refusal to entertain the suggestion that genetic inheritance or physical constitution play major roles in who we are, what we can do, and what we know.[7] Rejecting the nativist idea of inborn and unchanging potentialities, some social scientists began to argue that such cultural conditions as educational opportunities and social prejudices play the major parts in defining personal possibilities. A century ago, such a suggestion was radical.

The idea might be seen to arise in the meeting of humanist philosophy and evolutionary theory. As mentioned in chapter 7, humanism asserts that we are sufficient unto ourselves to make sense of our situations. The movement began in the Renaissance and was formalized into the prevailing academic attitude during the Enlightenment, especially as philosophy and science extended their interpretive reaches into the traditional realms of mysticism and religion. In the 1800s, with such contributions as Darwin's, humanism reached its zenith. It had found the sorts of interpretive and explanatory tools that rendered such abstract notions as deities or an ideal realm completely unnecessary.

The move away from the supernatural and the ideal as explanatory principles presented a major conceptual problem: What is knowledge if it is not an intuition, a reflection, or a glimpse into some eternal, transcendent realm? The humanist response was that concepts must be understood in terms of human products. For the humanist, knowledge does not descend from on high, it is not divined by mystical means, and it does not inhere in nature. It was deemed, as mentioned, a matter of collective agreement—and must thus be explained in terms of human relations.

The evolution of humanism away from its deistic roots was prompted in large part by the emergence of another philosophical movement—naturalism. Naturalism was a specific response to assumptions of a supernatural—literally, "above natural"—that are characteristic of every metaphysical system of thought. As a worldview, naturalism asserts that knowledge about both how things work (episteme) and meaning (gnosis) is best achieved through the sciences. Knowledge of humanity and humanity's place in nature is understood as the product of a collective effort to assemble a consistent worldview—one that enables social cooperation while it permits a certain level of prediction and control.

The correspondence between naturalism and 19th-century humanism is not coincidental. American pragmatism, Marxism, psychoanalysis, continental philosophy, and other departures from rationalist thought that began to appear at the end of the 1800s drew explicitly on humanist and naturalist sensibilities. Karl Marx, for instance, suggested that his conception of communism, "as fully developed naturalism, equals humanism, and as fully developed humanism equals naturalism; it is the genuine resolution of the conflict between man and nature and between man and man—the true resolution of the strife between existence and essence".[8] The resolution, for Marx, occurred in the newly developed idea that essence could be understood as a product of existence, not as the definer of existence.

Over the past century, humanistic naturalism (or naturalistic humanism) has come to dominate discussions of legal structures and educational systems. However, the rejection of the supernatural by 19th-century thinkers was not without its problems. In particular, it prompted serious questions around matters of morals, meanings, and values. If order and ultimate purpose are neither inherent in nature nor imposed by a creator, on what basis might humans define and justify codes of appropriate behavior? If humanity is the product of historical accident and evolutionary coincidence, how are we to construe meaning in existence? What are right and wrong? Is consciousness just a chemical reaction? Is free will an illusion? These and similar questions were the prompts for a number of ideological movements that appeared in the first half of the 20th century, including Marxism, anarchism, and existentialism.

This is one of the points where the image of a bifurcating tree is inadequate to map out the relationships and disjunctures of emergent interpretive systems. In terms of image, something more like an intricate web would be needed to even begin to illustrate the relationships among the obsessions that came to be represented in philosophy—but of course this sort of analysis exceeds my purposes for this text. What is important to my purposes, however, is the shift in wordview that gave rise to the strew of discourses at the turn of the 20th century. Of key relevance, the conceptual movement from theism to deism, begun in the Enlightenment, was completed in an explicit movement toward atheism in many areas of inquiry. Perhaps the most familiar instance of this shift is found in the work of Marx, who famously criticized religion as the "opiate of the masses"[8] and who boldly asserted that God is a human product, not the other way around. With the erasure of the transcendent realm, the assumptions of rationalism fell to the wayside. Truth was no longer seen to be out there, and logic was no longer embraced as the sole means to insight. Indeed leading thinkers undertook to highlight the profound illogic of humans and their institutions. Modes of thought other than deductive and inductive reason must be at work, it was argued.

Across these discussions, the word *interpretation* began to figure prominently. Derived from the Latin *inter-*, "between" or "among", and the Sanskrit *prath*, "to spread about", interpretation was used to point to the human tendency to construe coherences amid the spray of experiences that constitute existence. The main criterion for an interpretation is that it be adequate to enable the interpreter to cope with the immediate situation. It need not be objectively true or rationally defensible, merely subjectively adequate.

The attitude here is one of adequacy or *satisficing*, a term that combines *satisfying* and *sufficing*. The word was introduced by economist Herbert Simon in 1957 in a move to incorporate Darwinian thought into and to exorcise metaphysical belief from the social and human sciences. Just as Descartes is said to have prompted an "epistemological turn" in his insistence that only those things that can be logically argued can be considered true, 20th-century philosophers led by Martin Heidegger, Jean-Paul Sartre, Simone de Beauvoir, and Maurice Merleau-Ponty are said to have prompted an "interpretive turn" by which knowledge is framed in intersubjective terms.[10] Through this movement, discussions shifted more toward the ways that humans construe reality through means that include, but that exceed, rational argument. A particular focus is language. The roles of metaphor, metonymy, allegory, personification, and other analogical devices figure prominently in these examinations of language and language-effected realities. As well, intersubjectivist discourses give special attention to nonconscious cognitive processes, which were ignored in Cartesian analytic philosophy with its exclusive concerns with explicit and logical assertions. In fact one of the major conclusions of the last century of inquiry is that humans are consciously aware of only a tiny portion of their cogitations.[11]

These more recent academic foci serve to underscore the important point that intersubjectivist discourses are concerned with matters of immediate human interest and interactivity. The orienting principle here might be framed as a distinction between *the world* and *descriptions of the world*. For the intersubjectivist, only the latter can be legitimately studied—and for reasons that are similar to those used by Descartes to champion rational derivation: Human perception is fallible. The world we see is not the world as it is, but the world as we have learned to see it, oriented in large part by an inherited language with its already established obsessions and webs of association. The key shift wrought by intersubjectivists is the realization that habits of perception evolve, subject to changing social needs and cultural preoccupations. In other words, intersubjectivists argue for a shift in emphasis away from analytic philosophy's obsession with human subjectivity toward the examination of our collective hallucination about the nature of reality. Intersubjective phenomena are those that are experienced and interpreted similarly by many sensing agents—that is, those phenomena that are agreed (tacitly or explicitly) to be of shared relevance. Significantly, there is (usually) no denial of a physical reality. The point is simply that we pick and choose which aspects of that reality that matter the most to us. As Rorty concisely states the point: "The world is out there, but descriptions of the world are not".[12]

Once again, and as might be inferred from such statements, the major focus among intersubjectivitist discourses is language—a technology that not only connects one brain to another, but that can reach across great distances and through generations. Other prominent foci are the culturally privileged means to establish consensus or consonance among many subjects, such as analytic philosophy and science.

INTEROBJECTIVITY:
MORE-THAN-HUMAN PARTICIPATION

As the focus in the humanities through the 20th century shifted from subjectivity to intersubjectivity, within the sciences the emphasis has begun to move from the desire for objectivity to the phenomenon of interobjectivity. An important conclusion of both intersubjectivist and interobjectivist discourses is that there are no objective—that is, free-standing, eternal—truths. Phrased differently, there are no observerless observations or measurerless measurements. Any and every identification entails and implicates an identifier. In reflexive terms, acts of observing and measuring generate observers and measurers at the same time that they generate observations and measurements.

Current discussions of the nature of science have come to be oriented by a realization that this cultural project must be understood in terms of the complicity of the observer in knitting the fabric of relations through which observations are rendered sensible. Science (and all efforts at the generation of knowledge) is suggested to be not just a matter of intersubjective accord, but of interobjectivity—that is, of the mutually affective relationships between phenomena and knowledge of phenomena.

An important principle here is that descriptions of the universe are actually part of the universe—and, hence, the universe changes as descriptions of the universe change. It is for this reason that these attitudes toward the generation of knowledge are known as participatory epistemologies. Knowledge, in this frame, is understood to inhere in interactions—that is, to be embodied or enacted in the ever-unfolding choreography of action within the universe. In other words, knowledge isn't out there. What we know is acted out in what we do, and what we do contributes to the unfolding of the cosmos.

As is no doubt apparent from the last few paragraphs, the notion of interobjectivity is difficult to describe briefly. One of the reasons for this difficulty is that the idea of interobjectivity relies on a rejection of some of the most deeply engrained assumptions about the nature of the universe—like, for example, the separation of descriptions of phenomena from actual phenomena. More important, the point here is not that things change by virtue to how we describe them, but that our actions are altered by virtue of our descriptions. As our actions shift, the physical texture of the world is affected—a point that has been dramatically demonstrated over the past century. For example, the climates that we study today, the illnesses that are currently of greatest concern, and the social issues that occupy our imaginations are emergent and, in obvious ways, prompted by previous habits of observation, interpretation, and action.

In more conceptual terms, the notion of interobjectivity entails a shift in the figurative devices used to describe the universe. One of these is the space-as-container metaphor. Popularly, space is conceived in terms of a vast emptiness that preceded the universe and that is gradually being filled up by the objects of universe. An alterative—and the current tendency within physics and astronomy—is to think of space as a relational quality. So framed, space isn't something that exists on its own, but a sort of interobjectivity; it results from the relationships and interdependencies among things.[13] (This idea was originally proposed by Gottfried Wilhelm von Leibniz, 1646–1716, a contemporary and rival of Isaac Newton.)

Although the notion of interobjectivity has not captured the collective imagination, some aspects of the principle have been incorporated into public debate through a few discourses that have recently gained some popularity. In particular, ecology has established a significant foothold, spurred along by mounting evidence that that knowledge is not inert: There are consequences to the ways that we humans embody our construals of the world in our actions-in-the-world.

As a variety of participatory (interobjectivist) epistemology, ecological discourses share many of the assumptions of intersubjectivist discourses. This is particularly true around the issues of nonlogical modes of thought, nonconscious cognitive processes, and Darwinian dynamics. However, whereas intersubjectivist discourses tend to maintain a deeply entrenched separation of the human from the nonhuman—and sometimes the mental-interpretive from the physical-biological—these sorts of distinctions are rejected within most ecological discourses.

The word *ecology* is derived from the Greek *oikos*, "household", and usage of the term has evolved to encompass the webs of relationships in which we find ourselves and out of which our identities are established. Ecology is about interrelationships and interconnections. It involves an attunement to co-dependencies, mutual affect, and co-determinations. In brief, ecology is concerned with the fundamental intertwining of all things. To speak of the ecology of an entity or phenomenon is to speak of everything that influences it and everything that it influences.

Over the past several decades, there has been a tendency to use the terms *ecological* and *environmental* as if they were interchangeable, particularly within popular media. Their meanings are actually quite different. The word *environment* derives from the Old French *en-*, "to place inside", and *viron*, "circle". The term is thus rooted in a sense of separation and enclosure, not relationship and implication. Ecologists worry about webs of interconnections within particular systems, whereas environmentalists tend to be concerned with their surroundings, which points to a non-interobjective world view. As Wendell Berry explains, "once we see our place, our part of the world, as *surrounding* us, we have already made a profound distinction between it and ourselves".[14]

The emergence of ecological discourses within the physical sciences roughly paralleled the rise of intersubjectivist discourses in the humanities through the 20th century. Toward the close of that century, these two movements began to be more commonly entangled in one another, helped along in part by the emergence of the field of complexity science. Complexity science is oriented by the realization that some phenomena do not lend themselves to Newtonian or statistical analysis, as formally announced in Weaver's discussion of different sorts of systems (presented at the start of this chapter). Those phenomena that arise in the interactions of autonomous or semiautonomous agents, rather than in the interactions of inert objects, cannot be well understood in the terms of their parts or in terms of global averages. Indeed in the frame of positivist science, such phenomena are not comprehensible at all because they can defy prediction and efforts at control.

Technically speaking, complexity science is the study of adaptive, self-organizing systems. More colloquially, it is the study of life and living systems. Relative to the concerns of teaching, complexity science can be appropriately construed as the study of learning and learning systems. This is because a complex system is one that is capable of responding in novel ways to dynamic circumstances—circumstances that, by the way, are dynamic partly because of the actions of the learning system. The relationship between context and learning agent is not a matter of object and subject, but of interobjectivity.

Perhaps the most important contribution of complexity science to discussions of learning and teaching has been the notion of self-organization. Complexivists point out that, for reasons not yet fully understood, complex unities emerge spontaneously from the co-specifying activities of agents. There is no need for an orchestrator or creator for a complex collective. It is a bottom–up phenomenon that can give rise to new levels of order—for free. By way of familiar examples, the flocking of pigeons, an anthill, mob mentality, and fads and customs are all examples of self-organization—that is, of the cohering of autonomous agents into discernible unities that cannot be reduced to the actions of those agents.

In the context of social systems, the notion of self-organization was represented in the social sciences literature well before it appeared as a formal principle in complexity science, particularly around intersubjective matters of social action and cultural trends. The contributions of complexity science have been to extend the idea to *all* forms of adaptive systems, to situate humanity amid other systems, and to discern some of the qualities and characteristics that are common to all cases of emergence, extending at least from the level of organelles that cohere into cells to the level of species that are intertwined in the biosphere. With regard to education, this particular shift is of tremendous significance because it, in effect, suggests that the individual human is not the only locus of learning. In fact, complexity science compels an expansion of the notion of *learner* to encompass a range of nested bodies, including the social cliques and other clusters that arise in any student body, the classroom collective, the school, the community, and so on.

An implication of this extension of the notion of learner into both micro- and macrodirections is that we humans are nested in— shaping and shaped by—both cultural and biological systems. As will be developed in chapters 14 through 16, this attentiveness to the biological has tremendous consequences for what we imagine knowledge, learning, and teaching to be. For millennia, the biological bases of knowing have been ignored and even actively suppressed within Western discussions of knowledge and Western efforts to teach.

COMMON ROOTS, DIFFERENT BRANCHES

Interpretivist (intersubjectivitist) discourses and participatory (inter-objectivist) epistemologies both arise in the reluctance to explain things in terms of any sort of supernatural force, entity, or realm. These antimetaphysical tendencies are prompted and supported by both the spectacular failures and the tremendous successes of modern science. Analytic science comes up short in such domains as situating itself in the matrix of human activity and making sense of human collectivity, and such lapses contributed to the formulation of interpretivist discourses that are built around notions of intersubjectivity. At the same time, however, the prying gaze of science has illuminated some of the darkest mysteries, including its own contributions to shaping the forms that it studies. Such is the main prompt for participatory epistemologies that are structured around notions of interobjectivity.

Within these movements, one of the principal breaks with metaphysics has unfolded around understandings of perception. From Plato through Descartes, perception was seen as inaccurate and easily deceived, and this fallibility contributed to a preference of rational thought over empirical observation. Bacon also saw perception as fallible, but his response was to focus on replicable measurement as the starting place for systems of knowledge. Both attitudes presume a separation of subjective and objective, with rationalism seeking to tame the former and empiricism seeking to entrap the latter.

Both intersubjectivist and interobjectivist discourses recast perception as the locus of connection of agent to the world, not as the site of separation. For example, concepts such as motion-and-rest, inside-and-outside, and big-and-small are argued to be meaningful because they are rooted in physical, bodily experiences of encountering others, putting fingers and toys into our mouths, as so on.[15] In this frame, the body is not a biological prison that holds back the mind from direct access to pure knowledge. Rather, the perceiving body is the root of all meaning; it is the experiential source of the mind. (More important, however, the mind is not equated to the body. As is further developed in chaps. 11 and 14, within both intersubjectivist and interobjectivist discourses, the mind is seen as dependent on the interactivity of many bodies. Hence, mind and consciousness are understood as intersubjective and interobjective phenomena.)

Three of the most influential movements in the early development of this notion of the embodied mind—understood in contradistinction to the disembodied mind of metaphysics—were psychoanalysis, phenomenology, and pragmatism. From their beginnings, psychoanalytic, phenomenological, and pragmatist theories spanned both the physical and social sciences. In terms of the discourses that would follow, these theories helped frame notions of intersubjectivity and interobjectivity. Psychoanalysis, in particular, made some important contributions to both intersubjectivist and interobjectivist discourses. For example, Sigmund Freud's (1856–1939) thoughts on the unconscious have been echoed in almost every 20th-century academic movement. The suggestion that our conscious mind is more a passenger than a pilot was revolutionary, introduced as it was at a time when conscious thought was the principal and sometimes exclusive focus of philosophy and psychology. Freud helped foreground the roles of social habitus and nonconscious processes in the shaping of individual and collective characters. An important contribution of psychoanalysis to contemporary thought is its refusal to separate the individual's constitution of the world and the world's constitution of the individual. This move is hinged to a reframing of individual subjectivity. Freud rejected the radical individualism of modernism, arguing instead that human identities are transitory, fragmented, and interlocked. According to psychoanalysis, our experiences of subjectivity are actually manifestations of intersubjective processes.

On these counts, psychoanalysis was aligned with the Gestalt movement in psychology that arose at about the same time. Gestalt theorists asserted that psychological, physiological, and behavioral phenomena could not be reduced to one another or to other elements such as sensation or response. Such phenomena were "more than the sums of their parts", to invoke a popular Gestalt phrase. Reacting to behaviorist psychology, Gestalt theorists argued that perception is an abstract cognitive achievement, not a cause–effect reaction to physical stimuli. Despite considerable criticism of the premises and methods of psychoanalysis and Gestalt theory over the last century, their core assertions have received considerable popular and empirical support. In particular, a substantial body of evidence has been amassed around the influence of the unconscious, including the perhaps surprising result that humans may be aware of less that one millionth of the perceptual possibilities that impinge on their senses at any given moment.[16] Our actions in the world are largely oriented by events about which we could never be aware—a fact that prompts the assertion that learning is much more about discarding or ignoring possibilities than it is about accumulation.

Similar notions were developed within phenomenology, which was first articulated in the early 1900s by Edmund Husserl (1859–1938). He sought to study phenomena by turning toward "the things themselves"—a choice of vocabulary that has proved unfortunate. The phrase has prompted some critics to dismiss phenomenology as focused on essences and as radically dichotomous. "The things themselves" has been taken as a suggestion that things should be studied in isolation, an interpretation that is actually the opposite of the actual intention.

Husserl's use of "the things themselves" was in response to the still-pervasive metaphysical assumption of ideal forms—that is, the tendency to deflect attention from things themselves to imagined essences and ideal forms. Husserl sought to develop a means to study how it is that the world becomes evident to awareness, the ways things first come to be present for us through direct sensory experience. His phenomenological theory was thus about physical engagement with the world, about the complex intertwinings of concept and percept—about interobjectivity.

At the same time that phenomenology was emerging in Europe, pragmatist philosophy was emerging in North America. It too was greatly influenced by Darwinian thought—in fact, probably more so. Some of its principal authors, including Charles Sanders Peirce (1839–1914), William James (1842–1910), and John Dewey (1859–1952), made explicit use of evolutionary notions to describe knowledge and its production. Succinctly, for the pragmatist, truth is what works—a definition that is grounded in Darwin's notion of fitness and that foregrounds the roles of context and timing. During the late 1800s and early 1900s, when pragmatism was cohering as a formal philosophy, there was no shortage of examples to illustrate this suggestion. Most prominently, Darwin's *The Origin of Species* was toppling libraries of scientific treatises, and Einstein's theories of relativity were poking holes in Newton's seamless fabric of the universe.

The pragmatist movement is notable for its immediate and emphatic assertion that questions of collective knowledge cannot be dissociated from matters of morals, ethics, personal meaning, and cultural standards. No claim to truth was permitted to be construed as benign—simply because all truth was understood to exist in an intricate web of collective meaning. It is thus that truth, the world, and existence, to the pragmatist, are understood as sorts of collective hallucinations. They are contrivances in which we all participate and to which we all contribute.

There is a pronounced tendency to define both intersubjectivist and interobjectivist discourses in terms of what they are *not*. This tendency is evident in the recent popularity of the prefix *post-* —as in postmodernism, postformalism, postpositivism, and posteuclideanism. In almost every case of current usage, post- is used to flag a rejection of metaphysical assumption.[17] Postmodernists, for example, argue that modernism's hope for a unified and fully knowable universe has collapsed. Instead we live in a world of partial knowledge, local narratives, situated truths, and shifting selves. The postmodern world is endlessly contemporary, a constantly emerging hyperreality of cyberspace, Disneyland, Simwold, Barbie, and so on. Many of these cultural forms originated in the modernist project of carving up and modeling reality. However, the resulting simulations have given rise to a strange new reality in which there are no universal truths, no grand unifying themes—apart from a rejection of metaphysics.[18]

Unfortunately, *postmodernism* explicitly announces itself as a reaction to modernism—that is, to the privileging of rationalism and empiricism—and not to the metaphysical roots of modernism. The term has thus been taken up by some in an embrace of mystical and theistic attitudes that were rejected by modernists—a rejection that is maintained by most postmodernists. The term has also been treated as an object of scorn by many who cannot untether themselves from the conviction that analytic science provides us with truly objective knowledge. With this sort of diffusion, some have come to regard postmodernism as a sort of anything goes relativism.[17] In other words, although it flags some important 20th-century intellectual and artistic movements, the term *postmodernism* has been distorted and abused by both friend and foe. For that reason, I do not use the word in subsequent chapters even though it would be appropriate to do so, philosophically speaking.

As for the branching points of intersubjectivist and interobjectivist discourses, one important bifurcation is apparent around the academic disciplines that are most commonly associated with the two branches. Using divisions that are in place in today's universities, intersubjectivist discourses are most represented among the arts and humanities, whereas interobjectivist discourses are more commonly represented within the natural sciences. There are many exceptions, but the tendencies are pronounced. I personally find this point of considerable interest given the origins of contemporary disciplinary boundaries in ancient traditions. As developed in chapter 3, the arts and humanities are more associated with gnosis, the physical sciences with episteme. The distinction lingers.

Yet it lingers in a sort of inverted way. Gnosis points beyond the realm of human experience, whereas intersubjectivist discourses are usually delimited to the realm of social and cultural activity. By contrast, episteme was originally focused on mundane everyday know-how, whereas interobjectivist discourses are concerned with the grander weaves of existence. To reiterate, intersubjectivist discourses are, in the main, focused on the human—on language and other symbol systems, on culture, on personal identity, and so on. Their shared concern is the social construction of knowledge. For the most part, thought and language are seen as inseparable. Interobjectivist discourses tend to work from a much-expanded understanding of knowledge—one in which knowing is equated with being and thought is understood in terms of ongoing adaptations of dynamic circumstances. Here humanity is understood not just in terms of linguistic and cultural productions, but as biological-and-cultural forms that are nested in biological systems.

WHERE TO NOW?

This chapter was concerned with divergent conceptions of knowledge that arose with the Darwin-inspired break from metaphysics. It is intended as an introduction to two divergent discussions of the nature of knowledge—specifically, those in which knowledge is understood in intersubjective terms (chap. 11) and those in which knowledge is understood in interobjective terms (chap. 14).

11

Intersubjectivity:

STRUCTURALISM
V
POSTSTRUCTURALISM

[The] sociology of knowledge must first of all concern itself with what people "know" as "reality" in their everyday, non- or pre-theoretical lives. In other words, commonsense "knowledge" rather than "ideas" must be the central focus for the sociology of knowledge. It is precisely this "knowledge" that constitutes the fabric of meanings without which no society could exist.

— Peter L. Berger & Thomas Luckman[1]

Formal mathematics has been popularly regarded as the epitome of knowledge and truth at least since the time of the ancient Greeks. Pythagoras went so far as to assert that the universe was woven of number, and Descartes developed his own philosophy around the uninterrogated assumption that logically derived mathematical truths are objectively real and beyond question.

Yet beliefs about the objectivity of mathematics began to erode in the early 1800s. At that time, mathematical systems were developed that generated truths that were logi-

cally valid, had real-world applications, but flatly contradicted conclusions of already established systems. In particular, some new geometries were created by tinkering with the axioms laid down by
Euclid.[2]

The implications were devastating for metaphysics, in general,
and rationalism, in particular—because, if contradictory but valid conclusions could be generated, then clearly mathematical truths are not
etched into the universe. Far from the metaphysical ideal, mathematics began to be described in terms of tautologies—that is, self-refer-
ential systems in which the conclusions are the consequences of the
assumptions. It followed that the same must be true of rationalist
philosophy. In fact every area of academic inquiry at the time was
implicated. Even empiricist science began to be seen as a peculiarly
human project, particulary insofar as it relied on mathematics for its
models and analytic tools.

The crisis of course was not actually experienced by or among
mathematicians and scientists. Most proceeded more or less as they
always had, working from the assumption that they were uncovering
objective truths about a human-independent universe. Philosophers
and theorists of knowledge, however, were compelled to construe a
new basis for truth. The supernatural had been ruled out. Now mathematics had lost its status of ideal knowledge. What options were left
to account for the seeming unshakability of such claims as "2 + 2 =
4" and "the earth revolves around the sun"?

As mentioned in chapter 10, one notion that rose to prominence
by the end of the 1800s was that objectivity is really a matter of
intersubjectivity. One might say that the world that we perceive is a
sort of collective fantasy, held together mostly by language's tight
weave of shared assumptions. This conceptual move set the stage for
thinking about thinking during the 20th century. Questions about the
nature of knowledge came to be dominated by discussions of the
nature and effects of language. This shift was a major one. In the
traditions prompted by Descartes and Bacon, language was treated
uncritically as a sort of tagging system. As developed in chapter 10, it

was assumed that words were meaningful because they corresponded to objects in the world. By the 20th century, the prevailing attitude in academia was that language was something other than a collection of labels. In brief, and as elaborated in this chapter, language came to be understood in terms of interpretation rather than naming.

Two principal schools of intersubjectivist thought evolved over the past century: structuralisms and poststructuralisms. Both focus on language, and both look to the tacit and deferred as the source of meaning in any utterance. Structuralists developed the case that the meaningfulness of language derives from the interconnectedness of vocabulary. These discourses thus focused on the internal structures of languages, mathematics, and other symbolic systems. Poststructuralists embraced the structuralist premise, but focused elsewhere. They looked neither to what language was thought to name nor to the internal structures of language, but to that which remains unnamed and unspoken—to the background that must be ignored for an object or event to be made the figure of perception.

Before pressing on, I'll mention that in a preliminary draft of this book, I used the term *semiotics* to refer to (and, in fact, instead of) *intersubjectivist discourses*. The word is derived from the Greek *semeion*, "sign", and the field of semiotics is thus, not surprisingly, the study of symbols and signs. Semiotics as a discipline is characterized by radical breaks in opinion. Not only are structuralist and poststructuralist sensibilities represented, but a good portion of research conducted under the banner of semiotics is oriented by metaphysical assumption. For instance, a prominent area of study is the relationship between linguistic signs and their referents—either in the physical world or the ideal realm. The phrase "intersubjectivist discourses" is used to avoid confusions around the current range of meanings associated with semiotics.

STRUCTURALISM: THE FABRIC OF KNOWLEDGE

The term *structuralism* refers to a general movement that swept across and through most academic discourses in the early 1900s. It had its most profound influences in linguistics, mathematics, psychology, and sociology, largely through the contributions of Ferdinand de Saussure (1857–1913), Nicholas Bourbaki,[3] Jean Piaget (1896–1980), and Lev Vygotsky (1896–1934).

Although considered a 20th-century movement, some of the defining sensibilities of structuralism were actually articulated centuries earlier. In particular, Giambattista Vico (1668–1744) had made some important conceptual contributions. Born into the conceptual climate that had been defined by the likes of Descartes and Bacon, Vico denounced their philosophies. He felt that their emphases on mathematics and the physical sciences undermined the important contributions of other facets of human knowledge, including art, rhetoric, history, and language. Vico saw knowledge-making as entailing a certain level of uncertainty rather than in terms of inevitable progress toward certainty. As such he felt that rationalist and empiricist systems served to limit invention and stifle thinking.

Vico also offered dramatically different views of rationalist mathematics and empiricist science. Departing from the millennia-old belief that mathematics was objectively real, he saw mathematics as the product of human minds—as convictions that existed only in human brains. Science he saw in terms of interactions between the brain and the natural world. For him, scientific truth was not totally created in the mind, but through experimentation that bridged mental construct and physical constraint.

Vico is often described as a person who was centuries ahead of his time. Perhaps more than any of his contemporaries, he offered a radically new way to think about knowledge—one that came to be incorporated not only into structuralist sensibilities, but that was to figure into the emergences of existentialism, phenomenology, pragmatism, psychoanalysis, and other academic movements that unfolded more than 150 years after his death. Perhaps his most significant contribution is the suggestion that knowledge is created, not discovered—a notion that was to gain considerable impetus when coupled with the evolutionary dynamics described by Darwin more than a century later.

This point was dramatically demonstrated in Saussurian linguistics, Bourbaki mathematics, and Piagetian and Vygoskian cognitive theories. Each of these projects might be characterized as an effort to describe and assemble a closed system in which terms, propositions, and other constructs are rendered meaningful by virtue of their relationships to other terms and propositions. Meaningfulness and validity in such a system is not a matter of match with external referents, but of the system's internal coherence. For example, according to Saussure, a word is meaningful not because of any direct association with objects or events in the real world, but because of associations and dissociations with other words.[4] The same thing can be said of Bourbaki mathematics with regard to facts and theorems.[5] This project is aimed at the creation of a unified axiomatic formulation of all mathematics—one that shuns the uses of diagrams, examples, applications, or other references that are seen as external or superfluous to formal statements. The goal is the generation of a fully coherent, fully consistent set of propositions that don't need to correspond to anything but themselves.

Because the word *structure* is subject to diverse, even contradictory, interpretations, a few comments are in order on the meaning that was (and is) at work in these movements. In English, structure is a prominent term in discussions of both architecture and biology. When used in reference to buildings, there are senses of preplanning and step following, which are in turn caught up in a web of associations that includes such notions as foundations, platforms, scaffolds, basics, hierarchies, and so on. This sense of structure—which is much less prominent in French, the language in which structuralist theory was first developed—is not the one intended within structuralist discourses.

The one intended—that is, biological meaning of structure—is quite different. Heard in such phrases as "the structure of an organism" and "the structure of an ecosystem", the word points to the complex histories of organic forms. Structure in this sense is both caused and accidental, both familiar and unique, both complete and in process. This sense of structure is closer to the original meaning of the word, as suggested by its etymological links to *strew* and *construe*. Indeed when the word was first applied to architecture, it was at a time when most buildings were subject to continuous evolutions as parts were added, destroyed, or otherwise altered. The structure of a building was not understood in terms of original intent, but emergent product.

This more biological sense was woven through Saussure's understanding of language, which he framed in terms of a living, organic form composed of ever-evolving and intertwining parts. For him languages are the products of circular (recursive) interactions between two or more brains. Linguistic symbols were the go-betweens that allowed the minds to connect.

An example might be useful here. Consider the word *knows*. For this term to have meaning, it must first be set apart from phonemically similar words, such as *no's*, *nose*, *knolls*, *gnosis*, and *noise*. Its meaning is also dependent on its place within a matrix of synonyms and close associations, such as "understands", "is aware", "apprehends", and "gets it". The nexus of associations spreads out even further into such phrases as "knows the score", "knows in the biblical sense", "know-it-all", and "know-how"—phrases about confidentiality, sexual relations, self-assurance, and basic competence. A review of any of the terms or phrases listed will result in a similarly intricate web of association and difference—one might say there is a certain fractal-like scale independence that reaches out to encompass the entire language. Oriented by such analyses, Saussure described the emergence of meaning in terms of a "system of difference", by which he asserted that meaning arises in the contrasts and gaps among words, not in their references to external objects or events.

The biological sense of structure is also useful to interpret the way Piaget used the term to describe learning and the emergence of personal understandings. Piaget shared the structuralist assumption that knowledge arises within closed, self-referential systems. That is, just as Saussure saw language in terms of a self-contained set of cross-references, and just as Bourbaki mathematics aimed to restructure mathematics in such terms, Piaget saw such qualities as self-reference, self-containment, internal coherence, and no need for external correspondence as aspects of the individual's construed world.

On some of these counts, there are clear resonances of earlier sensibilities. For instance, on first hearing, Piaget may seem to be echoing Descartes and Locke in the assertions that one's knowledge is rooted in experience and that anything outside the domain of experience cannot be known. However, there are two big differences. Although both Piaget and Descartes saw the individual's thought as isolated from reality, Descartes focused on the achievement of unearthly metaphysical truths, and he saw formal logic as the means to get there. Piaget, by contrast, focused on individuals' sense-making, and he attended to learners' ongoing efforts to revise understandings of the world as they met up with novel circumstances. With regard to Locke, although Piaget shared the conviction that bodily experience is the basis of all knowing, he rejected Locke's assumption that truth is objective and fixed. Individual truth, for Piaget, was about fitness in the Darwinian sense, and he framed it in terms of adequate and evolving subjective construals. If a personal interpretation allowed the individual to maintain her or his coherence in a given situation, it would persist. If it threatened coherence, it had to be revised—or the person had to revise the situation. Put differently, Descartes' and Locke's theories of knowledge could be appropriately described in terms of architectural notions of structure, whereas Piaget's theory of knowing only makes sense through a more biological interpretation of the term.

Piaget's work has helped trigger a proliferation of what have come to be called *constructivist* discourses within the fields of psychology and education. Unfortunately, many of these discourses do not really reflect Piaget's work. The word *construction*, like its cognate *structure*, can be interpreted in different, conflicting ways. For instance, rationalists and empiricists alike can embrace the constructivist maxim that "individuals construct their own understandings". Although intended as a critique of Cartesian worldviews, the assertion doesn't seem far removed from his core premise that proper and valid knowledge must be logically assembled (read: constructed or structured, in the architectural sense) on foundations of certain truth. By contrast, in Piagetian terms, the phase is used as a rejection of the notions of objective validity and certainty. For this reason, a distinction is often drawn between *trivial constructivism* and *radical constructivism* in the research literature.[6] For the more Piagetian radical constructivist,[7] personal knowledge is framed in terms of ongoing adaptations that are conditioned—but never determined—by the knower's context. The determining influence is the knower's structure, which in Piaget's work was understood in terms of the learner's history of experience. To underscore this critical point, Piaget's (and radical constructivist) theory revolves around the assumption that the sense a person makes of an event is less a function of the qualities of the event and more about the complex history of the agent's linguistically effected, biologically enabled, and culturally framed structure.

An immediate implication of this sort of assertion is that there is no possibility of common or shared knowledge between knowers. Each person is compelled to construe the world in her or his own way, and so radical constructivists have tended to discuss collective knowledge in terms of compatible, rather than identical, interpretations. So framed, provided that nothing happens to rupture the illusion, we humans are quite content to move along as if our perceptions and understandings are identical to one another's when they might actually be knitted out of entirely different sets of experience.

It shouldn't be surprising that this interpretation is often criticized as being solipsistic—that is, of asserting that there is no world beyond the ones we construct in our minds. The criticism is a persistent, but an unfair one. Constructivists have repeatedly acknowledged that the individual is not free to construct the world in whatever way she or he pleases. Personal interpretations are subject to constraints of physical experience, the associations built into language, and so on. The point is not that the individual is free to construct any world, but that the individual is compelled to construe a reality that fits with the context or circumstance.

Other structuralist discourses have emerged that are concerned with precisely the sorts of phenomena that contructivists set aside as context or circumstance. These phenomena include language, disciplinary knowledge, and social habitus—and the associated discourses are known as *constructionisms*.[8] Whereas constructivisms tend to focus on subjective interpretation and relegate matters of objectivity to other discourses, constructionist discourses are generally concerned with the simultaneous and interdependent creations of subjectivity and objectivity. That is, the core concerns of constructionist discourses are more toward the manner in which the world is jointly construed and the manner in which the world constructs the individual—in contrast to the manner in which the individual construes a personal sense of the world.

At present the figure most commonly cited in discussions of constructionism is Lev S. Vygotsky, a contemporary of Piaget. It is not really correct to identify this perspective so strongly with Vygotsky, however. His writings only began to reach the English-speaking world in the early 1960s,[9] by which time discourses on the social construction of knowledge were already well-established. Most theories that are currently identified as constructionist are actually rooted in French structuralist and American pragmatist (discussed in the next section) philosophies. For the most part, Vygotsky's work was absorbed into an existing literature—evidenced by the fact that he never used the vocabulary of construction in his own writings. In fact the core notion of Vygotsky's work was shared labor, not biological structure. The principle is drawn from the work of Karl Marx, and its centrality in Vygotsky's writings reflects the Soviet context of his work.

One of Vygotsky's particular interests—and a main reason for his current popularity among those interested in questions of learning and knowing—was the process by which individuals come to interiorize the world into which they are born. Departing from the assumption that learning is about taking things in, he felt that one came to a coherent personal understanding of the world by mimicking, parroting, rehearsing, and otherwise acting out observed social roles. In particular, he attended to the contributions of parents and teachers in nudging learners to more sophisticated understandings of their worlds. These foci also prompted his attentions toward, for example, the ways that language and other cultural tools work to delimit interpretive possibilities, enable conceptual reach, and contribute to a social corpus that is united in its common sense.

Over the past few decades, many, many pages in many, many research journals have been given to comparisons of Piaget's and Vygotsky's theories. For the most part, this literature has been devoted to some sort of effort to reconcile the two bodies of work—a move that is prompted and frustrated by the fact that they were interested in different phenomena. Piaget studied the continuous processes by which learners incorporated new experiences into their expectations of the world. Vygotsky studied the incorporation of the individual into the body politic. Different processes are at work, and different concerns emerge at these two different levels of activity. In point of fact, both theories were directly influenced by structuralist philosophy, and both are developed around such core structuralist principles as internal coherence, self-reference, and ongoing adaptive evolution.

Almost all constructionist discourses, including those based in Piaget's and Vygotsky's theories, share one more element—namely, use of body-based metaphors to describe their particular interests. Examples include a body of knowledge, a social corpus, the body politic, and a student body. This similarity, of course, also foregrounds some significant divergences among constructionist theories because the bodies studied vary considerably in structure and form. Of particular relevance to this discussion are those theories that are concerned with the social construction of systems of knowledge like science and mathematics. Some prominent theorists on these topics include Karl Popper (1902–1994), Thomas Kuhn (1922–1996), and Imre Lakatos (1922–1974), who studied the evolutions of different areas of academic inquiry along with the mechanisms of proving and disproving that serve as the impetus for such evolutions.[10] As with the case of Piaget and Vygotsky, the differences among these theorists and their departures from other structuralist discourses have been topics of considerable discussion. Unfortunately, commentators have tended to focus on obvious but somewhat superficial points of departure, thereby ignoring the increasingly transparent, but nonetheless revolutionary points of agreement.

On this issue, it's safe to say that by the end of the 20th century, structuralist discourses had become so transparent and commonsensical that they dominated academic discussions of knowledge, learning, and teaching. Yet other discourses—historically related, but conceptually divergent—had also risen to prominence. These poststructuralist discourses sometimes support and sometimes challenge structuralist sensibilities.

POSTSTRUCTURALISM: THE LINING OF KNOWLEDGE

I'll begin this section by defining *discourse*—a word that I've already used several dozen times in this text without any explicit references to my intended meaning.

Poststructuralists are critical of this sort of unqualified usage of key terminology. They follow the structuralist argument that terms are rendered meaningful through systems of difference and differentiation, not through unambiguous reference to something real or ideal. However, poststructuralists tend to concern themselves more with the power structures at work—deliberate and accidental, explicit and tacit—within these systems of difference.

One might say that the focus is not so much the weave of a garment of knowledge, but its lining—the usually invisible structures that give it its shape. Discourse is one of the terms used to flag this focus.

Discourse refers to the intertwining structures—linguistic, social, and so on—that frame a social or cultural group's preferred habits of interpretation. A discourse organizes and constrains what can be said, thought, and done. The emphasis here is on language, but poststructuralist discourses are also attentive to the activities and traditions that are prompted and supported by specific vocabularies and patterns of language use. Each discourse has its own distinctive set of rules and procedures—mostly tacit—that govern the production of what is to count as meaningful or senseless, true or false, normal or abnormal.

Discourses always function in relation or opposition to one another, as illustrated by the many discourses (i.e., all the *-isms*) addressed in this text. Those discourses that might be labeled as *poststructuralist* have the particular quality of being discourses about discourses. For example, they are attentive to the theoretical commitments and personal and social implications of their own and other discourse systems.

Unlike most other discourses that use the prefix *post-* in their titles, the post- of poststructuralism is not meant to signal a rejection of structuralist sensibilities, but an elaboration. Saussure actually set the stage for the emergence of poststructuralist discourses by arguing that language must be understood as a set of relations rather than in terms of discrete word units. Poststructuralists have extended Saussure's emphasis on structural analyses of languages, asserting that these structures must not be considered in decontextualized or dehistoricized terms. Poststructuralists argue that it is immersion in culture that defines our modes of consciousness. For instance, Michel Foucault (1926–1984) sought to demonstrate how systems of meaning are inextricably entangled with the cultural beliefs around sexuality, sanity, and social order.[11]

Perhaps the most prominent site of poststructuralist work is the field of literary criticism. Oriented by Saussure's work, literary structuralists in the mid-1900s began to reject the early 20th-century assumption that the author's intended message somehow resided in the text. For structuralists, a text's meaning surpassed the author's deliberate intentions. Meaning was recast as something that always exceeds the author—as a structural phenomenon caught up in metaphors, archetypes, and tropes that give shape and context to a piece of writing.[12] This point has been elaborated in the poststructuralist assertion that meaning emerges more from what is deferred than from what is made present. Perhaps the most familiar articulation of this notion is Jacques Derrida's (1930–) neologism *différance*, which he used both to nod at Saussure's notion of systems of difference and to point to how these systems depend on absence or deferral.[13]

Derrida argues that *différance*—that is, difference plus deferral—is always and already present in every event of meaning-making. It is thus that a central project of poststructuralist literary critics is deconstruction—an interpretive practice used to study the usually-not-noticed aspects of language, images, and practices and that is intended to support new understandings of how meaning is always enabled and constrained by one's ability to perceive (or not perceive) such aspects. Deconstruction is always an elaborative process, and it should not be confused with the analytic and reductionist emphases of rationalism and empiricism.

Such efforts to show how absences, slips, misalignments, and other deferrals contribute to the productions and evolutions of meaning are common within poststructuralist discourses. In general, they are also tied to examinations of *power*—a term that is actually a translation of the French words *pouvoir* and *puissance*. The principal meanings of these words have to do with "ability", "wherewithal", "means", and "capacity to act". However, they can also be used to refer to "force" and "strength", and the specific connotation varies across poststructuctural discourses. By way of illustratration, a rough—but not at all reliable—distinction might be drawn between *cultural studies* and *critical theory*, two currently popular movements within poststructuralist thought. *Cultural studies* is a title applied to various cross-disciplinary efforts to interpret texts, events, and other cultural phenomena. As a field, it is largely oriented by the notion that popular media and everyday events offer rich sites for making sense of what we believe and why we believe it. Within cultural studies, usages of the word *power* tend more toward "capacity to act". Critical theory is an older movement that is actually rooted in studies of textual interpretation in the 1800s.[14] In contrast to cultural studies, within critical theory references to power tend more toward the dominance-seeking, force-based senses of the word. Once again, however, this distinction is hardly a clear or fully consistent one. In fact in some discourses, cultural studies and critical theory are treated as synonyms.

In more general terms, power might be described in terms of influence on prevailing conceptions of natural and normal—and of course on what is unnatural and abnormal. For instance, until the last half century, *normal* within medical science almost always meant "adult white male"—often giving rise to procedures and interventions that were inappropriate for the majority of people outside this category. Another example is the notion of "normal family". In popular political rhetoric, the normal family consists of a middle-class married couple, usually White, with two to three of their own children—despite that this particular arrangement is a historic anomaly that is not at all representative of the current diversity of familial structures. A further example, currently at work in North American discussions of schooling, is a formal definition of *normal* that is based in statistical methods. As developed in chapter 7, normal achievement, normal ability, normal development, and so on are all articulated in terms of calculated averages. Those who deviate from those averages are formally defined as *abnormal*.

Such examples point to an array of influences that are at work within discourses, including religious convictions, scientific assumption, media portrayals, and political rhetoric. For instance, these and more subtle influences are manifest in the convictions that women are naturally more nurturing and caring than men, that homosexuality is unnatural, that public nudity is wrong, that adolescents should be barred from drinking and voting, and that public schools are benevolent institutions. These sorts of beliefs float on the surface of hegemonic discourses—that is, discourses that, at the moment, have the greatest influence on the collective imagination.

The fact that hegemonic discourses operate to define what is natural and normal means that poststructuralist discourses can never become dominant discourses. By definition, poststructuralist discourses must be attentive to and suspicious of the discourses that give shape to commonsense—and, hence, can never be commonsensical. Rather, they must be attentive to what has slipped into transparency, what is taken for granted, and what is embodied and enacted. In a phrase, poststructuralist discourses are concerned with what is deferred or ignored in any claim to truth. Poststructuralist commentaries are about the partialities of knowledge, where *partial* is intended in the dual senses of "biased" and "incomplete" and *knowledge* is understood to encompass both the explicit and the tacit.

COMMON ROOTS, DIFFERENT BRANCHES

Structuralist and poststructuralist discourses should be read as complements. Their departures from one another tend to be around matters of emphasis, not conceptual commitment.

For instance, across both sets of discourses, formal logic is seen as an important tool in the generation of new ideas and the validation of old ones. Logic, however, is not seen as the sole or even the principal means to these ends. In fact logic is not even seen as a self-contained or discrete mode of thought. Rather, like all modes of sense-making, logic is understood to be co-dependent with other interpretive devices, like narrative and analogy. Metaphor—the process of mapping one category of experiences onto another—figures particularly prominently across these discourses. Some have gone so far as to argue that humanity's most sophisticated conceptual achievements are matters of elaborations of metaphors that are anchored in such primary bodily experiences as walking, climbing, and eating.[15]

Of course we are rarely aware of the bodily experiences and linguistic structures that support our abstract understandings, which is precisely the point made by structuralist and poststructuralist discourses. Meaning is argued to arise not in what is made present and explicit, but in what is absent and tacit. Meaning and truth are not so much about the correspondences between references and referents, but the coherences in the forgotten and the no-longer-noticed.

WHERE TO NOW?

This chapter dealt with discourses on knowledge that are principally concerned with the nature and role of language. These discourses began to emerge in the late 1800s. Although they have not yet captured the popular imagination, they now either dominate or are profoundly influential within many areas of academic inquiry across the arts and humanities.

Their influences in the physical sciences are decidedly less pronounced, although movements have arisen there that share some key conceptual commitments. The key break between contemporary discourses within the humanities and discourses within the sciences is around the centrality of language (see chap. 14).

In chapters 12 and 13, I examine the conceptions of learning and some of the models of teaching that have arisen, respectively, in structuralist and poststructuralist discourses.

Structuralism:

TEACHING AS FACILITATING

> *Education is not something which a teacher does, but ... a
> natural process which develops spontaneously in the human
> being. It is not acquired by listening to words, but in virtue of
> experiences in which the child acts on the environment. The
> teacher's task is not to talk, but to prepare and arrange a
> series of motives for cultural activity in a special environment
> made for the child.*
>
> — Maria Montessori[1]

Perhaps the most important conceptual break between 20th-century
discussions of knowledge and previous sensibilities has to do with
the matter of explicitness. In mystical, religious, rationalist, and empiricist traditions, to know something was to be able to bring it to
conscious awareness. These traditions differed according to their beliefs about the sources of knowledge, but they all agreed that knowledge, to be knowledge, had to be explicit.

Structuralist discourses, supported by phenomenology, psychoanalysis, and pragmatism, suggested something different: that formal, explicit propositional knowledge arises from a vast sea
of informal, tacit, embodied experience. Personal knowing
and collective knowledge are mostly nonconscious—a sus-

picion that has been substantiated by a century of research in the cognitive sciences. Explicit knowledge is the mere surface of a knotted tangle of experience and interpretation.

Another important conceptual break of structuralist theory was the use of evolutionary principles to describe the emergence of understanding. Having rejected the idea that learning is a matter of receiving or acquiring knowledge, theorists suggested that learning is a matter of modifying the knowledge that we already have. Such modifications occur when we uncover inadequacies that we hadn't previously noticed. So understood, learning is an ongoing, recursive, elaborative process, not an accumulative one. Learners are not incomplete beings, but cognitive agents whose universes are always and already seamless even if they are never fixed or finished.

Such conceptual developments began to have a recognizable influence on educational research in the 1960s, arriving under the banners of *constructivism* and *constructionism* (rather than structuralism). With references in the literature following steady exponential increases for the past 30 years,[2] these frameworks are currently predominant in many branches of educational research.

This being the case, it is important to underscore a point mentioned in chapter 11: The principal metaphors of structuralist discourses *do not* have to do with buildings or architecture. (These sorts of images, however, do figure prominently in rationalist and empiricist discussions of knowledge and learning. See chaps. 7, 8, and 9.) Rather, owing to their shared structuralist heritage, the main metaphors of constructivist and constructionist discourses have to do with the biological sense of structure. This more organic attitude prompts attentions to historical effect, evolutionary fitness, gradual unfolding, continuous coping, and internal coherence. These qualities are seen to inhere in a range of phenomena, including personal understandings, social collectivity, and bodies of knowledge. Respectively, among educational researchers, these topics have come to be associated with the discourses of radical constructivism, activity theory, and constructionism (or social constructivism).

For the most part, it is problematic to identify one person or another as a principal author of any of these theories. For instance, Giambattisto Vico (1668–1744), Jean-Jacques Rousseau (1712–1778), John Dewey (1859–1952), and Jean Piaget (1896–1980) are all commonly cited as progenitors of radical constructivism, but they didn't refer to themselves as constructivists in their own writings. Piaget came the closest, making frequent written references to structuralism, structures, and constructions, all oriented and informed by his background in biology.[3] His genetic epistemology is by far the most influential theory in current discussions of constructivism.

As developed in the previous chapter, constructivists describe individual cognition in terms of closed (but dynamic) systems of intertwining understandings that are meaningful by virtue of their relationships to each other, not because of any sort of match to the world beyond the knower. Constructivists reject mentalist and cognitivist models of personal knowledge that are based on metaphysical assumptions. Instead of describing knowledge in terms of internal models of the external world, constructivists speak more in terms of potentials to action.

This point is pivotal. For constructivists, bodily action is not evidence of understanding—it *is* understanding. It is this particular notion that most presses attentions to the wealth of tacit knowing that is enacted in every moment of our existences, but of which, most of the time, we are unaware.

I've found in my own teaching that a useful way to underscore some of the major principles of constructivism is to point to the successes and failures of research in artificial intelligence (AI). Since its origins in the 1950s, AI has been prone to overoptimistic, even grandiose forecasts. From the start, it was confidently predicted that electronic minds would soon surpass flesh-based intellects. Progress, however, has fallen spectacularly short of these projections. The reasons for this failure are informative, as they foreground some important aspects of commonsense beliefs around knowledge, learning, and teaching.

Early on AI researchers had great success in programming computers to outperform people on logical tasks—that is, on the sorts of tasks that the programmers personally found difficult. Based on that success, it seemed only reasonable to expect that computers would soon be able to speak, recognize faces, and assist in moral and political decision making. The dominant belief was that developments of such competencies were matters of accumulating immense databases of information and building powerful processors.

In fact such predictions were rooted in the rationalist assumption that thought was logical and the metaphysical assumption that knowledge is objectively real and out there, independent of knowers. As it turns out, language use, moving through the world, moral judgment, and other everyday competencies that humans master in the first few years of life are not much rooted in logic, nor do they require an immense store of inner knowledge. Quite the contrary, humans have been shown to rely much more on analogical modes of interpretation, such as metaphor, than on logic. Further, it also appears that humans "store" very little information about the world in their memories. Far from building an inner world, most of the information that we need to survive is left out in the world.

More recently, some AI researchers have abandoned rationalist assumptions in favor of more constructivist notions—specifically, using associative rather than strictly logical processes, and equipping machines to explore the world rather than trying to program the world into them. Although still a long way from the creation of electronic geniuses, these researchers have begun to manufacture computers that are capable of innovative responses to unexpected conditions—even though they generally have limited databases and relatively weak processors.[4]

The point here is that, behind the surface of such everyday competencies as being able to formulate a new sentence or survive a shopping trip, there is a body of personal knowledge that has become transparent. We know more than we know we know. Constructivists are interested in the sources and dynamics of this knowing, as well as the manner in which it is interwoven and elaborated into more abstract understandings. On these counts, constructivists assert that all formal, explicit knowledge is abstracted from physical, bodily sensations that occur as one moves through the world—touching, being touched, hearing, being heard, and so on. Each and every action contributes to knowing, and each and every knowing orients action. Action, then, is more than a means to gather information about the world (as empiricists saw it). More profoundly, action begets self-knowledge. Our actions tell us about the edges of who we are, the reach of our influences, the things that we are not. In more direct terms, cognition is not trapped in the brain. For constructivists, the entire body is a cognitive system.[5]

It almost goes without saying that learning, to the constructivist, is a complex, uncontrollable phenomenon because it arises not just in experience, but in biologically enabled, culturally conditioned, and socially situated experience. Educationally speaking, an upshot is that teaching cannot be construed as causing or compelling learners to learn specific things in specific ways. Although learning is understood to be dependent on teaching, it is not seen to be determined by teaching. For the most part, then, within constructivist discussions, teaching is construed in terms of *facilitating* (from the Latin for "making easy"), *guiding* (in the sense of "prompting" or "steering"), or *enabling*. In fact some of the most prominent constructivist theorists tend to be quite reticent when it comes to matters of teaching, arguing that constructivism is a theory of personal sense-making that can at best tell teachers what they can't do, not what they can or should do.[6] For these theorists, teaching tends to be conceived in terms of chains of perturbation and construal in which the teacher attempts to prompt the learner toward a particular interpretation, then attempts to interpret the learner's actual interpretations to decide on the next prompt, and so on.

One of the most significant influences on such attitudes toward teaching is Rousseau's 1762 treatise, *Émile*, in which he translated his romanticist philosophy into several principles of what he called "natural education". Romanticism was an 18th-century reaction to the constraints of rationalist and empiricist thought. The movement might be described as an effort to reclaim gnosis because it emphasized matters of meaning over matters of epistemic fact. Romanticism was characterized by a heightened interest in the natural and by emphases on the individual's emotions and imagination. Rousseau argued that children were cognitively different from adults, that they were naturally good, that humans progressed through different stages of development, that individuals make sense of the world in their own ways and must therefore be encouraged to draw their own conclusions, that mental activity is rooted in bodily activity, and that education must be tailored to each learner. In brief, for Rousseau, the goal of teaching was to arouse in the student a passion to learn.

All of these points are prominently represented in the current educational literature. Another frequently cited source for recommendations on teaching is John Dewey. He also argued that learners must be allowed to explore, and that a key aspect of teaching is well-timed interpretive assistance. Dewey, like Piaget, also argued for carefully designed learning tools that would help focus learners' attentions while they provided learners with relevant experiences—an idea that has come to underpin current emphases on manipulative materials in mathematics classrooms.

Such recommendations, however, can be of limited value to teachers who must work with many learners simultaneously—and usually for only brief periods. This problem with constructivist theories, of course, is to be expected. They are explicitly concerned only with individual cognitive processes, not with interpersonal dynamics. For this reason, many educators have looked to other branches of structuralist thought. Prominent among these are various subdiscourses that trace back to the work of Vygotsky, including situated learning[7] and activity theory.[8]

Vygotsky was more concerned with interpersonal processes and the role of cultural tools (including language and the structures used to organize the human world) in learning. For him learning was a process of habituating to social practices through participation in those practices, and he saw personal cognitive processes as a sort of reflection or internalization of collective or external processes. In fact Vygotsky argued that internalized thought is something that must be learned; it is not there early in life. A child's first symbolic performances, he argued, are completely public—acted out—even to and for themselves. These operations come to be internalized only slowly, from the outside to the inside, from culture to the individual.

Working in the communist Soviet Union, Vygotsky's work was framed by metaphors of shared labor that pointed more toward the processes of the collective corpus than to those of the biological body. A basic unit of analysis in his research—and in the educational theories rooted in his work—is human interactivity. Such interactivity is seen as purposeful, driven by particular needs, embedded in an established community of practice, and generally mediated by specific tools. From these emphases, it followed that teaching would be mainly a matter of *mediating* (from the Latin for "to be in the middle"), *mentoring, modeling,* and *initiating.* In some cases, teaching is described in terms of *orchestrating* the experiences of learning by organizing tasks and situations that might resemble those of, for example, professional writers, scientists, mathematicians, and so on.

Often such conceptions of teaching are associated with Jean Lave and Etienne Wenger's "situated learning", a constructionist discourse that is centrally concerned with the processes by which individuals come to know the customs and to develop the competencies that are particular to different professions and subcultures. Teaching is such circumstances is usually a not-very-deliberate process; the onus for learning is on the learner who is understood as a novice, an apprentice, an initiate, or a neophyte. The teacher, as might be expected, is the *expert* or *master.*

Note that the way *master* is used here is different from mystical and religious traditions. To reiterate earlier points, in Western mysticisms, learners are oriented toward mastery of themselves and their destinies. In Western religions, the responsibility for mastery is shifted to the teacher and the term is generally used to refer to the authority of the teacher over the learner. In the case of constructionist discourses, mastery is a description of the teacher's relationship to a craft or a subject matter and is synonymous with expertise. The goal is for learners to develop a similar mastery.

Lave and Wenger are careful to indicate that their theory "is not itself an educational form, much less a pedagogical strategy or teaching technique. It is an analytical viewpoint on learning, a way of understanding learning".[9] Even so, many educational researchers have bypassed such qualifications and have interpreted this description-oriented theory of learning as a prescription-generating theory of teaching.

As for specific educational recommendations, theories informed by Vygotsky's work have tended to advocate project-oriented and group-based classroom structures, especially ones that emulate the practices and norms within and around particular cultural activities. A science class, for instance, might be organized around a particular topic of interest—and students would be expected to imitate scientists by gathering relevant background information, making hypotheses, designing experiments, verifying results, and reporting conclusions. Within this example, the teacher would act as a representative of the scientific establishment who is initiating novice scientists into the practices of scientific inquiry. Hence, the educational aim is not to impart established knowledge, but to engage learners meaningfully in the application and possible extension of established knowledge. In brief the teaching is understood to be a process of *enculturating* learners to specific communities of practice.

As mentioned in chapter 11, there is a tendency in the current educational research literature to pit Piagetian and Vygotskian theories against one another—a tendency that operates in ignorance of the fact that these theories are concerned with two different categories of phenomena. Nevertheless, it is important to emphasize that

Vygotsky's work did help elaborate the discussions of learning and teaching that were first prompted by Piaget's research. For instance, Vygotsky offered a more expansive account of human consciousness. Whereas Piaget's work continued to be framed by the ancient assumption that all thought resides in the head of an insulated and isolated learner, Vygotsky contended that individual consciousness is actually dependent on social engagement and cultural tools, especially language. Consciousness, for Vygotsky, was not principally an individual phenomenon, but a reflection of collective human phenomena. As understood by Vygotsky, the relationship between a teacher and learner (or among any humans engaged in social interaction) is a sort of mind sharing. In effective pedagogy, there is a reciprocal dance in which the teacher regulates the learning processes of the student while the student tracks the intentions of the teacher. This choreography is fluid. Further, in contrast to the constructivism-rooted conception of teaching as a cycle of perturbations-and-interpretations, constructionists highlight that the teacher's actions are not always matters of conscious decision making. In fact they're not often matters of conscious decision making.[10]

Vygotsky's work prompts a suggestion that, in terms of the implications of structuralist theory for schooling, the major break with previous thinking is not so much on the matter of what learning is (although this issue is an immense one), but on the matter of what learners are. For structuralists, the individual is not a monad locked in a biological prison, but an emergent and evolving form entangled with other emergent and evolving forms. Learners are understood in much the same figurative terms as words and mathematical propositions—as autonomous aspects of grander unities that are rendered coherent by virtue of relationships with other aspects, not via innate forms or external referents.

In developing these notions, Vygotsky helped open discussions of knowledge, learning, and teaching to the sorts of concerns are announced by poststructural critics—including, for instance, the partialities that are implicit in any body of knowledge. Over the past several decades, such matters have been at the center of perhaps the most lively of recent discussions of teaching.

WHERE TO NOW?

This chapter was concerned with the origins and conceptual implications of synonyms for teaching that are associated with structuralist theory—specifically, the terms *facilitating, guiding, enabling, mediating, mentoring, modeling, initiating, orchestrating,* and *enculturating.* In chapter 13, I undertake a similar discussion of terms associated with poststructuralist theory.

Poststructuralism:

TEACHING AS EMPOWERING

> *There is no such thing as a neutral educational process. Education either functions as an instrument which is used to facilitate the integration of the younger generation into the logic of the present system and bring about conformity to it, or it becomes "the practice of freedom", the means by which men and women deal critically and creatively with reality and discover how to participate in the transformation of their world.*
>
> — Richard Shaull[1]

For both structuralists and poststructuralists, truths are matters of social accord. Yet whereas structuralist discourses tend to be more concerned with the mechanics of knowledge production, poststructuralist discourses are attentive to the implications and complications of those claims to truth that come to be taken as *the* truth. Poststructuralist discourses are not principally concerned with how individuals shape personal understandings of the world, but how understandings of the world are shaped for individuals—indeed how individuals' own identities are shaped.

Three prominent and intertwining themes of the poststructuralist literature are language, identity, and power, all of which are understood in terms of fluid, intersubjective phenomena. Significantly, the main interests of poststructural theorists in these regards are not with the obvious and explicit imbalances among individuals and groups, which are of course of concern, but the hidden and implicit structures that support imbalances, oppressions, and aggressions among humans.

These concerns are brought to bear on a range of issues. For example, one currently prominent topic has to do with the nature, social role, and the cultural consequences of Western science. The popularity of this theme is hinged to the fact that science has displaced religion as the arbiter of truth in the modern world. Rejecting the idea that science is progressing toward totalized knowledge, poststructuralist theorists argue that science "advances" only in the sense that it expands its own interpretive reach as successive generations of researchers elaborate, correct, reinterpret, or disprove the works of their predecessors. The movement is not forward or upward, but outward toward newly opened horizons of possibility.

As mentioned in chapter 10, Thomas Kuhn[2] used the word *paradigm* to refer the webs of belief and assumption that prompt researchers in a particular discipline to agree on the issues (but not necessarily the details around those issues) within that discipline. A paradigm might be described as the commonsense of an era or setting. It consists of entrenched habits of association that render some ideas sensible, others silly, and still others unthinkable. This tacit accord is understood to be in large part rooted on the prevailing language, which imposes on speakers already established sets of interpretations and associations. Hence, for knowledge to evolve, language must change. We must learn to speak differently—to invent new words or appropriate old words—to open new interpretive possibilities. In brief knowledge production is profoundly poetic.

Personal knowing, in this frame, is understood in the same terms as collective knowledge: embedded in, enabled by, and constrained through the social phenomenon of language; carried along by the momentum of centuries of history and tradition; mostly invisible to itself. To have an acceptable identity is to master the prevailing set of identifications—that is, to embody or enact culturally privileged habits of interpretation and preference. Those who cannot master these identifications are marginalized as odd or, in the extreme, banished as insane.

Every act of identification is primarily an act of ignorance—of carving out a focus of attention by discarding a multitude of interpretive possibilities. These sorts of ignorances and discardings—or, more specifically, their social and cultural consequences—are used to orient critical and liberatory discourses in education. These discourses are framed by different sorts of ideological commitments (e.g., Marxism, democratization), cultural movements (e.g., corporatism, globalization), social issues (e.g., racism, classism, sexism, and/or heterosexism), and educational structures (e.g., age appropriatism, linearized curricula, preset lesson plans). Among the most prominent themes in the critical education literature are condemnations of political oppressions, reactions to instances of biological essentialism, and interrogations of lingering metaphysical beliefs about the natures of knowledge and identity. Despite these variations in specific concern, the discourses share a tendency to be critical of the conventional school as an agent of enculturation caught up in the perpetuation of existing social orders. That is, far from the rhetoric of benevolence and opportunity typically used to describe schooling, formal education is argued to be wholly complicit in the maintenance of an economically stratified culture in which the middle-class, middle-aged, married, White, Christian male is the *normal* person.[3]

For the most part, critical theorists do not frame their conceptions of good teaching in strictly—or even primarily—political terms. Teaching is perhaps better described as an attitude that is oriented toward "making the familiar strange"[4]—and, in particular, of challenging what tends to be taken-for-granted as *normal*. In response to the extensive and uncritical uses of the word in today's culture of schooling, critical theorists have argued that phenomena such as normal intelligence and normal families are not pregiven qualities of the universe, but imposed interpretations. To underscore this point, theorists often replace the adjective *normal* with *normative* or *normalizing*. There is, for example, no normal child, merely a set of normative standards generated by various assumptions and measurements that are deployed to shape and organize the experiences of all learners. A critical education is thus concerned with the simultaneous tasks of uncovering normative structures and developing counternormative strategies.

Discourses of normality are closely related to and sometimes synonymous with discourses of power. A power structure is a means by which sensibilities are established and maintained. Power structures are both subtle and blatant, both covert and overt, both nonconscious and conscious, both accidental and deliberate. Male privilege, for instance, is asserted through a curriculum developed around the products of dead White males,[5] through a professorate that is mainly female in the early grades and increasingly male as one moves toward postsecondary institutions, through discourses and social practices that cast males as analytic and rational and females as intuitive and emotional, and so on. The hidden curriculum[6] of male privilege operates simultaneously on all levels, personal through cultural. The same is true of White, wealthy, heterosexual, and other current categories of privilege. Consequently, critical theorists argue, these sorts of issues compel responses on all levels, from the pedagogical through the political, simultaneously.

The main pedagogical strategy of those educators whose teaching and research are oriented by poststructuralist sensibilities is to turn language onto itself—to invite learners into critical examinations of the conventions that frame their experience and into similarly critical examinations of their own complicity in those conventions. Critical or liberatory educational movements began to rise to prominence during the 1960s in a climate of social upheaval and radical cultural change. In keeping with these movements, educational theorists began to argue that teaching did not need to operate in the service of the established social order. Rather, teaching could be *emancipating, liberating,* and *empowering*—a subversive activity.[7]

One of the most influential figures in the liberatory pedagogy movement was Brazilian Paulo Freire (1921–1997), who offered the term *conscientização*[8] to describe the process of engaging with others in critical dialogues about their situations. The version of critical pedagogy developed by Freire is much more than a matter prompting the oppressed to awarenesses of their oppressions. It is more a matter of the poststructuralist notion of deconstruction applied to the circumstances of one's existence. Freire argued that teachers and learners must transgress one another's boundaries—teachers must become learners, and learners must become teachers—in a shared and dialectical project of overturning old structures and inventing new ones that are more egalitarian. The contrast between structuralist and poststructuralist conceptions of teaching is perhaps most evident around this particular point. Within structuralist discourses, there is an acknowledgment that teaching is about enculturation; within poststructuralist discourses, there is an admonition to become conscious of and to work to affect the processes of enculturation. In such critical terms, teaching becomes a matter of *giving voice*[9] and *advocating*.

Another term that has been broadly embraced within the movement is *pedagogy*—a word that has had a conflicted status in its long history. Derived from the Greek words *pais*, "child", and *agogos*, "leader", a *paidagogos* was a slave who escorted children. When incorporated into Latin, the meaning of *paedagogus* was expanded to include general supervisory responsibilities. The meaning was broadened again with the Old French *pedagogue*, which is usually translated as "teacher of children".

In some European languages other than English, *pedagogy* is paired up with *didactics* to describe the role of the teacher. Neither word has a direct English translation. Didactics is roughly synonymous with instructional techniques or methods, but is also used to refer to the teacher's command of the subject matter knowledge, ability to interpret student responses, and other personal competencies. Its complement, pedagogy, is more a reference to the teacher's interpersonal competencies, and is thus used to refer to the moral and ethical—as opposed to the technical—aspects of the teacher's work with learners. It is this sense of responsibility to learners that prompted many critical education theorists to adopt the noun *pedagogy* and to drop such adjectives as *critical*, *emancipatory*, and *liberatory*.

There is an irony with critical education discourses. For the same reason that poststructuralist discourses can never be the dominant voices in academia, critical education attitudes can never prevail in schools. They are concerned with interrupting the status quo, with deconstructing the structures of dominance—always interrogating how we might limit or be limited, disenfranchise or be disenfranchised by habits of action and interpretation. Such habits are moving targets, and pedagogy that is critical must move with them. It can never fall into a naive belief that it has succeeded in its goals.

WHERE TO NOW?

This chapter was concerned with the origins and conceptual implications of synonyms for teaching that are associated with poststructuralist thought—specifically, the terms *emancipating*, *liberating*, *empowering*, *subverting*, *giving voice*, *advocating*, and *pedagogy*. It completes the branch of the discussion around interpretivist discourses—that is, those attitudes toward knowledge, learning, and teaching that are framed by the notion of intersubjectivity. In chapter 14, I turn to a discussion of participatory epistemologies—that is, those attitudes toward knowledge, learning, and teaching that are associated with the notion of interobjectivity.

14

Interobjectivity:

COMPLEXITY SCIENCE
V
ECOLOGY

Caught up in a mass of abstractions, our attention hypnotized by a host of human-made technologies that only reflect back ourselves, it is all too easy for us to forget our carnal inherence in a more-than-human matrix of sensations and sensibilities.

— David Abram[1]

The notion of interobjectivity is radically different from the notion of objectivity within empiricist science. Bacon, Newton, and their contemporaries were oriented in their work by the faith that a God's-eye view of the universe—that is, a detached and totalized knowledge—was not only imaginable, but ultimately accessible by humans.

The concept of interobjectivity is presented as a direct challenge to the metaphysician's desire for objective or observerless observations. Humberto Maturana makes the point in the concise statement that "Everything said is said by an observer".[2] An act of observation entails more than something that is observed; there must also be something observing. Further, observed and observer are not two forms separated by space. It's more the converse: The concept of space only becomes necessary when there are objects that are separated—that is, the notion of space is already suggestive of interobjectivity.

As indicated in earlier chapters, this departure from modernist thought can be traced to several influences over the past century or two. One major conceptual influence has been phenomenology, particularly the work of Maurice Merleau-Ponty (1908–1961). His principal interest was perception, which he understood as an interface between actor and acted-on. For him, a sensory perception was an instance of unification of perceiver and perceived, not a separation. He thus described perception in terms of engagement rather than detachment.

This particular emphasis sets Merleau-Ponty apart from many 20th-century structuralist and poststructuralist theorists—a departure that is particularly evident in his discussions of language. For him language was rooted not only in social action, but also in nonverbal exchanges that are always going on between our physicalities and the flesh of the world. As David Abram summarizes the point, Merleau-Ponty concluded that human languages "are informed not only by the structures of the human body and the human community, but by the evocative shapes and patterns of the more-than-human world".[3]

Merleau-Ponty's work on this matter might be interpreted as a response to linguistic determinism—an idea that arose within structuralist discourses and that has underpinned many poststructuralist discourses. The extreme form of linguisitic determinism, sometimes referred to as the Sapir–Whorf Hypothesis, asserts that what we perceive and experience is strictly constrained by the linguistic habits of our culture.[4] In this frame, language is argued to specify the possibilities for both interpretation and perception. Merleau-Ponty suggested almost the opposite—that human interpretive systems, including language, are rooted in and conditioned by our primal engagements in the world.

Merleau-Ponty was not in any way attempting to resurrect corre-spondence theories of language that had been so effectively critiqued by structuralists (see chaps. 10 and 11). Yet he did seek to interrupt the sense that languages are hermetically sealed and strictly self-refer-ential, as posited by structuralists. He also sought to foreground that humans are biologically coupled to the cosmos—indeed that humans are part of the cosmos. He thus argued that human knowledge con-sists of more than systems of internally consistent propositions. Knowledge entails contextually appropriate action. It is situational and embodied. Departing from language-focused discourses on knowl-edge, Merleau-Ponty advocated attentiveness to both the cultural and the biological,[5] as well as to both the announced and the enacted.

For many the question that follows this sort of move is: If lan-guage and other aspects of human knowledge have physical-biologi-cal bases, how did they come to support the dichotomizations of human from nature, mental from physical, civilized from savage, knower from knowledge, explicit from tacit, and self from other?

Let me frame emergent responses to that question by describing my own situation, at this moment. I'm sitting at the kitchen table. My writing is punctuated by glances out the window at the thousands of bohemian waxwings that have been flocking—swarming—in the trees of our and our neighbors' backyards for the past hour. It's −23°C outside, so the windows are shut tight. Even so, the chatter of birds presses through the triple panes of glass. I can't ignore them (or per-haps *it*—they comprise an undeniable unity), and that's not just be-cause they're noisy. It's because, although we are separated by walls and windows, I am part of their unfolding choreography and they are part of mine. Most of the time, the majority of them are perched in trees, with a few dozen shuttling about like envoys among divided populations. As if prompted by these movements, every now and then a caravan rises and sweeps from one tree to another, and some-times such missions appear to trigger grand social uprisings. Every bird seems to take wing, to weave about in ways that are unmistakably patterned, but whose orders vastly exceed my capacities to consciously interpret—except through the sorts of tools that I've used in this paragraph. Narrative. Metaphor. Anthropomorphism. Causal logic. I also use gesture to understand: I find myself swaying with their collectivity, moving as they move, moved by their movements. And suddenly I realize that my actions are contributing to the shape of the grand collective. I peek around a corner of the bay window and a small flock, perched in a nearby tree, takes wing. With the suddenness of their movement, many more nearby also take to the air.

The birds outside my window seem to be communicating an exuberance. Their individual gestures do not go unanswered. Acts trigger other acts, and the collectivity that arises in these millions of events of mutual specification is a dance of communication. Yet of course this communication isn't language. It lacks many important qualities of human symbolic interaction. For instance, this sort of gestural choreography is immediate and situationally specific, with no relevance or discernible echo beyond the moment. Language, by contrast, provides a means to preserve aspects of the dance. It enables me to recall being in the event after it ends. More dramatically, language enables me, however imperfectly, to invite others into it—others who may be separated by time, distance, and climate. With language one need not experience things directly. One can borrow others' narrations and project from their experiences.

Much has been written about what language is, how it might have begun, and how it acquired its capacity to reach across space and generations. There is no consensus on the matter, but one broadly accepted hypothesis is that language began with gesture.[6] Merleau-Ponty developed the idea and suggested that communicative meaning arises first in the body's affective responses to changes in its environment. Yet for language to be language, an expression must move beyond context-specific action to context-independent gesture—perhaps with such portable, interobjective motions as nodding or pointing or swaying, perhaps through vocalizations that mimic aspects of encounters with other living forms. This power of language—that is, its capacity to move us beyond the actual, immediate, and present into the possible, past or future, and absent—is often cited as one of its distinguishing qualities (and the feature that most underpins the human abilities to abstract and imagine).

Yet language is more than gesture and utterance. In fact the technology that has the most dramatic effect on our language-effected realities might be the written symbol. Walter Ong,[7] David Olson,[8] and others have argued that, with the invention of writing, words were transformed from transient vocal gestures that were attached to a speaker into durable visual objects that might seem to have an independent existence. As representational systems evolved from pictographs to alphabets, word-objects ceased to require a context because an idea that's encoded in alphabetic writing retains little or no trace of its grounded origins. It does not have to be memorized, rehearsed, acted out, embodied. Alphabetically inscripted knowledge can be seen as some *thing* in and of itself.

It's probably not coincidental that the two cultures most closely associated with the rise of Western metaphysical traditions, the Semitic and the Greek, are also the ones in which alphabetic writing was first developed. The Hebrew God, who transcends this fleshly realm and who ordered man to set out to "fill the Earth and master it",[9] would seem to be implicated in the deeply engrained conceptual separation of the human from the natural. Similarly, Plato's assertion that this world is an imperfect shadow of a nonsensorial ideal realm would seem to be implicated in the conceptual separation of mind and body. (Christianity, a co-mingling of Hebraic religion and Hellenist philosophy, served as a vehicle to spread these sensibilities across much of the Western world.) The lever that pried apart human from natural and mind from body rested on the fulcrum of alphabetic literacy— a technology that was being popularized during Plato's life. Through writing, one could engage *ideas* directly because those ideas were detached from other people and from direct references to the sensible world. Indeed the original sources of ideas came to be seen as the shadows or consequences of the Ideal.

Given alphabetic writing's profound influences on humanity's attitudes toward the physical and biological, one might expect the issue to have been a major topic of discussion within philosophy. In fact such has not been the case. As developed in chapter 11, the overwhelming emphasis among 20th-century philosophers was on the contributions of language to the organization of human experience. Issues of biological constitutions and physical contexts were all but ignored. A question that follows is how we, as alphabetized citizens of modernist culture, might make a different sense of the relationship of the human to the more-than-human world. Among the conceptual orientations that have been taken up in efforts to address this question, two closely related branches of thought have risen to prominence over the past few decades: complexity science and ecological discourses.

COMPLEXITY SCIENCE:
SELF-ORGANIZATION AND KNOWLEDGE

Unlike analytic science, *complexity science* is defined more in terms of its objects of study than its modes of investigation. It has only come together as a coherent field of inquiry in the past 30 years or so, having arisen in the confluence of several areas of research that first appeared as branches of physics and biology in the mid-20th century. These included cybernetics, information science, systems theory, and artificial intelligence—and later catastrophe theory, connectionism, fractal geometry, and nonlinear dynamics. More recently, certain research emphases in the social sciences have come to be included under the rubric of complexity.

In one popular account of the emergence of the field, M. Mitchell Waldrop[10] introduces the diverse interests and diffuse origins of complexity research through a list that includes such disparate events as the collapse of the Soviet Union, trends in the stock market, the rise of life on Earth, the evolution of the eye, and the emergence of mind. This list could be extended to include any phenomenon that might be described in terms of a living, adaptive system—including, with regard to immediate human interest, such nested levels of organization as cells, bodily organs, individuals, social groupings, cultures, societies, species, and the biosphere.[11] These phenomena share two key qualities. First, each is adaptive—that is, a complex system can change its own structure in response to internal or external pressures and is thus better described in terms of evolutionary processes than in terms of the laws of physics. More concisely, a complex system embodies its history in its structure. Second, a complex phenomenon is self-organizing, meaning that it is composed of and arises in the co-implicated activities of individual agents. It is not the sum of its parts—an object; it is the product of its parts and their interactions—an interobject.

Complexity scientists (or complexivists) often describe such adaptive, self-organizing phenomena as *learning systems*,[12] where learning is understood in terms of ongoing, recursively elaborative adaptations through which systems maintain their coherences within dynamic circumstances. These discussions are often accompanied by such illustrative examples as the flocking of waxwings, the spread of ideas, or the unfolding of cultural movements. Such self-maintaining phenomena transcend their parts. They present collective possibilities that are not represented in the individual agents. Self-organized, self-maintaining forms can arise and evolve without goals, plans, or leaders.

This quality of transcendent collectivity is useful for drawing a further distinction between analytic and complexity science. Complexity is not just an acknowledgment of a new category of non-deterministic phenomena, but an assertion that analytic methods are not sufficient to understand such phenomena. Different attitudes and means are needed to make sense of the ever-shifting characters of complex phenomena and that allow researchers to appreciate such systems, simultaneously, as coherent unities, as composed of coherent unities, and (possibly) as subagents to grander unities.

Interest in what are now described as complex phenomena pre-date the emergence of complexity science by more than a century. For example, complex sensibilities are represented in Charles Darwin's studies of the intertwined evolutions of species, in Frederich Engel's discussions of social collectives, and in Jane Jacobs' characterization of living (and dying) cities. Many dozens of examples could be cited in both the physical and social sciences.[13]

Significantly, although these researchers framed their studies in terms of evolutionary dynamics, none of them proposed the notion of self-organization. For reasons that are not well understood, under certain circumstances, agents can spontaneously cohere into func-tional collectives. That is, they sometimes come together in unities that have integrities and potentialities that are not represented in them-selves. These events of self-organization are bottom–up, as emer-gent macrobehaviors (i.e., collective characters, transcendent abili-ties, etc.) arise through the localized rules and actions of individual agents, not through the imposition of top–down instructions. For example, there is no overarching regulator of food supplies in North America. Somehow through the actions and interactions of produc-ers, processors, distributors, and investors—who operate on local rules and on the basis of local information—hundreds of millions of people have ready access to the food they require or desire. Com-plexity science is an example of what it aims to understand—namely, the emergence of transcendent possibilities through some sort of phenomenon-specific boot-strapping process.[14]

Through most of its brief history, complexity science has been focused on efforts to better understand self-organization mainly through close observations of complex systems and computer mod-eling. (Classical experimental methods are not particularly useful be-cause complex systems are self-transformative. That presents a two-pronged problem with their study. For reasons that might never be apparent, similar systems can respond very differently to identical circumstances, or the same system can respond differently to virtu-ally identical situations.) For the most part, this work has been descriptive in nature. Researchers have attempted to identify features and conditions that are common to complex systems. More recently, there has been an increased emphasis among complexivists on the creation and maintenance of complex systems such as the restoration of an ecosystem.[15] To this end, several key conditions that are necessary for self-organization and ongoing adaptation have been identified. For example, for complexity to arise, systems must have considerable redundancy among agents (to enable interactivity), some level of diversity (to enable novel responses), a means by which agents can affect one another, and a distributed, decentralized control structure. (These points are elaborated in chap. 15.)

Within the arts and humanities, complexivist sensibilities have shown up in an array of new subdisciplines whose titles transgress institutionalized disciplinary boundaries, including, for instance, social cybernetics, biosemiotics, neurophenomenology, and biological psychiatry. In the process, new ways of talking about knowing and knowledge are emerging—ways that are explicit in their acknowledgment of the biological roots of personal knowing, the cultural roles in collective knowledge, and the more-than-human contexts of human activity.[16] In terms of knowing and knowledge, several neurophenomenological discourses—studies of human consciousness that couple neuroscientific research with phenomenological methods—have emerged. One of the most prominent of these is Francisco Varela's (1946–2001) enactivism.[17]

Enactivism begins with a redefinition of cognition in terms similar to the scientific definition of *complexity*. Cognition is understood as ongoing processes of adaptive activity. As with complex systems, the cognizing agent can be seen as an autonomous form and/or as an agent that is coupled[18] to other agents and, hence, part of a grander form. An implication is that cognition is not seen to occur strictly inside an agent. Rather, cognition is used to refer to all active processes—internal and external to the cognizing agent—that are part of its ongoing adaptive actions. The processes of cognition are the processes of life. In other words, although framed in a different way, an enactivist understanding of cognition has some important correspondences to the ancient Greek gnosis, including the notion that cognition inheres in the dynamics of the cosmos. (Recall that *cognition*, *notion*, and *knowledge* are all derived from the word *gnosis*.)

As with all complexity (and most intersubjectivist) discourses, enactivism rejects the assumption of a core, essential, inner self. Instead personal identity is seen to arise in the complex mix of biological predisposition, physical affect, social circumstance, and cultural context as the agent copes with the contingencies of existence. The aphorism "knowing is doing is being"[19] is often used to foreground this point. The term *enactivism* is also intended to highlight the notion that identities and knowledge are not ideal forms, but enactments— that is, embodied in the nested interactivities of dynamic forms. Life and learning are thus understood in terms of explorations of ever-evolving landscapes of possibility and of selecting (not necessarily consciously) actions that are adequate to situations.

A further aspect of enactivism, and one that is particularly relevant in discussions of human cognition, is the notion of languaging. Understood in complexity terms, language is an emergent phenomenon that exceeds the agents who language. It arises in the interactions of agents and, in turn, conditions the interactions of agents— and thus exerts a certain influence over its own evolution. The gerund *languaging* (vs. the noun *language*) is used to point to the open-endedness of language. Like knowing-knowledge, doing-action, and being-existence, languaging-language is in no way a finished form. It is constantly arising and adapting.

A key aspect of languaging is recursivity. Humans have the capacity to language about language—an endlessly elaborative process that seems to be vital to knowledge production and the emergence of consciousness.[20] Our abilities to self-reference—that is, to cleave our individual selves from one another and from our contexts—is clearly amplified by, if not rooted in, our language. In this regard, enactivism has much in common with intersubjectivist discourses.

The main differences have to do with attitudes toward scientific inquiry and persistent reminders that we are biological beings whose habits of interpretation, while enabled by sophisticated languaging capacities, are conditioned by way that humanity evolved in and is coupled to a physical world. Many of the remnants of metaphysical assumption are refuted here. Even humanity's most abstract conceptual achievements are understood to be tethered to the ground of biologically conditioned experience.[21]

One further quality of enactivism is a concern for ethical action—which, in fact, makes it an example of a theory that spans both complexivist and ecological sensibilities.

ECOLOGICAL DISCOURSES: BEING AND KNOWING

Complexity science has helped legitimate a topic that had almost become taboo in Western academia: transcendence. The idea of "order for free"[22]—that is, that higher order unities can emerge spontaneously—simply does not fit with the mindset of analytic science, oriented as it is by quests for fundamental components and causal explanations.

One break in sensibilities between complexity science and analytic science was acted out in public in the early 1970s. James Lovelock, a research scientist, proposed that Earth's biosphere might be considered a superorganism—a grand unity that maintains itself far from equilibrium. Lovelock posited several phenomena—such as transcendent wholeness, self-organization, and life as a matter of constant disequilibrium—that challenged the orthodoxy of analytic traditions. Lovelock, in fact, lost a position as a research scientist for proposing an earlier version of this Gaia Hypothesis.[23]

Despite its contribution to the relegitimation of notions of interconnection and grand unity, the discourse within complexity science research has tended to be very similar to that of analytic science in terms of rhetorical strategies, standards of proof, and so on. This is not to say that complexity scientists are unaware of their participations in cultural and natural forms. Quite the contrary, such issues are prominent.[24] Nevertheless, the moves to collect humans, hearts, social collectives, and the biosphere (among other forms) into the same category and redescribe them in terms of systems rather than machines reveal that, conceptually, complexity science has maintained aspects of the detached modern scientific attitude. In particular, it tends not to concern itself with questions of meaning.

In many ways, this continued evasion is odd. Complexity science asserts that our knowledge systems are rooted in our physical forms—and that those forms, in turn, are engaged in ongoing cyclings of matter with all other living forms. Oriented by this realization, science has mounted a case against itself in the accumulation of evidence that many current personal, cultural, and planetary distresses can be traced to scientifically enabled human activities.[25] It does not seem unreasonable to suggest that something other than an explanation-seeking scientific attitude is required for an effective response. Knowledge is useful here, but wisdom is needed.

In particular, an ecological philosophy or ecosophy (from the Greek *sophia*, "wisdom") is needed. This is the sort of thinking that underpins deep ecology, a movement that encourages a shift in how we experience the more-than-human world. Departing from most environmentalist discourses, which continue to frame humanity's relationship to the more-than-human in terms of management and overseeing, deep ecology begins with the assertion that life in all forms is inherently valuable. In other words, within deep ecology, the role of humanity is not understood in terms of stewardship, but of mindfulness and ethical action. A tenet of deep ecology is that humanity has the right to draw on planetary resources only to satisfy vital needs, which is a much more radical stance than the one taken within more popular sustainability discourses.[26] For many deep ecologists, there is also an explicit political agenda that includes calls to reduce human populations, rethink the Western corporate obsessions for endless economic growth, move toward smaller scale modes of production, and embrace more local governance structures.[27] A major recommendation in the deep ecological agenda is bioregionalism—a movement toward region-appropriate lifestyles and production activities.

Attentiveness to situation is a prominent theme in ecological discourses. Ecopsychology, for example, is oriented by the assertion that widespread feelings of personal isolation and collective dysfunction are mainly rooted in people's separation from the natural world. The main therapeutic tool of ecopsychologists is reconnection to nature.[28] Another emergent discourse is ecofeminism, in which it is argued that prevailing worldviews are not just *anthropocentric* (human-dominant), but *androcentric* (male-dominant). Proponents note close correspondences between the beliefs and structures that contribute to the oppression of women and those that contribute to the oppression of nature.[29] In effect, ecofeminists, along with deep ecologists, argue that anti-oppression discourses and movements should include the category of nature along with race, class, gender, and sexuality.

The issue of how humans discriminate themselves from other living forms is common across traditions. In fact I encountered it repeatedly while researching the conceptual commitments of the various movements represented in this book. For example, within Western mystical and religious systems, the human tends to be distinguished from the nonhuman by virtue of a soul. In rationalist and empiricist sensibilities, the means of differentiation is the faculty of reason. Across structuralist and poststructuralist discourses, humans are set apart by language and other capacities for symbolically mediated interaction. For complexivists, the human brain is frequently cited as the most sophisticated structure that is known, and human consciousness and social systems are often described as the highest known forms of organization.

Across most ecological movements, this apparent need to discriminate between the human and the nonhuman is interrupted. This point is true of ecosophy, deep ecology, ecopsychology, and ecofeminism. It's particularly true of those ecological discourses that are clustered under the umbrella term of *ecospirituality*, some of which have pressed toward modes of description and engagement that are highly reminiscent of ancient mystical traditions.

I'll frame this brief introduction to ecospiritual movements with recent neurological research into what might be described as the biology of belief. There is mounting evidence that humans are physiologically predisposed to mystical and spiritual experiences—that is, to such feelings or sensations as timelessness, boundlessness, transcendence, and oneness that have been commonly associated with spiritual events.[30] Until quite recently, the scientific explanation for mystical and religious experience was that the experiencer was in some sort of pathological state, such as a neurosis, a psychosis, or another problem with brain function. (In fact the American Psychiatric Association listed "strong religious belief" as a mental disorder until 1994.) The associated assumption—that the mystic or religious zealot is prone to losing touch with reality—has proved problematic on several levels. As Newburg, D'Aquili, and Rause indicate, science has been unable to prove the assumption that spiritual experience is the product of delusional minds. On the contrary, it appears that those who experience genuine mystical states or who live devoted religious lives tend to have much higher levels of psychological health than the general population.[31] There is further evidence that mystical experiences are quite unlike psychotic states. The latter tend toward confused and even terrifying hallucinations; the former tend to be described with such terms as serenity, wholeness, and love.[32]

Such events, in fact, may not be all that unusual. Virtually everyone can recall an experience of being lost in a book, immersed in an activity, or swept up in a crowd. Such experiences can also be induced and enhanced through repetitive, rhythmic activity—which should perhaps not be surprising. The explicit purpose of most rituals is to lift participants from their respective isolations into something greater than themselves. As it turns out, there is a neurological basis for these sorts of responses. Such activities affect parts of the brain that are associated with reason and the imagined boundaries of the self.[33] To oversimplify, when the dichotomizing tendencies of logic and self-identification are relaxed, the sensations associated with mystical experience emerge.

It's one thing to say that something of this sort can happen and quite another to address the questions of why it happens at all and why it is so common.[34] Why might humans be physiologically predisposed to feelings of transcendence? Among the many answers that are possible to these questions—depending on whether one adopts mystical, religious, rationalist, empiricist, interpretivist, complexivist, or ecological stances—one response has a particular intuitive appeal: It happens because there *are* transcendent unities of which we are always and already part. In being aware of their selves and of nature, humans are one of the means by which nature is conscious of itself. Human thoughts are not merely about the cosmos; they are parts of the cosmos—and so the universe changes when something as seemingly small and insignificant as a thought changes. These convictions are at the core of emergent ecospiritual movements. The defining feature of ecospirituality is an attitude of respect and entanglement with all living forms. This sort of attitude is represented in almost every ancient spiritual tradition, theistic and nontheistic alike.

The word *spiritual* has been redefined somewhat within ecospiritual movements. Classically, in modern and Western settings, spiritual is used in contradistinction to the physical and is associated with disembodiment, ideality, and denial of the worldly. This sense of spirituality also tends to be framed in contrast to a scientific attitude in which spirituality is thought to be about unquestioned faith, whereas science is seen to be concerned with unquestionable evidence.

This cluster of distinctions is usually erased in ecospiritual discourses, which are structured around the recollection that matters of the spirit are, literally, matters of breathing. Derived from the Latin *spiritus*, "breath", the spiritual is about constant physical connection to and material exchange with an animate world. (The word *psyche* has a similar root, from the Greek *psukhe*, "breath".)

Once again this attitude seems to be as much about a recovery of an ancient understanding as it is about the emergence of a new one. Historians, anthropologists, and cultural commentators have reported on many indications of deep ecological sensibilities across cultures and societies. Unfortunately, when these sorts of beliefs were interpreted by the first Europeans to reach indigenous cultures— evangelical Christian missionaries—references to spirits and souls could only be heard in terms of the other-worldly forms of Western spiritualist discourses. To a listener who imagined him- or herself a servant to the supernatural and eternal, the suggestion that a tree or river was somehow inspirited and caught up in every aspect of one's being was an indication of ignorance and mystical delusion. Outside the frame of metaphysical assumption, however, such a belief is very much in keeping with emergent ecological understanding. It is about lateral or outward relationships as opposed to forward or upward grasping.

The underlying attitude is one of *participation*—a word used by Lucien Lévy-Bruhl (1857–1939) nearly a century ago to describe the animistic aspects of indigenous people's and oral cultures' world-views.[35] The term has been picked up in the current phrase "participatory epistemology"—which, as developed in chapter 10, is used to refer to any theory that asserts that all aspects of the world, animate and inanimate, participate with humanity in the ongoing project of knowledge production. The whole is understood to unfold from and to be enfolded in the part(icipant). In a word, within participatory epistemologies, the central issue is meaning.

COMMON ROOTS, DIFFERENT BRANCHES

Conceptually, complexivist and ecological discourses are closely aligned. Both are attentive to the intertwinings and co-dependencies of phenomena, both understand the universe as constantly unfolding, both foreground the roles of agents in the emergence of collectives, and both are attentive not just to the realm of human interest, but to the more-than-human world.

Further, both might be described as responses to the modern (actually metaphysical) neglect for context. This neglect is manifest, for example, in scientific technologies that are deployed in ignorance of their environmental consequences, in medical practices that are fixated on responses to disease rather than the support of good health, in legal systems that protect individuals' rights and ignore collective responsibilities, and in educational systems structured around age-appropriate (versus situation- or person-appropriate) standardized curricula. It wouldn't be difficult to extend this list.

Complexivist and ecological discourses diverge in ways that are curiously reminiscent of the ancient distinction between episteme and gnosis. Complexity science, for the most part, describes itself in the detached rhetoric of modern science and concerns itself more with the workings than with the meanings of things. Ecological discourses, by contrast, are more oriented to questions of meaning, ethical action, spiritual entanglement, and mindful participation in the evolution of the cosmos.

Another way of making this point is to mention that ecological discourses have reasserted the role of human consciousness. Through the 20th century, several key theoretical movements either dismissed or diminished the consciousness as a largely illusory, inconsequential epiphenomenon. From orientations as diverse as behaviorism, psychoanalysis, and poststructuralism, many theorists argued that consciousness had little or no control over one's actual existence—although it somehow manages to dupe conscious beings into believing that we are autonomous, aware, and free agents.[36]

Ecological discourses acknowledge that consciousness may not be all that it is popularly imagined to be. However, these discourses foreground the role of consciousness in affecting the conditions of existence—a faith that is supported by a considerable body of neurological, psychological, and sociological research.[37] It is this reclaimed faith in the role of consciousness that frames the emphases on ethical responsibility and mindfulness awareness.

WHERE TO NOW?

This chapter was concerned with the common ground and differences in emphases of complexity science and ecology. In chapters 15 and 16, I examine some of the implications of these theories for teaching. Because these discourses are relatively new, widely accepted principles and vocabularies have yet to emerge, but there are some discernible trends. Chapters 15 and 16 complete the discussion of conceptions of teaching that are rooted in evolutionary sensibilities.

15

Complexity Science:
TEACHING AS OCCASIONING

*Since Darwin, we have come to think about organisms as
tinkered-together contraptions and selection as the sole source
of order. Yet Darwin could not have begun to suspect the
power of self-organization. We must seek our principles of
adaptation in complex systems anew.*

— Stuart Kauffman[1]

One of the major contributions of intersubjectivist discourses
to education—via constructivist, constructionist, and critical
discourses—is an interruption of persistent dichotomization of self
and society. Structuralist and poststructuralist discourses have rejected
the metaphysical notions that such forms are distinct, fixed, and
pregiven and have recast individual and collective in terms of nested,
dynamic, and emergent phenomena.

As noted in chapters 12 and 13, this manner of reframing the
self–society tension has some important educational implications. At
the same time, however, the constructs of self and society continue
to bookend discussions of teaching and schooling within intersubjectivist discourses. At one end of the discussion, constructivists are concerned with the individual's construal of socially effected reality; at the other end, critical theorists fo-

cus on how intersubjectively effected reality delimits the possibilities of the individual.

In many ways, this constraint on discussions of learning and teaching is ironic. Even as structuralist and poststructuralist discourses have incorporated biology based evolutionary metaphors, there has been a tendency to ignore the realm of the biological. Specifically, in these discourses, concepts such as *fitness* and *adaptation* have been used to describe individual thought and collective knowledge, not the biological structures that support and are implicated in thought and knowledge. Piaget, for example, was clear that his theories were strictly about the emergence of personal interpretations, not about the biological processes at work in cognition. He did not, however, deny the relevance of the biological, although some poststructuralist discourses do precisely that. One reason for this sort of rejection has to do with the lingering tendency to interpret references to biological constitution as indications of essentialism or determinism in the metaphysical senses.

The tendency to deny the role of the biological in matters of human subjectivity is most pronounced in those discourses that seek to interrupt cultural prejudices that are based in physical difference. Most prominently, these discourses include some versions of feminism and antiracism. However, the rejection of the biological on political bases would seem to rely on the dichotomizations human/nature and mental/physical.

To appreciate the position of complexity discourses on this issue, it's useful to frame the relationships among structuralist and poststructuralist discourses in terms of fractal geometry (see Appendix B). As already developed, constructivist, constructionist, and critical discourses are each concerned with a particular body— individual, epistemic, and politic, respectively. These bodies are nested, and each is described as dynamic and adaptive. They might be further described as self-similar. That is, regardless of which one is brought into focus, similar sorts of recursive, self-maintaining processes seem to be at work. Understood in fractal terms, individual knowing, collective knowledge, and cultural identity are three intertwining, self-similar aspects of one whole. These phenomena, however, cannot be collapsed into one another. At each level, different possibilities arise and different rules emerge. Complexivists thus avoid debates around matters of the relative worth of different intersubjectivist discourses. Instead they are more oriented by the question: On which levels (or in which domains) is a particular theory an explanation? Radical constructivism, for instance, does not help to explain much on the level of cultural evolution. Similarly, the field of cultural studies tends to offer little to help make sense of an individual's construal of a mathematical concept.

As mentioned in chapter 10, this fractal interpretation of the nested sites of cognition can be extended in both micro- and the macrodirections. On the subhuman level, for instance, recent complexity-oriented medical research has underscored that the body's organs are relatively autonomous and cognitive unities. For example, the immune system isn't a cause–effect mechanism, but a self-transforming agent that learns, forgets, hypothesizes, errs, recovers, recognizes, and rejects in a complex dance with other bodily subagents.[2] The brain, similarly, is not a static form, but a vibrantly changing system that is fractally organized: Neurons are clustered into minicolumns, minicolumns into macrocolumns, macrocolumns into cortical areas, cortical areas into hemispheres—and at every level agents interact with and affect other agents.[3] This is one of the reasons that the cognitivist brain-as-computer metaphor is problematic. Each event of learning entails a physical transformation of the brain; hence subsequent events of learning are met by a different brain. On the biological level, personal learning is not about acquisition, processing, or storing, but about emergent structuring.

On the supracultural level, to understand humanity as a species, one must attend to the web of relationships in the global ecosystem. Metaphorically, humanity might be understood as one among many organs in the body of the biosphere, engaged with other organ-species in the emergence of collective possibility. Invested in every human—woven through our biological beings—is a trace of our species' history and its implicatedness in the planet. By way of simple example, it is no accident that human lungs are so perfectly fitted to Earth's atmosphere. They evolved together.

An individual's cognition, then, is not just the product of her or his experiences. It is also a reflection of the emergence of the species. To ignore or downplay the biological, in the complexity view, is to seriously restrict any discussion of what learning is and how it might happen. This is not to say that the biological must be given priority, merely that humans are both biological and cultural beings. Each of us is, all at once, a collective of agents, a coherent unity, and a part of other emergent unities. It is for this reason that complexity science is a useful discourse for those interested in matters of knowledge, learning, and teaching. Complexity science straddles the classical institutional break of the sciences and the humanities.

Educationally, complexity science has also prompted attentions to levels of structural unity that lie *between* the individual and society, not just beyond them. For instance, a common, everyday conversation turns out to be a complex event. Although participants in a conversation are rarely aware of it, slowed videorecordings of their interactions reveal a complex choreography of action. Speech patterns are precisely synchronized with subtle body movements that are acutely sensitive to events in the surroundings. The choreography is so tight that a conversation can properly be described as a *coupling* of individuals' attentional systems.[4]

The same sort of structural coupling—that is, of intimate entangling of one's attentions and activities with another's—is observed in parents' actions as they assist in their children's learning of language and various fine motor skills. Exquisite choreographies of activity emerge as a parent offers subtle cues or assistance, maintaining a delicate balance between too much and too little help. What is surprising, as highlighted in follow-up interviews with parents, is that this extraordinary process of coupling one's actions to another's can occur without conscious knowledge. When asked about prompts given and assistance offered, most parents are unable to provide rationales for their actions. In fact parents are often at a greater loss when asked to explain how and when they learned to teach in this complex, participatory manner—an observation that has prompted the suggestion that humans are *natural* teachers.[5] We are biologically, not just culturally, predisposed to engage with others in ways that can properly be called teaching.

Joint attention—that is, the interlocking of two or more consciousnesses—is the foundation of all deliberate efforts to teach. As Merlin Donald points out, "human cultures are powerful pedagogues because their members regulate one another's attention, through a maze of cultural conventions".[6] However, it is one thing to note that humans have these capacities to engage, and it is quite another to assert some sort of utility for the rigidly organized and prescriptive context of the modern classroom. How might the teacher go about structurally coupling with 30 students at the same time around an issue that may not be a particularly engaging topic of conversation?

On the first part of this question, it turns out that we are always already structurally coupled to one another. Judith Rich Harris makes this point in a review and reinterpretation of a substantial literature around the emergence of individual identity.[7] To perhaps overtruncate her argument, the evidence seems to suggest that the major influences in the emergence of identity are genetics and one's peer group. Compared to the influences of friends and agemates, parents and early family life play minor roles. Harris reasons that this difference in influence arises in the fact that the child's main task is not to become a successful adult, but to be a successful child—to fit in, to be part of the group, to not stand out. In other words, the child (and for that matter the adult) is oriented toward structurally coupling with others. This phenomenon is perhaps better examined on the group level as a tendency toward social self-organization.

The classroom teacher can thus count on this tendency to already be in place. Eavesdropping on almost any lunchtime school staffroom conversation will confirm this point.

Teachers commonly refer to classrooms of learners as coherent unities that have intentions, habits, and other personality traits. The difficulty, however, is that such collectivity rarely emerges around engagements with a subject matter, but around the common and continuous project of fitting in. The question thus remains, how might a teacher concerned with a prescribed curriculum topic invoke the capacities and tendencies of learners to come together into grander cognitive unities? This is a question that is only starting to be answered. One strategy that seems to hold some promise has been to structure classroom activities in ways that ensure the presence of the conditions that are necessary for complex emergence, as mentioned briefly in chapter 14.

For instance, for complex co-activity to arise that surpasses the possibilities of the agents on their own, there must be a certain level of *diversity* among them. Such variation is the source of novel responses. It is argued to be the reason behind, for instance, the vast amount of unexpressed DNA in the human genome, the range of vocational competencies in a community, and the biological diversity of the planet. When a complex system is faced with a problem, an adequate solution might be found in these pools of diversity.

Such diversity is useful only to the extent that it can be appreciated by other agents in the system, which points to a second key condition—*redundancy*.[8] To engage in joint activity, to structurally couple, agents must have sufficient common ground to be able to interact. In fact, in most cases, they need to be much more the same than different because a system's robustness is linked to its agents' abilities to compensate for one another's lapses. Although the teacher can usually assume that the condition of diversity will be met in the classroom, some work might be required to ensure adequate redundancy. For example, to engage in productive discussions of global politics or explorations of fractions concepts, some familiarity with issues or some common experiences would be necessary. Such background—or the provision of opportunities to develop such background—is one important category of pedagogical decision making.

A further category of decision making, and the real challenge in my own experiences of teaching, is the development of tasks that are rooted in redundancies and that allow for the expression of appropriate diversities. For instance, a lesson on adding fractions might be developed around cutting, folding, and reassembling pieces of paper, which could serve as the source of common experiences and a basis for a common vocabulary while allowing learners to adapt their activities to their specific interests and understandings.[9] Such tasks involve the imposition of constraints—or, more precisely, the imposition of *liberating constraints*.[10] These are guidelines and limitations for activity that are intended to provide enough organization to orient students' actions while allowing sufficient openness for expression of the varieties of experience, ability, and interest represented in any social grouping. Liberating constraints must not be overly prescriptive because the result of a complex emergent event cannot be fully anticipated. By the same token, the notion of liberating constraints is not an embrace of an anything goes attitude. (Indeed one way to ensure that complexity will *not* emerge is to remove all limitations.)

At least in part, the activity must be emergent—that is, defined in the process of engagement. This quality points to a fourth condition of complex emergence—*decentralized control*. In classroom terms, the understandings and interpretations that are generated cannot be completely prestated. Rather, to some extent they must emerge and be sustained through shared projects, not through prescribed learning objectives, linear lesson plans, or rigid management strategies. Complexity can't be scripted.

Applied to schooling, the condition of decentralized control should be interpreted neither as a condemnation of the teacher-centered classroom nor as an endorsement of the student-centered classroom. Rather, it represents a critique of an assumption that is common to both those structures—namely, that the site of learning is the individual. As complexity science asserts, the capacity to learn is a defining quality of all complex unities. Thus one must be clear on the nature of the complex unities that are desired in the classroom. Such unities are concerned with the generation of knowledge and the development understanding—meaning that the focus should not be on teachers or learners, but on collective possibilities for interpretation.

I realize that these sorts of statements may well be more obfuscating than illuminating, owing in large part to the fact that the ideas represented here depart quite radically from the structures of and rationales for modern schools. On the suspicion that illustrations might be useful, in an endnote[11] I have identified some texts that develop these principles in greater detail and that include accounts of teaching episodes that were deliberately structured around principles of complexity.

Unfortunately, a vocabulary to frame complexivist teaching has yet to emerge. At the moment, it's much easier to talk about what such teaching isn't rather than what it is or might be. For example, it isn't prescriptive, detached, or predictable. It can't expect the same results with different groups. It can't assume that complex possibilities will in fact emerge. Further, this manner of teaching is not a matter of orchestrating; once again, complex emergence cannot be managed into existence. However, a teaching informed by complexity science might be described as a sort of *improvising* in the jazz music sense of engaging attentively and responsively with others in a collective project.

Another term that I find compelling as a synonym for teaching is *occasioning*. In its original sense, occasioning referred to the way that surprising possibilities can arise when things are allowed to fall together. The word is thus useful for foregrounding the participatory and emergent natures of learning engagements as it points to both the deliberate and accidental qualities of teaching. For similar reasons, teaching might also be described in terms of *structuring* in the biological rather than the architectural sense (see chap. 11).

Another word that might be associated with the act of teaching is *framing*, which has the same roots of the word *from*. The original sense of both terms had to do with movement oriented by particular conditions and histories. The notion of framing might thus serve as a reminder of the ways that complex histories are knitted into intentions and expectations while it points to the teacher's role in ensuring that the conditions necessary for complex emergence are present.

A quality that is common to notions of improvising, occasioning, structuring, and framing is the participatory role of the teaching. For complexivists, teaching is *participating*—in the production of personal knowing and collective knowledge, in the evolution of personal identities and collective forms, and in the shaping of personal activities and collective possibilities.

Just as the teacher's role is reconceived by complexivists, so is the role of the student. Departing from structuralist and poststructuralist discourses, complexity science does not use notions of margins, fringes, and peripheries to describe complex systems. In fact such constructs make little sense when systems are understood as nested within systems. This alternative geometry prompts the suggestion that students are not neophytes, initiates, or novices to be incorporated into an established order. Rather, like teachers, they are participants—and in fact they play profound roles in shaping the forms that are popularly seen to shape them.[12]

WHERE TO NOW?

This chapter was concerned with the origins and conceptual implications of synonyms for teaching that are associated with complexity science—specifically, the terms *improvising, occasioning, structuring, framing,* and *participating.* In chapter 16, I undertake a similar discussion of terms associated with ecological discourses.

16

Ecology:
TEACHING AS CONVERSING

*When we try to pick out anything by itself, we find it hitched
to everything else in the universe.*

— John Muir[1]

As noted in chapter 14, ecological discourses have a good deal in
common with complexity science. They share a worldview.
Where they tend to part company is around the same sorts of issues
that separated gnosis from episteme: concerns and questions about
meaning.

On this count, although it has abandoned the metaphysical assumptions of empiricist science, complexity science has retained the
emphasis on the production of explicit knowledge. The belief in a
totally predictable universe has been left behind, as has the desire for
totalized control. Nevertheless, the work of complexity science continues to be oriented by the thought-to-be neutral question of "What
can be done?" rather than the ethically saturated question of "What
should be done?" In other words, although complexity science has
rejected the philosophical commitments of episteme, even though
the desire for objectivity has been interrupted by the realization of interobjectivity, the field continues to be oriented by
the concern for practical know-how.

Ecological discourses tend to pull in a different direction. They share with complexity a conviction that all forms and events are intimately intertwined, but this conviction has prompted more of a concern for ethical know-how than practical know-how.

The topic of ethics has been the subject of extensive debate for millennia. Like matters of knowledge and learning, conceptions of ethics are hinged to beliefs about the nature of the universe and the sources of truth. Within metaphysical traditions, for instance, ethics are understood as ideal, universal, and enduring principles that are somehow inscribed into creation. Mystics see ethics as woven into the fabric of the universe, religious adherents consider ethics to be matters of divine revelation, and rationalists see ethics as logically deducible.

Common to these conceptions is the assumption that ethics are matters of conscious and explicit knowledge. The sources of conviction vary, but across metaphysical traditions a tidy line is drawn between what is right[2] and what is wrong. By contrast, within ecological discourses, ethics are understood not in terms of formal principles or propositions, but in terms of action. Ethical action is understood as contextually appropriate behavior that may or may not be—and usually isn't—consciously mediated.

The suggestion that ethics may not be consciously mediated was actually first developed within intersubjectivist, and particularly poststructuralist, discourses. Ethics have been argued to be matters of collective accord, of tacit social contract. Ethical codes are seen by some structuralists and poststructuralists as largely arbitrary sets of rules deployed to maintain existing social orders. However, despite the departure from the metaphysical conviction that ethics are ideal and universal, these interpretations of ethics maintain one ancient assumption. For metaphysician and intersubjectivitist alike, ethics tend to be understood in terms of interactions of humans with other humans. One might say that ethical concerns have been seen to operate only in intersubjective space.

What might it mean to frame ethics in terms of interobjectivity rather than intersubjectivity—to consider questions of ethics within the more-than-human world, rather than delimiting discussions to the space of human concern? Not only does this move prompt departures from metaphysical worldviews and intersubjectivist discourses, it also moves beyond notions of complexity into matters of complicity. This sort of shift is timely given such developments as the now-apparent role of human activity in ecosystems, the prospect of pulling biological evolution into the space of the conscious and the volitional through genetic engineering, and the emergence of technologies that amplify our potential impact on the planet. These concerns are added to those already foregrounded within poststructuralist discourses, including, for instance, the decline of cultural diversity, ever-widening gaps between have and have-not nations, and persistent social inequities rooted in perceived differences among races, classes, and other means of distinguishing one human from another.

A mere 25 years ago, along with 150 other preservice teachers, I listened to a professor of psychology as he explained that (nonhuman) animals could not think—that their limited capacities to learn were strictly matters of stimulus–response, cause–effect associations. Knowledge, for him and within the anthropocentric academic discourse that he represented, was a strictly human phenomenon. In another lecture, he explained the evils of anthropomorphism—that is, of ascribing such qualities as intentions and knowledge to anything other than singular human beings, the only site of knowing that was permitted.[3] Questions of ethics did not come up in that class. They couldn't. If everything in the realm of the nonhuman operates on a cause–effect, mechanical logic, and if there are no transcendent unities, it hardly makes sense to engage with matters of meaning, value, and conduct.

I'm dismayed to report that the same sensibilities continue to be represented in the text used in the only course on learning that is required in the preservice teacher education program at my home university. I suspect this situation is not at all unusual. It seems to fit with the increasingly anachronistic phenomenon of the public school—an artifact of modernism that in some ways persists in its centuries-old emphasis on equipping learners with the attitudes and knowledge appropriate to 16th-century society.

How could it be that a cultural institution that defines itself in terms of preparing for the future could have so tenuous a connection with the present? Part of the answer, I believe, is that schooling has been oriented by matters of practical action, not ethical action.

Varela[4] explains that ethical action arises from a deep appreciation of the virtuality of one's own identity—a knowledge that one's self is a fluid, always-emergent, biological-and-cultural form. Knowing, doing, and being are inseparable. One might thus embody a conception of the self as pregiven and eternal and, hence, not implicated in the events of the physical realm. One might also embody a conception of self as situated and emergent and, hence, complicit with events in the physical realm. Ethical action flows out of this latter sort of enactment. Ethical know-how is neither instinctive nor based on principles that are woven into the fabric of the universe. Rather, it is a mode of ongoing coping—a responsiveness to what is appropriate here and now.

As for what this ethical action might mean for living, generally, and teaching, specifically, many ecological discourses advocate an attitude of *mindful participation*[5] in the unfolding of personal and collective identities, culture, intercultural space, and the biosphere. In some important ways, the notion of mindful participation harkens back to the mystical traditions that prompted teaching to be described in terms *educing* and *educating*—of drawing out (see chap. 5). A teaching that is informed by ecological sensibilities might be understood in similar terms, although selves would be understood as emergent possibilities rather than pregiven but unactualized potentials. Further, and also resonating with mystical traditions, a teaching that is informed by ecological sensibilities would be attentive to the place of the individual within grander unities.

As might be expected, a consistent and broadly accepted vocabulary has not yet emerged for this sort of teaching. Some terms have been suggested that are resonant with the principles of ethical know-how, such as Sylvia Ashton-Warner's *conversing*,[6] Nel Noddings' ethic of *caring*,[7] Max van Manen's *pedagogical thoughtfulness*,[8] and Chet Bowers' *eco-justice*[9] (which he offers as an elaboration of poststructuralist emphases on social justice). In previous work, I have described this conception of teaching as *hermeneutic listening*.[10]

These notions point more to teachers' attitudes than to the pragmatics of teaching. To that end, the one I find particularly useful for describing the teacher's activity in the classroom is *conversing*. The word is derived from the Latin *convertio*, "living together", and thus resonates with the notion of *oikos*, "household", which is echoed in the contemporary prefix, *eco-*. A conversation is an emergent form, one whose outcome is never prespecified and is sensitive to contingencies.

An exploration of what the metaphor of teaching as conversation might mean for life in the classroom is provided by Sylvia Ashton-Warner in *Teacher*, an account of her work with Maori children. Published in 1963, Ashton-Warner anticipated many aspects of current complexivist and ecological attitudes toward teaching. For example, she describes the learner and the classroom as organic—that is, in the terms I've used here, as emergent structures. Perhaps most significant, in the context of describing specific teaching strategies and emphases, she communicates a sense of deep ethical responsibility in a manner consistent with ecological sensibilities.

She also talks about "harnessing children's sociality" and "communal mind" in ways reminiscent of the discussions of structural coupling and collectivity in the previous chapter. It is in reference to such notions that she describes teaching as conversing. Recent neurophysiological research supports her use of the term. When engaged in conversations, our working memories are vastly larger than they are on our own. We are able to recall more detail, juggle more issues, represent more complex ideas, and maintain better focus than when alone.[11] Part of the reason is that conversations involve interlocking consciousnesses—a quality of interpersonal engagement that is all but ignored in the traditional, radically individuated classroom.

Extending this notion of interlocking subjectivities, and as developed in chapter 15, another suggestion that I find compelling is an elaboration of the complexivist suggestion that the classroom might be productively recast as a collective unity. However, a problem with this suggestion is that it says little about the role of the teacher beyond responsibilities for ensuring that the conditions necessary for complex emergence are in place. In ecological terms, the role of the teacher in the classroom collective might be understood as analogous to the role of consciousness in an individual.

To reiterate some earlier points, despite popular assumption, our consciousnesses do not direct our thoughts and actions. In fact, for the most part, human consciousness operates more as a commentator than an orchestrator.[12] However, consciousness does play an important role in orienting attentions—that is, through differential attention, in selecting among the options for action and interpretation that are available to the conscious agent. Succinctly, consciousness doesn't direct, but it does orient. Such is the role of the teacher in the eco-minded classroom: attending to and selecting from among those possibilities that present themselves to her or his awareness. In this sense, teaching is about *minding*—being mindful in, being conscious of, being the consciousness of—the collective.

WHERE TO NOW?

This chapter was concerned with notions and vocabulary associated with teaching that have emerged among ecological discourses—specifically, the terms and phrases *mindful participation, conversing, caring, pedagogical thoughtfulness, eco-justice, hermeneutic listening,* and *minding.* This chapter ends both the discussion of teaching emphases that arise from the notions of interobjectivity and the discussion of educational attitudes that are rooted in evolutionary dynamics.

17

Reinventions of Teaching:

EXPANDING THE SPACE OF THE POSSIBLE

A good simulation, be it a religious myth or scientific theory, gives us a sense of mastery over our experience. To represent something symbolically, as we do when we speak or write, is somehow to capture it, thus making it one's own. But with this approximation comes the realization that we have denied the immediacy of reality and that in creating a substitute we have but spun another thread in the web of our grand illusion.

— Heinz Pagels[1]

The temperature this morning was −32°C, which is more than 20 degrees below the average low temperature for this time of year. My initial response to reading the thermometer was, "It's *supposed to be* −10!"—an assertion which reveals, despite my best efforts, that aspects of metaphysical belief (e.g., the way the universe is *supposed to be*) and mathematized notions of normality (e.g., that an *average* temperature is somehow an *ideal* temperature) continue to frame my unguarded habits of interpretation.

I'm comforted by the fact that I'm not alone in this tendency to maintain diverse, even conflicting, sensibilities. In the course of researching aspects of this book, I came across a great many examples of our human capacity to hold incompatible beliefs—in fact not just to hold them, but to freely combine them into notions that are imagined to be coherent. For example, I've encountered references to evolutionary determinism, naturalist metaphysics, eco-Christianity, and numerous New Age movements—all of which, in one way or another, involve the merging of a belief in an ideal realm with an embrace of an evolutionary dynamic. Descartes was clearly way off the mark in his assertion that we are principally rational creatures.

It's hardly surprising, then, that there is an enormous diversity of belief represented in contemporary discussions of learning and teaching. The rationale statements at the start of virtually any current curriculum document can be used to underscore this point. It's not unusual to find references to nurturing individuals toward their full potentials, guiding them to their proper places in society, instructing them in sound habits of mind, measuring educational achievement, modeling appropriate behaviors, and empowering learners—despite the incoherences that emerge when such statements are clustered together.

Although the diversity of belief around matters of learning and teaching should not be unexpected, I must confess that I'm troubled by the fact that the phenomena of teaching itself is rarely the site of contestation in debates of educational reform. True, teaching *methods* are popular topics, but one hardly ever encounters discussions on what *teaching* is. Instead arguments tend to swirl around the specific curriculum topics that should be covered, the levels of proficiency that should be demonstrated, and the classroom structures that are more or most effective. The point is brought home to me each year at an annual meeting of educational researchers, where upward of 15,000 conference attendees spread their attentions across more than 3,000 research reports. As I move from session to session, I'm repeatedly reminded that we have few common undestandings of learning and teaching—despite the pretense that the meanings of these terms are settled.

Almost all of my formal educational experience has been oriented by the question: How do we make people learn what we want them to learn? This common concern relies on the transparent assumption that entrenched perspectives on learning are appropriate to the task of teaching. Such was certainly the premise of most of the courses in my own undergraduate teacher education program. I distinctly recall, for example, an item on the multiple-choice final examination in one class: "What is learning?" The correct answer, which I still have memorized, came directly from the text: "Learning is modification in behavior due to experience". Taking the next step along this line of thought, it follows that teaching must be the provision of experiences intended to induce those modifications in behavior that are desired.

At the time I was unaware that these ideas are driven by some deeply rooted cultural assumptions about causality and independence—two issues that have been recast through intersubjectivist and interobjectivist accounts of knowledge. These discourses frame learning in terms of change in the being of the learner, not simply "modification in behavior". They also problematize the assertion that learning is "due to experience"—a formulation that places the responsibility for the things learned on events outside the imagined boundaries of the learner. Within intersubjectivist and interobjectivist discourses, experience is understood in terms of triggers, not causes. Learning is a matter of structural change of the learner, which, while conditioned by particular circumstances, is "due to" the agent's own complex structure. Such conclusions represent a rejection of the notions of linear causality that were transposed from the analytic sciences onto discussions of teaching. Cause–effect interpretations make little sense when learners are understood to embody their own histories.

Pragmatically, this sort of thinking compels reconsiderations of many of the structures and artifacts that have been prominent in discussions of teaching. For instance, such fundamental contrivances as prespecified learning objectives and formal lesson plans do not fit with embodied understandings of learning. One of the current challenges is thus to develop new vocabularies that might support new habits of acting. To recap a few points made in this text, learning objectives and classroom activities might be usefully framed in terms of liberating constraints—that is, in terms of establishing a balance between sufficient organization to orient learners' actions and sufficient openness to allow for the varieties of experience, ability, and interest represented in any classroom. The classroom might be reframed as a collective learner—that is, as a self-organizing, coherent, and evolving unity—as opposed to a collection of assumed-to-be independent and isolated learners. This shift prompts a redescription of lesson plans as thought experiments rather than itineraries or trajectories—as exercises in anticipation, not prespecification. So framed, a lesson plan is distinct from a lesson structure, the latter of which can only be realized in the event of teaching. (These sorts of ideas are developed in greater detail elsewhere.[2])

However, my main purpose for writing this book was not to propose a new vocabulary for teaching. Rather, the intention was to underscore that there is a surprising variety of opinions represented in current vocabularies. I believe that we must be careful not to allow this diversity to fade into the backdrop of debates on educational reform. Ours is a teaching species. We act out our beliefs about who we are and who we might be in the structures that we build around efforts to teach. For instance, the modernist assertions-turned-assumptions that humans are rational and radically individuated have been embodied in four centuries of prescriptive technique-driven models of teaching.

Another example, perhaps more profound, is the way that diverse metaphysical beliefs are sustained and concealed by habits of speech. As I researched the histories of many of the synonyms for teaching discussed in the first half of this book, I repeatedly came across the Indo-European root, *deuk-*, "to lead, draw, drag, tug"— present in *educe, educate, induce, induct, introduce, introduction, deduce, deduction, induction, reduce,* and *reduction.*[3] Themes of control, grasping, and prelimited potentials are foregrounded in this family of terms. Mystical, religious, rationalist, and empiricist beliefs about the nature of knowledge, the processes of learning, and the implications for teaching are all represented in this particular mesh of association and dissociation.

Another cluster of terms that is woven through the sorts of sensibilities discussed in the first part of the book is one rooted in Euclid's geometry of the plane. Notions drawn from Euclid infuse many premodern and modern worldviews, evidenced by the prominence and privilege of straightness, rightness, directness, normality, and standardness (all of which originally had to do with lines or right angles; see Appendix B). The root of plane, the Latin *planus* for "flat", is echoed in such terms as *plan*, *plain*, and *explanation*—the last of which originally meant "to lay flat".

The belief that teaching is mainly a matter of explanation—of flattening things out—continues to prevail in contemporary discussions of education. Yet the notion has recently given some ground to suggestions that teaching is more about explication than explanation. Derived from the Indo-European *plek-*, "to weave, plait, fold, entwine"—also echoed in *explicit, implicit, implicate, complicit, complicate, complex, complexity*[4]—explication is part of a family of terms that points to a world that is more tentative, to possibilities that are emergent rather than prelimited, to actions that are more about interrupting or dispersing control that acquiring it. While conducting etymological searches for terms presented in the second half of this text, I often encountered members of this family. This cluster of words is knitted through structuralist, poststructuralist, complexivist, and ecological discussions of knowledge, learning, and teaching.

Different senses of the goals and purposes of schooling are entailed here. In the sorts of classrooms described through the last half of this book, the possibilities for interpretation and action are not predetermined. Rather, such classrooms might open new spaces of possibility—a proposition that is utterly incompatible with the ends-oriented, test-driven culture of modern schooling. It's not clear to me whether conventional structures of formal education are flexible enough to accommodate the conceptions of teaching that are associated with intersubjectivist and interobjectivist sensibilities, although there are nontraditional institutions that have found ways to embody many of these sensibilities.[5]

In an earlier book, Dennis Sumara, Rebecca Luce-Kapler, and I wrote that there was one point of agreement across the diversity of opinions on the nature of teaching—namely, that teaching has to do with one group's desires, conscious and unconscious, to have another group see things the same way they do.[6] I now find myself disagreeing with that assertion.

Oriented by complexivist and ecological discourses, teaching and learning seem to be more about expanding the space of the possible and creating the conditions for the emergence of the as-yet unimagined, rather than about perpetuating entrenched habits of interpretation. Teaching and learning are not about convergence onto a pre-existent truth, but about divergence—about broadening what is knowable, doable, and beable. The emphasis is not on what *is*, but on what might be brought forth. Thus learning comes to be understood as a recursively elaborative process of opening up new spaces of possibility by exploring current spaces.

Learning is the dynamic of existence; when it happens on levels other than the individual, we tend to notice it as evolution (of species, societies, cultures, knowledge, social movements, etc.). Teaching reaches through and across the layers of these entangled, evolving forms. Teaching, then, is never simply a personal or an interpersonal act. It touches the subpersonal through the planetary. Teaching is participating in the transformation of what is.

In this way, teaching participates in the invention and reinvention of itself. Unlike many of the forms that contribute to the structures of our existences, teaching has a say in what it becomes.

A GENEALOGICAL TREE
of Contemporary Conceptions of Teaching

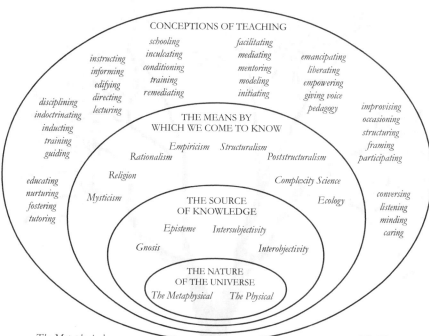

The Metaphysical

The universe is seen to be complete and unchanging—and, hence, understood in terms of other-worldly ideals and essences.

Collective knowledge and personal learning tend to be framed in terms of convergences onto ultimate truths. They are thus understood as acquisitions and accumulations of absolute facts. Thought is seen to be uniquely human.

WESTERN
WORLDVIEWS

The Physical

The universe is understood to be emergent—and, hence, described in terms of transformations and diversifications.

Collective knowledge and personal learning tend to be framed in terms of divergences—that is, as opening up of new possibilities. They are understood as processes that occur constantly, on and across many levels of organization.

APPENDIX B

A Brief Introduction to
FRACTALS

COMMONSENSE AND EUCLIDEAN GEOMETRY

For most English speakers, the word *geometry* conjures images of lines, triangles, circles, and other forms that are studied in one of the less popular strands of traditional secondary school mathematics. Geometry tends to be understood as synonymous with *Euclidean geometry*, a system developed in the third century BCE.

Euclid didn"t invent geometry. Rather, he systematized a particular class of mathematical forms—specifically, those that could be constructed on a plane by using such instruments as a compass and a straightedge. Euclid"s great contribution was the application of deductive logic to demonstrate that everything that the ancient Greeks knew about planar forms could be traced to and knit from five axioms.

This development actually prompted a narrowing of the definition of *geometry*. A century earlier, the term was understood more broadly to refer to "reasoned thought". This was the sense intended by Plato in the famous inscription above the door to his Academy, "Let no one ignorant of geometry enter here".[1] Plato"s geometry wasn"t focused on figures drawn on the plane, but on a mode of argumentation that he believed could be used to gain access to truths that were assumed to exist in a realm beyond this physical world (see chap. 2).

Despite the fact that Euclid"s usage of the term was more restricted than Plato"s, his geometry of the plane actually helped to entrench the formal logical argument in Western mindsets. Euclidean geometry currently serves as a sort of transparent backdrop of commonsensical understandings of the world and academic discourse. For example, our living spaces are structured by right angles and parallel lines, our lives are organized by linearized conceptions of time, and virtually every university researcher has struggled with demands for plain language and straightforward arguments.

It might be tempting to dismiss these observations as related to, but not really rooted in, Euclidean geometry. After all the most efficient way to build a house or a city is to organize things around a rectangular grid—axioms or no axioms. The connection between *plain* language and *plane* geometry seems to be little more than a case of homonyms. However, examinations of the histories and inherited meanings of terms derived from and associated with Euclidean geometry demonstrate that contemporary commitments—physical and conceptual—to the forms of the plane are neither benign nor inert. They are anchored in and project a particular worldview.

The influence of Euclidean forms on the collective imagination might be illustrated through the web of associations that has arisen around the straight line. The Latin word for straight, *rectus*, is heard in many current English words, including *correct, direct, erect, rectangle, rectify,* and *erect. Right* is also a derivative of *rectus*, and so straightness is also echoed in such phrases and dyads as "right of way", "right and wrong", "right and left", "rights and responsibilities", and "right angle". *Regula*, Latin for "straightedge", is the root of regular and regulate, as well as rule and ruler. The word *line* is derived from the Latin *linum*, "flax (linen) thread", and is prominently represented in some key notions: "time line", "line of argument", "linear causality", and "toeing the line" are just a few of many common expressions. *Straight*, from the German *streccan*, "to stretch", is just as well represented in contemporary phrases: "straight talk", "straight and narrow", and "straight-laced", for example. *Normal,* from the Latin *norma*, "carpenter"s (right-angled) square", is heard in the popular constructs of "normal family", normal child", "normal development", and "normal life". I could go on.

In fact I could go on and on. Terms such as *standard, normal, orthodox,* and *plain* are also rooted in Euclidean geometry. So are *truth, justification,* and *ordinary*. But the point might be better made by looking at some antonyms. For instance, things that aren"t planar are warped, distorted, or not on the level. Things that aren"t straight are bent, kinky, perverse, or twisted. Things that aren"t normal are deviant and aberrant. Things that aren"t pointed or to the point are dull or blunt.

Euclidean geometry, through both its mode of argumentation and its forms, has been a significant influence in the emergence of modern philosophy and modern science. Most prominently, it served as the model for Descartes in his articulation of his philosophical methods (see chap. 7). It also served as the principal source of interpretive tools within modern research—especially notions associated with lines. In fact until recently, almost all research into complex and dynamic phenomena was structured around efforts to define linear relationships among the objects studied.

This quest for linear models was originally a matter of computational necessity, not representational accuracy. Newton, for example, was well aware that many phenomena were not linear. He and the generations of scientists who followed were obliged to substitute linear approximations for nonlinear events simply because the calculations required for nonlinear models were much too demanding for pen and paper.[2] Unfortunately, the practice of imposing linear interpretations on nonlinear phenomena became so automatic and pervasive that many scientists (and the public at large) eventually came to believe that virtually all phenomena could be appropriately represented with line-based constructs.

The situation has begun to change in recent years. With the advent of powerful calculation technologies, science is coming to interpret nonmechanical aspects of the universe in terms of relentless nonlinearity (see chaps. 11 and 14). Even so entrenched beliefs about linear causality and linear relations linger. Such beliefs are as prevalent among educators and educational researchers as among any other group. For example, oriented by assumptions that linear relationships exist between particular aspects of teaching behavior or classroom context and student performance, teachers have been assaulted with advice and imperatives on lesson structures, question-posing, seating arrangements, explanation styles, practice exercises, wall colors, lighting levels, class sizes, and so on. Closely related, it is not unusual to come across reports on linear-relation-seeking studies in which statistical methods were used to "control for" such "confounding variables" as "teachers, schools, and classrooms". The mind boggles.

Such studies are lodged in rationalist and empiricist attitudes toward knowledge, learning, and teaching. As I develop in this text, other interpretive frames are possible—and almost all of them invoke nonlinear interpretive tools. One source of nonlinear images that I find personally compelling is fractal geometry.

UNCOMMON SENSE AND FRACTAL GEOMETRY

In the early 1800s, mathematicians realized that Euclid"s was not the only geometry. By tinkering with one of his five axioms, new possibilities emerged—ones that gave rise to new forms and new conclusions that proved to be every bit as valid and useful as those rooted in Euclid. (For instance, one of these new branches of mathematics was spherical geometry, which is of tremendous value in projects that involve spherical rather than planar forms, such as mapping the planet.) Toward the end of the 1800s, in a different branch of mathematical study, some mathematicians began to generate and examine forms that departed so radically from the objects of Euclidean geometry that they were labeled as *monstrous* and *patho-logical.* Unfortunately, these forms are difficult to study because many, many calculations were needed to generate their images. For several decades, little attention was paid to them.

The reason that so many calculations were required is that these forms were generated through recursive processes. In contrast to Euclidean forms, which are built up through linear sequences of operations, to create one of these monstrous forms one had to apply a rule to generate a result, then apply the rule to that result to generate an new result, and then to continue in this manner. There are no end points to recursive processes, merely stopping points.

By way of example, if I begin with a seed of a simple line segment

SEED:

and apply a rule—in this case, whenever I encounter a form that resembles the seed, I draw two prongs on one end—

RULE (and ITERATION 1):

after a few *iterations* (i.e., applications of the recursive process), the emergent form begins to look a bit like a tree,

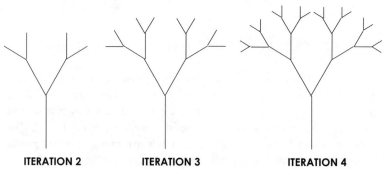

ITERATION 2   ITERATION 3   ITERATION 4

and after many iterations (a mere 16 in this case), it looks very much like a tree:

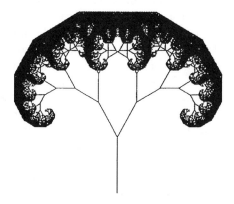

Minor variations on the seed and/or the rule can lead to some strikingly different results.[3]

Every stage in the generation of a fractal is an elaboration, and such elaborations can quickly give rise to surprising complexity. The resulting forms have some unusual properties—unusual, at least, when set against the backdrop of Euclidean geometry. A fractal, for instance, is *scale independent*, meaning that its bumpiness of detail remains constant no matter how much it is magnified or reduced.[4] Some fractals are also *self-similar*, a curious property by which a well-chosen part can closely resemble the whole—as in the tree above. Any of its branches, or branch of its branches, when magnified appropriately would be identical to the entire tree. Another feature, and the reason behind the adjectives *monstrous* and *pathological*, is that fractal forms slip between dimensions. For instance, the shape that traces out a coastline is neither 1-dimensional nor 2-dimensional, but somewhere between 1-d and 2-d.[5] Such transgressions and fragmentations of one of the most entrenched structures of classical mathematics—discrete dimensions—has prompted some dramatic developments in recent imaginings about the nature of the universe.[6]

Fractal geometry has been applied in many ways—in the medical sciences (e.g., to describe bone structures, circulatory systems, immune responses, brain organization, and neuronal interconnections), information science (e.g., to design the Internet, to compress data, to reduce noise in transmissions), economics (e.g., to represent market trends, to characterize the organizations of large corporations), and in the sociology of knowledge (e.g., to illustrate the tangled conceptual relations among and relative influences of different thinkers and philosophies), to name a few fields.

The list of applications is growing constantly and rapidly and is so diverse that fractal geometry has been dubbed "the mathematics of surprise", "the mathematics of complexity", and "the geometry of nature".

The "geometry of nature" reference is a particularly popular one, prompted in large part by a statement made early in the history of fractal geometry. Benoit Mandelbrôt, the mathematician who coined the word *fractal*, noted that "Clouds are not spheres, mountains are not cones, coastlines are not circles, and bark is not smooth, nor does lightning travel in a straight line".[7] In this statement, Mandelbrôt was making two points: First, modern science has tended, somewhat problematically, to describe natural forms in terms of Euclidean forms; second, natural forms seem to have much in common with fractal forms, including underlying recursive processes, surprising complexity on the basis of often-simple inputs, scale independence, some level of self-similarity, and a certain unpredictability. It is for these reasons that fractal geometry has been so broadly embraced across so many areas of inquiry. It"s simply a better fit than Euclidean geometry when it comes to efforts to represent and interpret complex phenomena.

The value of fractal geometry to studies of education is just beginning to be demonstrated. For example, in terms of description, the notions of scale independence and self-similarity are useful for making sense of the leveled and embedded natures of individuals, social collectives, bodies of knowledge, cultures, and societies. As discussed in this text, classical attempts to interpret these phenomena against one another have been frustrated by a tendency to dichotomize (i.e., focus on differences), a habit that is entangled with the sort of logic associated with Euclidean geometry.

A further contribution of fractal geometry to discussions of education arises in the fact that it is the geometry of complexity science. As discussed in chapters 14 and 15, complexity science is beginning to offer educators and educational researchers important interpretive tools and practical advice. In particular, it has provided a means of prying discussions of learning and teaching out of the frame of linear causality.

For more detailed discussions of fractal geometry, I recommended Mandelbrôt 1977, Gleick 1987, Stewart 1989, and Stewart 1998. For those interested in the relevance of fractal geometry to educational issues, I recommend Doll 1993 and Davis & Sumara 2000.

APPENDIX C

Clustered
GLOSSARY

The primary means of organization in this glossary is *association* rather than *alphabetization*. Terms have been clustered according to the shared assumptions around the natures of reality, knowledge, and learning—that is, according to the worldviews in which they are embedded and from which they emerged. To facilitate use, I begin with an alphabetized index.

Italics are used to indicate terms that are defined elsewhere in the glossary.

CONTENTS

Chapters 1 & 2 • Western Worldviews:
THE METAPHYSICAL V THE PHYSICAL

Bifurcation: an attitude toward distinction-making that is oriented by a desire to better understand the history and consequences of the distinctions that we tend to draw. This attitude might also be referred to as "the philosophy of the middle way". It is intended to prompt attentions to the shared assumptions that often underlie distinctions. The major products of this approach are *genealogies* (i.e., traces of the origins and interconnections of habits of inter-pretation). For example, a mental-versus-physical dyad is rooted in the ancient assumption that mental processes occur in the ideal realm and hence involve no physical processes—an assumption that neurophysiological and other *cognitive science* research has demonstrated as untenable. (Contrast with *dichotomization*.)

Dichotomization: a mode of distinction-making that is focused on the articulation of differences among the elements in a dyad—and that, in the process, can prompt senses of irresolvable tensions. For example, the prominent mind-versus-body and self-versus-other dichotomies are suggestive of radical splits.

Much of academic thought, at least since Aristotle, has been oriented by an attitude of dichotomization, the major products of which are taxonomies (i.e., systems of classification that seek unproblematic distinctions among species, races, questions, etc.). Indeed the privileged mode of academic engagement, the formal debate, is explicitly focused on the articulation of differences around superficially opposed claims to truth. (See *bifurcation* for an alternative attitude to distinction-making.)

Epistemology: the discussion of questions of knowing and knowledge. (Derived from the Greek, *episteme*—see below.)

Metaphysical/Metaphysics: a term with seemingly incompatible meanings in popular parlance—ranging from the *analytic philosophical* embrace of formal *reason* (i.e., *rationalism*) to the explicit rejection of formal argument in favor of the supernatural as a source of explanatory principles. The incompatibility is resolved in the recognition that both attitudes are rooted in the convictions that Truth is an ideal and incorporeal form and that we creatures of the corrupt and fallible flesh can only have access to it by denying, being deeply suspicious of, or otherwise ignoring our bodies.

Physical: a reference to the bodily or corporeal. In Western *metaphysical* traditions, the physical is distinguished from the mind or spirit, but this *dichotomy* is rejected within the theoretical and philosophical movements discussed in chapters 10 through 16. In this text, the modifier *physical* is used to refer to those discourses that do not rely on notions of the ideal or the supernatural to address questions of emergence and existence. This usage is consistent with the ancient, pre-Aristotelian origins of the term. Physical is derived from the Greek *physis*, "growth, nature", a cognate of *phyein*, "to bring forth"—which is also the root of the English infinitive, *to be*.

Chapter 3 • *The Metaphysical:* GNOSIS V EPISTEME

---

episteme: everyday, practical know-how. A complement to *gnosis*, which is more concerned with matters of spiritual meaning and divine truth, episteme is focused on the immediate and pragmatic. Unlike gnosis, as a category of knowledge, the truths of episteme must fit with observed realities. Whereas gnosis looks back at beginnings and asks big questions, episteme is more concerned with working through the details of current situations.

gnosis: Gnosis and *episteme* were once seen as complementary and distinct categories of knowledge—and both were considered essential. Until relatively recently, gnosis was seen as primary because it addresses what was thought to be the eternal and universal aspects of existence. Gnosis looks back to the origins of life, to the foundations of culture, and to the deepest levels of the human mind. In brief, gnosis is concerned with meaning, not with practical matters.

Chapters 4–6 • *Gnosis:* MYSTICISM V RELIGION

Alchemy: a variety of *hermeticism* that emphasizes the interconnectedness of all things. Alchemy is best known for the efforts of some alchemists to transform baser metals into higher ones, but it is more properly understood as a *mystical* tradition concerned with the transformation of base humans into higher spiritual beings.

Determinism: the idea that there are no accidents. Everything that is going to happen is absolutely determined—either by a higher power or order (as posited by mystical and religious traditions) of by what has already happened (as assumed within pre-20th-century science).

Fundamentalisms: efforts to fortify beleaguered *religious* identities by means of a selective retrieval of certain doctrines and practices of the past, coupled to an absorption of *rationalist* or *modernist* sensibilities (or, at least, the façade of rationalism—because fundamentalisms tend to operate from the assumption that the truth of existence has already been divinely revealed and is therefore not in need of rational interrogation). For the most part, fundamentalisms (across most of the world's major religions, albeit that the specific obsessions vary across different fundamentalist movements) have arisen as responses to perceived crises, such as secularist policies, economic or military incursions, and rapid cultural transformations (especially those prompted and enabled by technological developments).

Hermeticism: a strand of *mysticism* that embraces a variety of influences and traditions. Hermeticists hold that the great work of humans and humankind is to return to a state of unity with the divine through creative and transformative engagement.

Mysticism: an umbrella term that refers to worldviews structured around the belief that reality exceeds human capacity to explain. Knowledge (*gnosis*) is understood to inhere in the cosmos and to be accessed through means of divination. Mysticisms tend to be *pantheistic* rather than *theistic*. (Contrast *religion*.)

Mythos: the complex of knowledge (*gnosis*)—including beliefs, values, attitudes, and so on—that are characteristic of a society or culture and that orient human interactions with one another and with the nonhuman world.

Neoplatonism: a *mystical*-philosophical tradition, originally derived from Plato's metaphysics. It has three key tenets: (a) a dichotomization of spirit and flesh, (b) a suspicion of sensory perception, and (c) the embrace of an ascetic lifestyle as a means to transcend one's base existence. Neoplatonism is regarded as one of the major influences of both *mystical* and *religious* belief systems in the modern Western world.

Pantheism: the identification of the supernatural with the natural. Rather than seeing nature as created and/or controlled by god(s), the divine is understood to infuse the natural world. (Constrast *deism* and *theism*.)

Religion: an institutionalized, usually *theistic*, system of belief. Religions tend to be developed around the assumption that divine knowledge is revealed by an all-powerful God. Humans are obligated to organize their lives according to the strictures with those revelations.

Religious myths and narratives are usually framed in terms of dichotomies that require some sort of resolution. These include creation stories (e.g., the separation of darkness from light, the divine from the mortal, the human from the natural, etc.), which are typically accompanied by stories of redemption.

Teleology: an explanation of a phenomenon that is based on the assumption that everything has an ultimate design or obeys an ultimate purpose.

Theism: a belief in God as a supernatural being who actively intervenes in the affairs of the world. (Contrast *deism*.)

Chapters 7–9 • *Episteme:* RATIONALISM V EMPIRICISM

Analysis: the separation of a unity—which could be an event, a claim to knowledge, a material object, and so on—into its constituent parts for study. The term that traces back to the Greek *analusis*, dissolving. (See *analytic philosophy*, *analytic science*, and *reductionism*.)

Analytic Philosophy: an approach to formal argument that is framed by an attitude of *analysis*—the logical reduction of a claim to truth to its basic premises. Analytic philosophy is associated with *rationalism*.

Analytic Science: the approach to knowledge generation and verification that, in the extreme interpretation, assumes that all phenomena can be understood in terms of logical and/or causal relations—which, ultimately, can be reduced to basic particles and fundamental laws. Analytic science is associated with *empiricism*. To really appreciate what analytic science is all about, it helps to know that both *analytic* and *science* have to do with taking things apart. (*Science* comes from the same root as *scissors*, *chisel*, and *incisor*. See *analysis* for an etymology of *analytic*.) More generously, analytic science is one of several attitudes in scientific inquiry—the one that is particularly well suited to the study of mechanical events. (Compare to *complexity science*.)

a posteriori: an inductive mode of argumentation, whereby conclusions are derived from observed events. This is the mode that is associated with *empiricism*. (Literally translated, *a posteriori* means "from the latter". Compare *a priori*.)

a priori: a deductive mode of argumentation, whereby conclusions are derived from self-evident propositions. This is the mode that is associated with *rationalism*. (Literally translated, *a priori* means "from the former". Compare *a posteriori*.)

Atomism: See *reductionism*.

Behaviorism: an approach to the study of learning that begins with (a) an *empiricist* (specifically, *positivist*) attitude and (b) an assumption of a *Cartesian subject*. By consequence, learning is understand as a change in observable behavior that is due to experience, which in turn prompts attentions to assumed-to-be-causal relations between actions and reward structures, chains (vs. webs) of associations, and so on. Notably, behaviorism does not deny the presence of mental processes and mental objects (in fact the theory assumes an edifice of stimuli–response connections in the brain); the point is simply that rigorous (empiricist oriented) research must focus on observable phenomena. (See *conditioning*.)

Cartesian (Modern) Subject: a conception of the human knower as an incorporeal entity that is entrapped in a physical body—insulated from the real world, isolated from one another. The notion of a Cartesian subject is generally associated with a cascade of dichotomies, including mental/physical, mind/body, thought/action, internal/external, individual/collective, self/other, knower/knowledge, subjective/ objective, observer/observed, and fact/fiction. (Compare to *postmodern subject* and *complex subject*.)

Cartesianism: loosely synonymous to *modernism*, but more strongly reflecting the Western tendency to attribute transitions in collective sensibility to individuals (in this case, the 17th-century mathematician and philosopher, René Descartes) rather than to broader and more gradual swellings in cultural attitudes.

cogito: abbreviated from Descartes' formulation *cogito ergo sum* (usually translated, somewhat inappropriately, as "I think, therefore I am"—but more appropriately phrased in the less causal terms of "I think, I am"), *cogito* is a reference to the *rationalist* project of deriving all truth from self-evident propositions.

Cognitive theory: See *mentalism*. (The term should not be confused with *cognitive science*.)

Cognitivism: (also known as computationalism) that branch of *mentalism* that is developed around the *metaphor*, "brain as computer". Attentions are thus oriented by notions of input, processing, storage, output, and so on. Internal representations are usually understood in terms of binary encodings of information, as opposed to formal propositions (as Descartes saw them) or as some sort of image- or language-based model of the world (as tends to be the conception in popular parlance).

Conditioning: The model of teaching that arises (logically) from *behaviorist* perspectives on learning. Psychologically speaking, conditioning (or training) is a process intended to alter the response of a learner to a particular stimulus or situation.

Correspondence theories: accounts of language in which it is asserted that words are meaningful because they correspond to objects or events in the real world. (Contrast with *structuralism* and *system of difference*.)

Deism: a belief that a supernatural entity—usually identified as a god (or *the* God)—created or was the principal cause of the universe, but no longer has any hand in its affairs. The suggestion is that the cosmos has a supernatural or metaphysical origin, but since the moment of creation it has unfolded according to natural or physical laws instituted at the moment of creation.

Empiricism: This is the other of the two major attitudes within the modernist stance (compare to *rationalism*). It asserts that any claim to truth must be demonstrable on the basis of objective and replicable physical experiments. Empiricism is rooted in the assumption that all of science is *analytic science*. In some ways, it is the opposite of rationalism, in that it seeks to derive basic principles and fundamental laws on the basis of observations of phenomenon, as opposed to seeking explanations of phenomenon in the logical knit of self-evident propositions. Both emphases, however, share an unquestioning faith in the power of *reason*. (See *a posteriori*.)

Essentialism: the belief that human identity pre-exists language, culture, and experience. (The term is also used to refer to the doctrine, inherited from ancient Greek philosophy, that material objects have an essence that can be distinguished from their physical attributes. Dogs, for example, are assumed to be dogs because of they have the essential quality of dogness.) Essentialism is rooted in the assumption that the universe is as it always was; it does not evolve.

Humanism: philosophically speaking, an attitude toward the development and justification of claims to truth that does not rely on notions of God or the supernatural. Humanism asserts that knowledge does not inhere in nature, but is a human product. More extreme versions of humanism hold that humans have the conceptual wherewithal to come to a complete understanding of the universe. (Contrast with *theism*.)

Idealism: the doctrine/belief, articulated by Plato, that thought or the mind is the only reality and that external objects consist merely of ideas. (See *essentialism*. Compare with *realism*, and note how both attitudes rely on a radical separation of internal from external. Also note how *idealism*, which originates with the philosophy of the ancient Greeks, is aligned with the *rationalist* project.)

Instruction: The model of teaching that arises (logically) from *mentalist* perspectives on learning and cognition. As any recent dictionary will highlight, *instruction* has to do with providing order and direction (note the underlying line-based assumptions). It's also interesting to note that *instruction* is now used to refer to the coded commands that direct a computer to perform specified functions—an extension of meaning that is likely hinged to the *cognitivist* assumption that brains and computers are alike (hence, one would instruct a computer as one would instruct a learner, and vice versa). (See chap. 8.)

Logocentrism: the modernist belief that the word (whether spoken or written) can represent presence, essence, truth, and/or reality, and which will act as the foundation of all human thought, language, and experience. Logocentrism presumes a *correspondence theory* of language.

Mentalism: an attitude in the study of learning that begins with the assumption of the *Cartesian subject* and that, in contrast to *behaviorism*, focuses on internal mental processes and structures rather than external actions of knowers. Learning in this frame is understood as a process of assembling an internal model/representation of an external reality. Personal knowledge and understanding are understood and measured in terms of correspondence to an assumed-to-be independent, objective, and inaccessible external reality. (Also referred to as *cognitive theory*. See also *cognitivism* and *instruction*.)

Method of (systematic) doubt: a tenet of Descartes' project, by which he insisted that any belief or assertion that presents the slightest reason for doubt must be discarded. (Compare this requirement for absolute certainty to the *pragmatist* criteria for truth claims.)

Modern Era: the period in Western civilization that commenced, roughly, in the 17th century with such co-implicated cultural events as the Industrial Revolution, the rise of capitalism, urbanization, democratization, and the Scientific Revolution. The era continues—and technically will never end because *modern* is a reference to recentness and currency. (See *modernism*.)

Modernism: Epistemologically speaking, a modernist attitude toward knowledge and knowledge-generation is in effect an unquestioned faith in the project of *metaphysics*. Key assumptions in the modernist attitude include: the truth is out there (albeit not directly accessible to us, owing to the fallibility of our senses); we can get at truth through careful and incremental processes of *reasoning* and experimentation (see *analytic science*); and we are gradually progressing toward a complete and total knowledge of the universe. Included among the prominent critiques of modernism are its assumptions of linear progress, its tendency toward totalized (master) narratives, its rejection of other epistemological attitudes and worldviews, and the blind spots created by its adherence to the knowledge-seeking question of "Can we ... ?" rather than the wisdom-oriented question of "Should we ...?" (Compare with *postmodernism*.)

Modernist attitudes can be subdivided into two main categories: *rationalism*, which is oriented to the internal and the abstract, and *empiricism*, which is oriented more toward the external and physical. The apparent opposition here is only superficial. *Rationalism* and *empiricism* share the same assumptions about the general structure of truth.

Nativism: the perspective that each brain or mind (the two terms are considered interchangeable) has a specific, innate structure that does not change through experience. This assumption underpins contemporary beliefs about personality types, learning styles, and multiple intelligences.

Normal/Normality: Within modernist frames, *normal* is most prominently understood in terms of statistical measurement—one is normal if one is within one or two standard deviations of the mean. (Compare with *normativity*.)

Positivism: a movement in *analytic science* that asserted that all claims to truth must be based on observable, measurable, and replicable phenomena. The term *positivism* is derived from the assertion that science must be focused on the generation of positive knowledge—that is, insights that affirm truths and are testable, as opposed to claims to truth that are based on denials and negations (such as those generated within *skepticist* traditions or through Descartes' *method of doubt*).

Rationalism: This is one of the two major attitudes within the *modernist* stance (compare to *empiricism*) that traces back to the *Idealist* school of ancient Greek philosophy. Both are given to an unapologetic faith in *reason*. In the case of rationalism, it is assumed that the route to unimpeachable knowledge is from first principles to the physical world—in effect, that self-evident propositions and their consequences form the basis of all knowledge, morals, conduct, and so on. (See *a priori*.)

Realism: the doctrine/belief that there are universal truths that exist independently of the mind—in a nutshell, "the truth is out there". The question of whether we can actually come to know that truth is another matter entirely. (Compare with *idealism*, and note how both attitudes rely on a radical separation of internal from external. Also note how *realism*, which originates with the philosophy of the ancient Greeks, is aligned with the *empiricist* project.)

Reason: Derived from the same roots as *rationalism*, reason is a reference to the formal logical argument. The Western privilege of this mode of deriving and defending truths extends historically at least to the ancient Greeks. Although it is most commonly associated with formal mathematics (Descartes, for instance, drew on Euclid's geometry as his model), the capacity and preference for formal reason appears to be strongly tied to literacy and literateness.

Reductionism: the attitude, within *modern* enlightenment modes of thought, that all phenomena and all claims to truth can be reduced to fundamental particles, basic laws, primitive assumptions, and essential causes. For instance, a reductionist economic theory would assert that economic events could be exhaustively explained in terms of the actions of individuals—which, it follows, could be exhaustively explained in terms of their constituent parts, and so on. (Also known as *atomism*.)

Representationisms: those theories of cognition in which learning and thought are seen to be matters of assembling internal models/representations of an external reality. The two key strands are *behaviorist* and *mentalist* perspectives. Both rely on the assumption of a *Cartesian subject*.

Scholasticism: a conceptual mix of Aristotelian philosophy, *neoplatonist mysticism*, and medieval Christian theology. Scholastism was the dominant school of thought in Christian theological and Western philosophical movements during the Middle Ages, and thus contributed greatly to the theoretical and philosophical movements in the time of Bacon and Descartes.

Skepticism: an ancient philosophical doctrine (dating from the 4th century BCE) that questions the notion and possibility of objective or absolute knowledge. The first skeptics argued that human knowledge is dependent on particular circumstances (which is why skepticism is sometimes, inappropriately, associated with *relativism*). The skeptics advocated a *method of doubt* as a means to assess the appropriateness of a claim to truth.

Chapter 10 • The Physical:
INTERSUBJECTIVITY V INTEROBJECTIVITY

Darwinism: mechanisms proposed by Darwin for the transformation of forms over time (including the evolutions as species, meanings, and customs) and increases in diversity and complexity (e.g., within an ecosystem, social collective, or culture). Epistemologically, the emergence of Darwinism triggered a profound break with modernist beliefs—in particular, *essentialism*, the assumption that the universe is pregiven and unchanging.

It is important to note that, although Darwinian or evolutionary processes are often assumed to be directional (e.g., from lower, simpler, or worse to higher, more complex, or better), Darwin's theory did not propose a direction, merely mechanisms for transformation and diversification. (See *natural drift* for a recent elaboration of Darwinism.)

Interobjectivity: an attitude toward knowledge that underscores the mutually affective relationships between phenomena and knowledge of phenomena. In interobjective terms, knowledge of the world arises in agents' actions within and interactions with the world. Knowledge is understood to inhere in interactions—that is, to be embodied or enacted in the ever-unfolding choreography of action within the universe. (Contrast with *intersubjectivity*.)

Interpretivism: Descartes is said to have prompted an "epistemological turn" in philosophy in his assertion that we should be spending our time on rational matters of how we know, not on questions of being and existence (which, to his view, were beyond our limited, perceptually corrupted reckonings). By contrast, many 20th-century discourses—in particular, the ones considered in this section of the glossary—are described as part of an "interpretive turn" in philosophy, whereby the focus shifted to matters of construals of reality through means that included, but exceeded, rational thought. In particular, the roles of *metaphor*, metonymy, and other analogical modes are taken seriously in interpretivist attitudes, as well as nonconscious cognitive processes that are all but ignored in Cartesian/analytic philosophy.

With the focus on language-effected realities, this category of discourses is focused on the realm of human interest and activity. (Contrast with *participatory epistemology*.)

Intersubjectivity: in simplest terms, the notion that all human knowledge is a matter of social accord—usually tacit and always enabled and constrained by the associations that are already established within language. (See *interpretism*. Contrast with *interobjectivity*.)

Participatory epistemology: any theory of knowledge that foregrounds the role of the knower's actions in and with the world. Participatory epistemologies are rooted in the assertion that all aspects of the world—animate and inanimate—are implicated in all aspects of knowing. See *interobjectivity*.

Chapters 11–13 • Intersubjectivity:
STRUCTURALISM V POSTSTRUCTURALISM

Activity theory: a *constructionist* theory that is rooted in the work of L.S. Vygotsky and his students (especially A.N. Leont'ev and A.R. Luria). Rejecting the individualistic foci of many psychological theories, including *behaviorisms* and *mentalisms*, activity theory foregrounds the role of artifacts in every-day life. It asserts that "mind" can only be understood in terms of goal-oriented, artifact-mediated, and culture-framed interactions between humans and their physical settings. Activity theorists call for the simultaneous study of agents, systems of artifacts (e.g., tools, language, signs), and other individuals—since these forms are tied together in ongoing processes of mutual specification.

Apprenticeship: the conception of teaching posited by *situated learning* theorists. The idea has been picked up by some educational researchers as a *metaphor* for interpreting and shaping schooling practice (e.g., elementary school science learners are described as apprentice scientists who are invited into the field by an expert—the teacher—who acts as a model or mentor).

Constructionism: (also referred to as *social constructivism*) a cluster of theories that is concerned with the manners in which collective knowledge is generated in the collaborative activities of individuals and how, in turn, that knowledge operates to frame the activities, understandings, and identities of those individuals. Learning is thus seen mainly in terms of socialization or enculturation—that is, of *embodying* collectively established sensibilities. A diversity of ideologies tends to be represented among constructionists, including *Marxist*, postcolonial, radical feminist, and other critical perspectives along with less politically oriented interpretive attitudes.

Constructivism: Usually traced to the work of Jean Piaget, (nontrivial) constructivist discourses might be characterized in terms of efforts to understand an individual's conceptual development in terms of *metaphors* of biological development. Concepts are thus seen as evolving and rooted in one's physical engagements with the world; learning is seen as an organic process through which a learner continuously adapts interpretations and expectations in order to incorporate new experiences into her or his system of understanding. (See *facilitation*.)

Continental philosophy: an umbrella term used to refer to philosophical discourses that rose to prominence in Europe during the 20th century, including *phenomenology*, *structuralism*, and *poststructuralism*.

Critical theory: a branch of *social constructivism (constructionism)* that finds its roots in critical *hermeneutics* from the late 19th century. Informed by several of the discourses mentioned in this section (in particular, *Marxism*), critical theorists tend to focus on the *metaphor* of power as manifest within particular knowledge domains and cultural practices. They note that power, for the most part, does not operate on conscious or deliberate levels, but tends to be tacitly inscribed in different systems of interpretation—especially those represented in modern curricula. (See *empowerment*.)

Cultural studies: an umbrella term used to refer to various efforts to discuss contemporary texts and cultural practices. Cultural studies draws from anthropology, sociology, gender studies, feminism, literary criticism, history, and all of the discourses mentioned in this section.

Deconstruction: an interpretive practice that aims to study usually-not-noticed aspects of language, images, ideas, and practices sponsor new understandings of how meaning is always constrained by *structures* and by one's ability to perceive and/or not perceive those structures. This is always an elaborative (vs. *reductive*) process that is aimed at bringing out what is excluded, concealed, or otherwise unsaid or unsayable.

Deference: a notion that highlights the necessary ignorances that are engendered when a particular detail is made the subject/object of attention. The idea is prominent in *postmodernist* discourses as they challenge the *modernist* quest for totalized understandings. Complete knowledge is unattainable, argue postmodernists, because all claims to truth are partial (both in the sense of "incomplete" and the sense of "biased"). Some discourses propose different mechanisms for partiality, including *psychoanalysis'* focus on repression and *critical theory's* worries about power.

Différance: a term coined by Jacques Derrida as a nod toward both the *structuralist* notion that meaning arises within *systems of difference* and the *poststructuralist* notion of *deference*.

Discourse/Discourse system: a unified and structured domain of language use (and the activities associated with language use) that organizes and constrains what can be said, thought, or done around such matters as schooling, gender, race, and sexuality. Discourses always function in relation or opposition to other discourses. Each discourse has its own distinctive set of rules and/or procedures that govern the production of what is to count as meaningful and/or true. Discourses change over time.

Discursive practices: specific uses of language and/or practices associated with language that function to create *discourse systems* (e.g., color-coding babies in pink or blue represents a discursive practice of gender).

Empowerment: the conception of teaching posited by *critical theorists*. Arising from concerns with *hegemony* and *power*, as inscribed in privileged disciplinary and educational structures, the teacher oriented by *constructionist (social constructivist)* attitudes seeks to alert learners to the structures that limit and enable their participation in society. The hope is that an awareness of these structures will empower learners to participate in the transformation of oppressive conditions.

Evolution: See *Darwinism*. (See also *natural drift*.)

Existentialism: a philosophy based on the assertion that neither perception (the basis of empiricism) nor logical thought (the basis of rationalism) is adequate for making sense of existence. Rather, existentialists hold that an understanding of existence can only arise by living—that is, in existentialist terms, by embracing the fact that existence is an unrelenting process of interpreting and reinterpreting being.

Facilitation: the conception of teaching posited by *constructivist* theorists. Oriented by the conviction that a teacher cannot cause a learner to learn anything in particular, teaching is seen as a circular facilitative process by which the teacher seeks to make sense of the sense the learner has made, perturb those understandings, make sense of the sense the learner makes of those perturbations, and so on.

Genealogy: a critical interpretive practice that aims to discern the ways in which *discourses* constitute the objects, practices, and/or subjects (*subjectivities*) that are available for study.

Genetic epistemology: a term used by Jean Piaget to refer to the development of personal understandings. Piaget invoked biological and evolutionary notions to describe the processes by which individuals continuously tinker with their understandings to make them fit with their experiences.

Gestalt: a term used to refer to theories that originally arose in psychology in the early 20th century in which perception was reinterpreted as an abstract cognitive achievement, as opposed to a straightforward interpretation of a physical stimulus. Gestalt theorists argued that objects of perception aren't given directly to the senses. Rather, they must be fished out of an immense sea of sensorial possibility.

Hegemony: the domination of one set of ideas and practices over others. Hegemony is achieved through political, ideological, *discursive*, and representational means (e.g., patriarchy is a hegemonic *discourse* with particular associated discursive practices).

Hermeneutics: a mode of inquiry that is oriented by two intertwining questions: What is it that we believe? How did we come to think that way? Hermeneutics seeks to trace out the *genealogies* of current understandings and practices.

Holism: a sensibility (as opposed to a field or movement) that arose in specific response to the *atomism* of *analytic science*. Holists endeavor to appreciate objects and entities in their functional wholenesses—that is, as more than the sums of their parts.

Linguistic determinism: the assertion that our language determines what we can and cannot think and perceive.

Marxism: the political and economic philosophy of Karl Marx (and Friedrich Engels). Marx saw cultural evolution in terms of an inevitable development, through class struggle, from capitalistic dominance of the bourgeois to a socialist, classless society.

Metaphor: a language-based means of interpretation and reasoning that involves the mapping of one category of experience onto another. In effect, what *reason* is to *modernism*, metaphor is to *postmodernism*. It is understood within most postmodernist discourses as the principal means by which humans elaborate their primal bodily experiences into more sophisticated, abstract understandings—which, in turn, might be further elaborated into even more abstract understandings. (An example is what Lakoff & Johnson 1999, call the "containment metaphor", which they demonstrate to be pervasive in our understandings of social, mathematical, and other concepts. They argue the notion to be rooted in such experiences as putting things in one's mouth.)

Naturalism: a category of theories in which consciousness and human life are understood as products of nature. In the 17th and 18th centuries, naturalists also sought to explain the emergence of society in terms of the effects of the natural environment. Naturalist philosophy helped set the stage for Darwin's theories of evolution, in part by disputing the then-prominent *humanist* emphasis on the active role of human beings in producing themselves through their own efforts. (Contrast with *humanism* and *theism*.)

Non-representationisms: those theories of cognition that reject the assumption that learning has to do with constructing and internal representation of an external reality. Non-representationist *discourses* tend to define cognition in terms of ongoing efforts by the cognizing agent to maintain fitness within ever-evolving circumstances. That is, this cluster of theories tends to agree that learning and cognition are *Darwinian* processes.

Different non-representationist accounts tend to part company around the matter of whether the individual is more responsible for construing a world (see *constructivisms*) or whether the world is more responsible for construing the individual (see *social constructionisms*).

Normativity: The establishment of mechanisms, procedures, disciplinary actions, measurements, systems of hierarchy, and regulations about what is to be considered the most correct representation of particular experiences (including experiences of identity). Categories of "abnormal" and "deviant" are understood as necessary to give form and shape to *normal*. Normative practices underpin the belief that what is considered normal is "natural". Current normalizing strategies have in large part been enabled and legitimated by statistics and statistical methods, which have been deployed in the social sciences to generate ostensibly scientific measurements of normal (and deviant) intelligence, sociality, sanity, and so on.

Phenomenology: a discourse through which one endeavors to better understand conscious experience (i.e., "lived experience") without recourse to *modernist* explanations or *metaphysical* assumptions. In brief, phenomenology is the study of the forms of consciousness in which researchers work to describe phenomena dispassionately with as few suppositions as possible. Phenomenology was among the first academic movements to develop research methods not founded on a *dichotomy* between objective reality and subjective experience.

Postmodern subject: Within *postmodern discourses*, when referring to human experience, "subject" is synonymous with "person" or "human being". The word *subject* implies agency, action, and authorship of identity, but it also points to subjection and deferral, thus rendering problematic the idea that human beings "choose" their identities and, as well, the idea that human subjects are determined by *discourses*.

Postmodernism: an umbrella term used to collect *discourses* that share one feature: a rejection of some aspect of *modernism*. For the most part, the term is applied retroactively to *discourses* that emerged in the 20th century. For the purposes of this text, the postmodern discourses that are of interest are the ones that reject the modernist principles of *essentialism*, *reason*, and *logocentrism*.

Poststructuralism: a reference to any *discourse* that involves critical interrogation of exclusionary procedures and/or mechanisms by which ideological, political, social, cultural, and/or personal standpoints or positions are established. Poststructuralist discourses also tend to involve efforts to construct *genealogies* of such positions.

Power: influence over collective beliefs about what is and is not natural. An example of the deployment of power is demonstrated in the perpetuation of the conviction that women are more nurturing and caring.

Pragmatism: To the pragmatist, truth is not ideal, eternal, or universal. It is rather what works—and hence practical, temporary, and contextually specific. In brief, practical consequences are seen to be the most important criteria for decisions around knowledge, values, and meaning.

Psychoanalysis: a method to study the mind that is based on investigation of the role of unconscious processes. As a discourse, psychoanalysis has helped foreground the roles of social habitus and nonconscious cognitive events in the shaping of the *subject*. Many of its constructs (e.g., the unconscious, the superego) and conclusions (e.g., cognition is mainly nonconscious) are echoed, if not explicitly invoked within, most *interpretivist* discourses.

Relativism: an embrace of the notion that the truth (or falsity) of a claim is relative to the person or group who makes the claim. A relativist attitude might involve a rejection of all modes of proof in favor of personal interpretation or cultural beliefs. Popularly, relativism is often (inappropriately) linked to *postmodernism*—usually by *modernists* who are unfamiliar with the philosophical commitments of postmodern discourses. (Note: A *complexivist* response to a relativist position is that different rules apply at different levels of organization. Hence, while on the personal level two individuals might be justified in their disagreement on a matter, owing to their different histories, at a social or cultural level, it may be that one of them must be considered correct and the other incorrect to maintain the viability of the collective.)

Romanticism: an artistic and intellectual movement that began in Europe in the late 18th century. Romanticism is characterized by a heightened interest in nature and an emphasis on personal expression of emotion and imagination. Romantics were critical of the sensibilities of *rationalism* and *empiricism*, and they rebelled against social conventions that were seen to be rooted in *metaphysics*.

Semiotics: derived from the Greek *semeion*, "sign", and the field of semiotics is the study of symbols and signs. Semiotics as a discipline is characterized by radical breaks in opinion. Not only are *structuralist* and *poststructuralist* sensibilities represented, but a good portion of research that is conducted under the banner of semiotics is oriented by *metaphysical* assumption.

Situated learning: a branch of *constructionist (social constructivist)* theory that is focused on the particular concern of how individuals become full members of subcultures (such as professions, communities, etc.). Theorists of situated learning tend to focus on the ways that novices or initiates are enculturated into existing communities of practice. (See *apprenticeship*.)

Social constructivism: See *constructionism*.

Structuralism: a method of investigation that is concerned with the structure—that is, the interconnections or internal coherences—of a phenomenon, such as a language, mathematics, personal knowledge, or a social system. For example, a structuralist interpretation of language would hold that meaning is a product of interrelationships among words, as opposed something that inheres in or is associated with individual words. Structuralism is often critiqued for its focus on form rather than content.

Subjectivity: refers to the self-conscious awareness of human subjects. As popularly used, subjectivity is a mode of awareness that is specific to modern Western capitalist culture. However, the experience of subjectivity is created in different forms, in different societies, and is informed by different *discursive systems and practices.* The use of the word *subjectivity* represents a way of conceptualizing discourse/subject relations without representing them either as fixed or unified categories. Instead subjectivity points to the fluidity through which subjects are created by *discourses* and, at the same time, create discourses.

System of difference: a *structuralist* notion, developed by Ferdinand de Saussure, associated with the assertion that the meanings of words and propositions arise in contrasts and gaps—differences—among them, not through any sort of direct correspondence to objects of events.

Chapters 14–16 • *Interobjectivity:*
COMPLEXITY SCIENCE V ECOLOGY

Artificial intelligence: the branch of computer science concerned with the simulation and/or production of intelligent behavior. Begun in earnest in the 1950s, AI research has fallen spectacularly short of early predictions, but its failures have helped to reveal deeply entrenched cultural assumptions about perception, language, learning, and intelligence.

There are several subbranches to AI research. At the moment, one of the most promising is robotics—or, more specifically, an approach to robotics in which many aspects of *complex agents* are built into the machines (including the *structural coupling* of *autonomous* subagents in an effort to prompt *emergent* possibilities, as well as capacities to explore the physical world in recognition of the *embodied*, situated, and distributed natures of learning and intelligence).

Autonomous: distinguishable from an environment—a definition that entails both an observer and an observed. (See also *complex subject/agent/system.*) The word *autonomous* literally means "self-ruled"—that is, in effect, *structure determined.* The laws governing the behaviors of a complex autonomous agent arise at the level of the agent's *emergence.*

Autopoietic: emergent (literally, "self-producing"). See *complex subject/agent.*

Catastrophe theory: a theory focused on the evolution of systems (mechanical and living), concerned in particular with occasional, sudden, and dramatic "jumps". Common illustrations for catastrophe theory include the triggerings of avalanches, landslides, and earthquakes—which highlight that the theory is attentive both to the internal structure of systems and contextual triggers and forces that help shape those systems.

Chaos theory: the study of unstable behavior in deterministic but non-linear dynamical systems. The title *chaos theory* has been appled to wide-ranging attempts to find qualitative and statistical regularities in processes that otherwise appear random, such as turbulence in fluids, weather patterns, predator–prey cycles, spread of disease, and onset of war.

Systems described as chaotic are extremely susceptible to changes in initial conditions. As well, the behaviors of chaotic simulations cannot usually be predicted far in advance. These are among the reasons that computer-based chaotic systems are often used to model *complex systems*.

Cognition: ongoing adaptation to dynamic circumstances—and, notably, adaptation that contributes to or otherwise affects those circumstances. Cognitive processes are the same as evolutionary (*natural drift*) processes, and they might be further described as life processes.

Cognitive science: an umbrella term currently used to reach across those discourses that address matters of human cognition. Cognitive scientific discourses are oriented by *complexivist* sensibilities. These discourses range from neurophysiology, through *ecopsychology*, through sociocybernetics, biosemiotics, ecopolitics, and beyond. (Note the habit of inventing names that deliberately transgress traditional disciplinary boundaries and that usually reach across the physical and social sciences.)

Complex subject/agent/system: an *autonomous* self-organizing, self-maintaining, self-renewing, *structurally determined* form that might be described as the product of its dynamic subagents and their interactions. Concisely stated, a complex system is a "structured structuring *structure*" (Dyke 1988).

Complexity (science): the study of adaptive, self-organizing systems—or, more colloquially, the study of living systems—or, more educationally, the study of learning systems. See *emergence, autonomous,* and *structure*. See also *new science, cybernetics, systems theory,* and *connectionism,* four major branches of inquiry that are among those that have cohered into complexity science.

Connectionism: an attempt to explain human cognition in terms of artificial neural networks or neural nets—which are simplified models of the brain that are composed of large numbers of randomly wired virtual neurons (actually nodes) whose connections change with experience. This model is seen by many as an alternative to the *cognitivist* model (i.e., "brain as computer that processes a symbolic language") because it reframes learning in terms of the *emergence* of relationships among nodes/agents, rather than the representation or storing of facts within existing structures. Computer simulations based on this model of the brain have demonstrated an ability to learn such skills as face recognition, reading, and the detection of simple grammatical structures.

While emergent, however, the resulting models lack some vital aspects of *complex agents*, most obviously the fact that living systems are bodies that move through the world. The cognition of complex agents is thus more than matters of internal connections. Cognition is also woven in and acted through the structures of the agent's relationships with other agents and with other aspects of the environment.

Cybernetics: an interdisciplinary study of the organization, pattern, and communication of/within systems— both complicated (mechanical) and complex (living). Cybernetics tends to be disinterested in the material structures of systems and is more focused on the flow of information (understood in terms of chains or webs of influence). This core interest underlies the most common definition of cybernetics: the science of communication and control.

    Early cybernetics was focused mainly on technology and developed ideas of circular causation, feedback, and (later) *recursion*. More recently, second-order cybernetics, a 1970s elaboration of the original 1950s movement, shifted the focus to the cybernetics of observing systems (as opposed to the cybernetics of observed systems). This move toward interobjectivity aligned the field much more closely with *systems theory* and helped set the stage for the emergence of *complexity science*.

Deep ecology: (also known as *ecosophy*) a discourse that begins with the assertion that all life is valuable. The relationship of humanity to the rest of the biosphere is thus understood in terms of *mindful participation* and *ethical* action, rather than in terms of the metaphysical notions of stewardship, mastery, or dominance. Deep ecology is a social movement with a sometimes political agenda to prompt transformations of societies in ways that minimize their impacts in the more-than-human world.

Ecofeminism: an *ecological* movement oriented by the assertion that prevailing worldviews are not just anthropocentric (human-centered), but androcentric (male-centered).

Ecology: Derived from the Greek *oikos*, "household", ecology is the study of relationships. It is often distinguished from "environmentalism", a term seen to imply a separation between agent and setting. Ecology assumes no such separation and understands agents to be aspects of their contexts.

Ecopsychology: a branch of psychology oriented by the assertion that most personal and collective dysfunctions are rooted in people's separation from the natural world.

Ecosophy: an abbreviation of "ecological philosophy"—otherwise known as *deep ecology*.

Ecospirituality: an umbrella term used to refer to movements that share one key tenet: Humans, who are constitutionally entangled with all living forms, must be mindful of and act with respect toward all aspects of the cosmos.

Embodied/Embodiment: There are two important aspects to the notion of embodiment (first articulated by Merleau-Ponty 1962, as "double-embodiment"). The first is the suggestion that human *cognition* is not strictly about brain-based processes. Bodily action is not simply an indication of thought, but an aspect of thought. Moreover, even the most abstract of thoughts can be demonstrated to be rooted in one's physical engagements with the world (e.g., containment *metaphors* implicit is schemes of classification; movement metaphors implicit in mathematical operations; force metaphors implicit in discussions of logic and social relations).

The second aspect of embodiment is the suggestion that individuals are actually part of a larger collective corpus—one that encompasses biological and cultural contexts. Stuart Kauffman (1995b) describes this relationship in terms of the oft-cited suggestion that the collective is enfolded in and unfolds from the individual.

Emergence: a process by which *autonomous complex agents self-organize* into a grander system that is itself an autonomous complex agent. Emergence is a bottom–up phenomenon through which transcendent unities arise without the aid of instructions or leaders. An emergent event is an instance of "order for free".

Enactivism: A perspective on cognition that its principal author (Francisco Varela—see Varela et al. 1991, Varela 1999) summarizes in terms of two intertwining principles: (a) perception is a recursively elaborative process, meaning that the possibilities for new perception are conditioned by the actions that are enabled by established perceptions; and (b) an agent's cognitive structures (which might be thought of as the "space of the possible" for the agent, as conditioned by its biological-and-experiential history) emerge from repetitions and patterns in the agent's engagements with its world.

At the level of human identity, enactivism rejects the assumption of a core (or essential, or inner) self, arguing instead that who we are arises in our moment-to-moment coping with the contingencies of our existences. The aphorism, knowing is doing is being, is often used to summarize this perspective. The term *enactivism* is intended to foreground the notion that identities and knowledge are not pre-existent, but enacted.

Learning is thus seen in terms of exploring an ever-evolving landscape of possibility and selecting (not necessarily consciously) those actions that are adequate to maintain one's fitness within that landscape. Learning is a *recursively* elaborative (vs. accumulative) process.

This is a difficult definition. It might help to look at the definitions of *embodied* and *complex agent.*

Ethical action: a Varelian idea that, in his terms, refers to "the progressive, firsthand acquaintance with the virtuality of self" (1999, p. 63).

Varela frames the notion by drawing a contrast between a *rationalist* conception of ethics (by which ethical principles are seen to be logically determinable if one begins with unimpeachable assumptions about the nature of reality) and an *emergent* ethics (by which what is ethical is understood in terms of contextually appropriate action that is not consciously mediated). So understood, ethical action is a *structurally determined* phenomenon that flows out of one's *embodied* being.

Fractal geometry: the branch of mathematics that studies extremely irregular curves or shapes (a) that are generated through *recursive* processes, (b) that are scale independent (i.e., the bumpiness of detail remains constant at all levels of magnification), and (c) that generally demonstrate some degree of self-similarity (i.e., a suitably chosen part will be similar in shape to a given larger or smaller part when appropriately magnified or reduced). Fractal geometry is often called "the geometry of nature" because fractal images tend to be reminiscent of natural forms, both in terms of appearance and manner of creation.

Information science: the field that deals with the collection, manipulation, storage, retrieval, distribution, and interpretation of information, in which information is understood as any phenomenon that has the potential to trigger actions or transformations of *complex systems*.

Languaging: a mode of structural coupling that involves more than symbollically mediated communication (language). Languaging refers to the recursively elaborative process of using language to understand language—a process that seems to be critical not just to our knowledge-generation abilities, but to our particular mode of consciousness.

A principal tool of human languaging is *metaphor*, by which one category of experiences can be mapped onto another.

Mind: an *emergent* phenomenon, noted to occur in humans and a few other social species, that is dependent on agents with sufficiently complex cognitive systems who are part of sufficiently complex collectives. In the case of humans, the mind that we talk about is an expression of the biologically and culturally conditioned *structure* of an *autonomous* human. We tend not to, but might just as well, talk about the mind of a collective (e.g., "The crowd had a mind of its own"), a species, and so on. In complexity terms, mind is immanent in and across emergent forms.

Mindfulness practice: A term derived from Eastern thought (particularly Buddhism and Taoism, often called the "Teaching Traditions"), mindfulness practice refers to one's efforts to develop a better awareness of the virtuality of self. Such awareness is understood to enable one's *ethical know-how*, which in turn is seen as the mode with which the teacher engages with learners.

As an attitude toward teaching, mindfulness practice is aligned with *enactivist*, *ecological*, and *ecospiritual* sensibilities. Pedagogically speaking, it thus engenders attitudes of *occasioning* and *conversing*.

Natural drift: a perspective on evolution used in contradistinction to "natural selection", which, in popular parlance, is taken to suggest a gradual evolution toward optimality or perfection (usually identified in biology as a weapon-toting White male or, in epistemology, as mathematics). Natural drift, by contrast to natural selection, might be described as operating by the principle of "good enough". Forms arise because they are possible; they survive because they are viable; they thrive because they are adequate. (Along with *self-organization*, natural drift is one of the key processes necessary for the emergence of a *complex agent*.)

Neurophenomenology: a coupling of neuroscientific and *phenomenological* methods (often along with meditative traditions) in the study of both conscious experience and corresponding neural patterns and processes. In brief, neurophenomenologists are oriented by the questions of how we, as conscious agents, come to have a world.

New sciences: (or, more specifically, new biology, new physics, new economics, ethnobotany, sociocybernetics, *ecopsychology*, neurophysiology, etc.) a broad scientific movement structured around at least two key principles: first, it is oriented by a logic of coherence or viability, whereby truth is understood in terms of utility of explanation (vs. the *modernist* logic of correspondence, whereby truth is understood in terms of some sort of match with an assumed-to-be pregiven reality); second, the observer is understood to be complicit in the observation (vs. the modernist desire to articulate observerless observations).

Occasioning: Derived from terms that originally meant "to fall together", occasioning is used to foreground the assertion that learning is dependent on, but not determined by, teaching. Teaching is understood to consist of efforts to establish the conditions necessary for learners to exceed themselves.

Some of these necessary conditions are identified as redundancy, diversity, neighbor interactions, organized randomness, and distributed control.

A consequence of this attitude is that teaching, while it might be oriented by specific intended outcomes, cannot be construed in terms of trajectories by which those outcomes might be best achieved—in large part because, if the conditions of complex emergence are indeed met, the outcomes may transcend expectations in ways that simply cannot be known beforehand.

Participatory pedagogy: See *occasioning*.

Proscription: Complex agents are rule-bound systems, but those rules are proscriptive, not prescriptive. That is, the space of possible action is defined in terms of what the agent must not do. By way of analogy, a soccer game is proscriptively structured. The rules tell players what they must not do, but the rules do not tell players what they must do. What must be done can only arise in the immediacy of the playing.

Recursion: a sort of repetitive process in which each step is an elaboration of the *structure* that was produced through the previous steps. Recursive processes tend to contribute to the growths of *structures*.

Santiago Theory of Cognition: See *enactivism*.

Self-organizing: a spontaneous, bottom–up process by which *complex agents* arise in the co-specifying (*structurally coupled*) activities of *autonomous* agents. For example, ants self-organize into ant hills, birds into flocks, and humans into various sorts of social collectives. (The other essential process for the *emergence* of a *complex agent* is *natural drift*.)

Structural coupling: (also referred to as co-evolution, co-specification, mutual specification, consensual coordination of action) the co-mingling of complex agents' ongoing histories; the intimate entangling of one's emergent activity with another's. (See *structure*.)

Structure: the embodied (and constantly unfolding) history of a *complex agent*. The structures of living systems are understood to be influenced by both biology and experience—with experience playing more significant roles in more complex systems.

Structure determinism: used to refer to the manner in which *complex agents* respond when perturbed. The manner of response is determined by the agent's *structure*, not by the perturbation. That is, a complex agent's response is dependent on, but not determined by, environmental influences. The same can be said of the components that comprise a complex unity. The properties of those components depend on the system in which they are located—in contrast to the components of a noncomplex system, in which the parts do not change depending on whether they are part of that system.

Systems theory: a scientific effort to understand some of the features that are common to living systems. In contrast to *cybernetics*, the principal interest in systems theory is with the physical organizations and evolutions of systems. The theory is holist—that is, living systems are studied as unities, not as amalgamations of parts. (Systems theory is also referred to as "general systems theory".)

ENDNOTES

Chapter 1 • *Inventions of Teaching:* STRUCTURES OF THINKING

1. Dewey 1910, p. 18.
2. Invent is derived from the Latin roots *in-*, "upon", and *venire*, "to come".
3. For the most part, my source for etymologies is *The Oxford English Dictionary*.
4. In fact the image is actually of a branch that was pruned from a tree—which is perhaps appropriate. The Western worldviews in this representation constitute only a fragment of the picture.
5. See Newburg, d'Aquili, & Rause 2001.
6. These examples are adapted from Hoffman 1998.
7. I do have a third reason for using V to mark bifurcations. Within logic, V denotes "or", the union or joining of sets. For me there is a certain rational appeal to such formulations as

ABSENCE OF COLOR: BLACK V WHITE

which might be translated as "The trait ABSENCE OF COLOR is manifest in those phenomena that are either BLACK or WHITE".

Chapter 2 • *Western Worldviews:* THE METAPHYSICAL V THE PHYSICAL

1. Dennett 1995, p. 18.
2. Aristotle divided inquiry into three strands—Logical (which included all the *rational* arts and sciences), Natural (which included all the *theoretical* sciences), and Moral (which included all the *practical* arts and sciences). Metaphysics was included in the Natural, along with Mathematics and Physics.
3. In my experience, Plato's views are most often presented and illustrated

through his allegory of the cave, developed in *The Republic*. In brief, Plato paints a picture of an ignorant humanity, imprisoned in the depths of a cave, able to see only a shadowy representation of reality (not reality itself) and unaware of its own limited perspective. The rare individual manages to escape the constraints of that cave. Through a long and arduous intellectual trek, he discovers a higher realm, a true reality, and an awareness of Goodness as the origin of all things.

One of the key assertions of the allegory is that invisible truths dwell beneath the visible surface of things. Another assertion is that only those who are enlightened can embrace the truth—and, by implication, that those who are seduced by the illusion of the cave will resist enlightenment. At the end of the passage, Plato develops the idea that teaching is not a process of pouring knowledge into empty minds, but of prompting people to actualize what they already know—a conception addressed in greater detail in chapter 5 of this book.

4. Aspects of this sensibility persist in contemporary theories of human development. In particular, some theories of physical, mental, and moral development tend to be structured around the assumption that children are imperfect or partial beings en route to completed or finished adults.

5. A prominent example of this approach is the modern system of biological classification developed by Linnaeus in the 1700s. He grouped species together in genera according to resemblances, genera into families, and so on until, at the apex of an organizational pyramid, he arrived at six kingdoms. Some of the conceptual difficulties with this sort of scheme are identified in the second half of this chapter. A more thorough discussion is provided in Mayr 1982/1942.

6. I return to this topic in chapter 3. For a fuller discussion of the conflation of Hellenist philosophy and monotheistic religious traditions, see Armstrong 2000.

7. The list of common words that are derived from the Latin *specere*, "to look", includes *aspect, especially, expect, inspect, introspection, perspective, prospect, respect, special, spectrum, speculate,* and *suspect*—to mention only those that I actually use in the first few chapters of this book.

8. Darwin actually proposed several mechanisms to explain the rise and spread of diversity. Most prominently, he offered different accounts for a species' transformation over time and the diversification of species within an ecosystem—a move that was perhaps necessitated by the fact that notions of genes and genetics, which can be used to explain both phenomena, were only just beginning to stir the imagination of Gregor Mendel (1822–1882) and were several decades from publication. See Gould 2002 for a fuller discussion of the elements of Darwin's theories and the evolutions of his ideas over the past century and a half.

9. The process of pushing out the borders of possibility and then filling up the space is known as *adaptive radiation*. A recent example of the phenomenon was the proliferation of dot.com ventures in the late 1990s. The Internet opened up the space of possibility, and diversity happened. Significantly, as with biological evolution, most ventures failed.

10. A second, related example of the unfortunate conflation of sensibilities is Social Darwinism, a discredited sociological theory in which wealth and power were taken as signs of inherent fitness, whereas the poor and disenfranchised were seen as naturally inferior. A century ago, Social Darwinism was used to justify racist and imperialist policies in the Western world.

    An influential proponent of the theory was Herbert Spencer (1820–1938), a British social philosopher. He was among the first to apply Darwin's theories to human societies, albeit that he framed this application in terms of inevitable progress toward optimality rather than ongoing coping with immediate circumstances. In fact Spencer was the person who coined the phrase "survival of the fittest". He also helped popularize the word *evolution*, which had been first used in the scientific sense by geologist Charles Lyell in 1830 and had been in general use prior to that to refer to tranformations (see note 6 of chap. 10).

    Spencer was in large part responsible for deflecting public debate from the issues raised by Darwin (around matters of biological, paleontological, and geological phenomena) onto issues that Darwin gave little or no close attention (including man's place in nature and the implications of evolutionary theory for the soul and the mind). See chapters 10 and 11.

11. See Gould 2002 for a detailed discussion of some of the academic precursors of Darwin's work.

12. Dewey 1910, p. 9.

13. Dennett 1995.

14. Ridley 1985 describes one such example: In Europe, the herring gull and the lesser black-backed gull are two species that are easily distinguished and that do not interbreed. If one were to trace out populations of herring gulls westward from Europe to North America, one would notice that their appearances change slightly. Continuing westward, by Siberia those changes collect into a gull that looks more like the lesser black-backed gull. By Europe, the transformation is complete.

Chapter 3 • *The Metaphysical:* GNOSIS V EPISTEME

1. From Blake's verse letter to Thomas Butts (written in 1802). The complete letter has been published in many places, including Erdman 1965,

p. 693.

2. In fact in English, a distinction is usually made between different types of knowing, but usually on a more implicit level. Relative to one another, English is often described as more noun-oriented and French more verb-oriented. The syntactic differences between the English and French versions of the sentences

> Je le connais. / I know him.
>
> Je le sais. / I know that.

present one example of this point. Whereas the two different types of knowledge are flagged by the verbs *connaître* and *savoir* in French, in English they're signaled by the objects in the sentences—that is, in these cases, the pronouns *him* and *that*. (Note that the pronouns are the same in the two French sentences, just as the verbs are the same in the two English sentences.) The point, then, is not so much that the distinction is not made in English, but that it is made in a less conscious, less explicit manner than in other European languages.

The distinction is also evident in two English nouns that are derived from French verbs. *Connoisseur*, from *connaître*, and *savant*, from *savoir*, are used to refer to people of two different sorts of expertise: the former more toward matters of art and good taste, the latter more toward matters of logic and fact.

3. For an interesting and somewhat controversial examination of *episteme* and *tekhne*, see Heidegger 1982.

4. Campbell 1991.

5. Armstrong 2000.

6. This point is powerfully demonstrated by Thompson 1989. He provides a compelling example of the power of myth through multilayered interpretations—literal, structural, anthropological, and cosmological—of the ancient fairy tale, *Rapunzel*. (*Rapunzel* is the story of a maiden trapped by a sorceress in a tower. The maiden is saved by allowing her rescuer to climb her long hair.) Thompson's analyses move through botany, history, astrology, and art.

7. See Berman 1984.

8. Gadamer 1989.

9. See Sloek 1996.

10. Armstrong 2000, p. xvii.

11. The complete title of Descartes' text, as it is most popularly translated, is *Discourse on the Method of Rightly Conducting the Reason, and Seeking Truth in the Sciences*.

12. Laplace 1951/1814.

13. The complete title of the work is *Novum Organum; or, True Suggestions for the Interpretation of Nature*.

14. The use of brain-as-computer metaphors are discussed in chapter 8. As for universe-as-computer, see Wolfram 2002. Wolfram is among those who use the notion literally.
15. See Berman 1984.
16. Berman 1984, p. 28.
17. A prime is a number with two factors, 1 and itself. A nonprime (or composite) has at least three factors. For example, 2, 3, and 5 are primes, whereas 4 (with factors 1, 2, & 4) and 6 (with factors 1, 2, 3, & 6) are composite. The number 1 is in a class by itself with only one factor.
18. This perspective is often attributed to Pythagoras (c. 569 BCE–c. 475 BCE) of ancient Greece. However, there is evidence that prime numbers had been noticed and recorded some 20,000 years ago. There is, of course, no way to know whether this noticing had any impact on conceptions of personal identity at the time. See Barrow 1993.

Chapter 4 • Gnosis: MYSTICISM V RELIGION

1. Campbell 1991, p. 53.
2. The study is summarized and discussed in Wilson 1999.
3. Greeley 1987.
4. This claim is supported by the results of a 1993 Gallup poll. In response to a question of the origin and development of human beings, Gallup reported that 47% of Americans polled expressed a belief that God created humans in their present form, 35% believed that humans developed under the guidance of God, and 11% indicated a belief that humans developed without a God. (Seven percent expressed no opinion.) In brief, and in terms of the branching worldviews discussed in this book, 82% of persons polled answered in terms of the metaphysical and 11% in terms of the physical.
5. Underhill 1990/1938.
6. Aristotle held that matter consists of four elements: earth, air, fire, and water. Different substances were thought to be composed of different ratios of these elements—hence transformations of one substance into another (e.g., mercury into silver) were understood as matters of properly readjusting the ratios.
7. The word *Gnostic* is, obviously, derived from gnosis, although it was only coined in the 1500s and applied retroactively to various mystical movements. Specifically, the term has been used to label a range of pre-Christian pagan, Jewish, and early Christian sects that claimed direct personal spiritual knowledge beyond the official texts or the hierarchies of their respective religions.

Kabbalah and Sufism are the main mystical branches of Judaism and Islam, respectively. Each is generally described in terms of the products of diverse philosophical and spiritual influences—including one another, neoplatonism, and Eastern traditions. As well, to varying extents, each is given to literal (versus allegorical) readings of sacred texts and to anthropomorphic understandings of God.

8. Armstrong 1994.
9. I use the word *archetypes* in the more historical sense of "typical specimen" or "constantly recurring motif", rather than in the more recent Jungian psychoanalytic sense of a product of the collective unconscious.
10. I do not mean to infer that Buddhism is a religion. As Watts 1957 notes, "Zen Buddhism is a way and a view of life which does not belong to any of the formal categories of modern Western thought. It is not a religion or philosophy; it is not a psychology or type of science" (p. 37).

    My point is merely that narratives of redemption and reparation are common across divergent worldviews.
11. Armstrong 2000. Armstrong frames her discussion in terms of *mythos* and *logos*, rather than *gnosis* and *episteme*. Although these pairs of terms are not completely interchangeable, the conceptual match is actually a good one.
12. Ibid.
13. In English, the most commonly preferred translation is the King James Version, first published in 1611.
14. Chapter 1, verses 28–38 of The Gospel According to Luke.
15. Chapters 2–4 of The Book of Daniel.
16. In fact one of the readers of an early draft of this book was bewildered and amused by this statement. From central Africa (and, hence, less encultured into Platonic sensibilities) and having never encountered a transfer-of-soul narrative, the reference simply made no sense to her.

Chapter 5 • Mysticism: TEACHING AS DRAWING OUT

1. Although I'm assured this is indeed a Buddhist saying, I actually get it from the title of Kopp 1974.
2. Bateson 1979.
3. The meaning of *epiphany* has changed little from its ancient Greek origins. The compound word *epiphainesthai* meant something like "to appear" or "to come forth". The prefix *epi-* has to do with proximity, and the stem *phainen* means, literally, "to bring light". Epiphany is etymologically related to fantasy, phantom, tiffany, and phenomenon.
4. The oldest known recorded uses of the terms in English with regard to

matters of teaching, according to the *The Oxford English Dictionary*, are as follows: *educate*, early 1400s; *nurture*, 1200s; *tutor*, 1300s. *Foster* is from Old English and hence needn't be dated.

Chapter 6 • Religion: TEACHING AS DRAWING IN

1. Proverbs 22:6, King James Version of *The Holy Bible*.
2. As with the synonyms for teaching within mystical traditions, the oldest known recorded uses of the terms mentioned here predate the mid-1400s. In fact all but *training* are dated to at least a century earlier.
3. See Armstrong 2000.
4. For further discussions of the knowledge-as-object and communication-and-conveyance metaphors, see Reddy 1979 and Lakoff & Johnson 1980.

Chapter 7 • Episteme: RATIONALISM V EMPIRICISM

1. Alexander Pope, "Epitaph Intended for Sir Isaac Newton" (circa 1737).
2. Agnosticism might be described as a sort of scientific mysticism. It embraces the mystic premise that God or the ultimate oneness must vastly exceed human comprehension. However, its response is not mystical practices, but empirical inquiry based on the assertion that only material phenomena can be known. See the "Rationalism" section of chapter 8.
3. This claim is not only made explicit in prominent critiques of modernist thought, such as Lyotard 1984 and Borgmann 1989, but it is also front and center in a number of popular books that criticize Descartes' cosmology (see, e.g., Damasio 1994, Davis & Hersh 1986, and Devlin 1998).
4. Although they withstood the assaults of many mathematicians for more than 2,000 years, it turns out that Euclid's five axioms are actually inadequate. In the early 1900s, German mathematician David Hilbert demonstrated the Euclid had missed several. As it turns out, and somewhat ironically, given Descartes' use of Euclidean geometric methods to argue for ideal, body-independent knowledge, the axioms of geometry as stated by Euclid can only seem mathematically complete if you have a body that can move in this universe. See Hilbert 1988/1899.
5. Some etymologies might be useful here. Rational, rationalism, and reason are derived from the Latin *ratio*, "calculation". A ratio, in its most formal sense, is a mathematical relationship among numbers. Fractions are ratios, which is why they're also called rational numbers. Numbers that cannot be written as ratios, such as π or $\sqrt{2}$, are called irrational. The deeply mathematized sensibilities of Western culture shine through in

these terms—underscored in the way that the words *rational* and *irratio-nal* have been coupled to *sane* and *insane*, *thoughtful* and *thoughtless*, and so on.

6. As mentioned in chapter 6, the word *induction* entered English through religion—specifically, through religious efforts to indoctrinate. The word *induction* here, while spelled the same way and sharing precisely the same Latin roots (originally meaning "to draw in"), appears to have been derived independently from those roots.

7. Bacon 1862/1620, p. 18.

8. Bacon 1620, Book XCVIII.

9. See Davis et al. 2000 (in particular, chapter 3A, "Discerning Abilities") and Foucault 1977 for more detailed discussions of the emergence of contemporary understandings of normality.

10. For an introductory discussion to experimental mathematics, see Borwein, Borwein, Girgensohn, & Parnes 1996.

11. That's, of course, the ideal. As science spread its influence and as knowledge grew, narrowed foci became more and more a necessity. The resulting culture of specialization has in many ways militated against new syntheses. Many examples of the consequences of specialization—indeed of overspecialization—could be drawn from medicine, teaching, and other professions.

12. At least since Descartes' time, learning and thinking have tended to be separated. Other species have been seen as capable of learning, but their learning was construed in terms of mechanical stimulus–response connections devoid of anything that might be called thought.

Chapter 8 • *Rationalism:* TEACHING AS INSTRUCTING

1. From Galileo 1623.

2. From, I Corinthians 13:12 of the King James Version of *The Holy Bible*.

3. From Descartes 1641.

4. One of the paradoxes with mentalist models of cognition is well illustrated by the example of mind-as-movie-theatre. Across these theories, a second, internal observer is almost always implied—in this case, someone is imagined to dwell inside the head and to watch the movie. Presumably, this knower must also have an internal observer, who in turn has an internal observer. The philosophical term for the problem is *cascading homunculi*. (A *homunculus* is a "small man".)

5. Glasersfeld 1995.

6. The earliest recorded English uses of all these words have been dated to the 1300s—and all of them in matters of religion. Current definitions

of the words, however, date from the 1600s and 1700s, when they were applied to schools organized around rationalist-informed curriculum structures.

7. From Plato, *Apology*, c. 395 BCE, §38A.
8. See, e.g., Howson 1982.
9. See, e.g., Anyon 1986.

Chapter 9 • *Empiricism:* TEACHING AS TRAINING

1. Locke 1693, §54.
2. Foucault 1977.
3. In fact this assumption of privilege as part of the natural order persisted for several more centuries, as demonstrated by Charles Dickens' writings in the 1800s.
4. For elaborations of this example, see Gauthier & Tardif 1995 and 1996. (The latter, an edited collection, is in French. The conceptions of teaching that are taken up present an interesting contrast to the conceptions I discuss in this book. As it turns out, synonyms for *teaching* in English simply do not match up with those in French. This is especially true of currently popular French terms that seem to rooted in sensibilities that are quite different from the ones in which the more popular English terms are rooted.)
5. See Calvin 1996, Johnson 1997, Kotulak 1996.
6. Another flaw of these sorts of nativist discourses is the assumption that particular competencies are housed in specific regions of the brain. Once again, this notion has a grain of truth, in that studies have shown that region-specific damage will consistently lead to losses of particular capacities, such as those associated with simple mathematics, recognition of faces, and interpretation of written symbols. However, recent research with advanced brain-imaging technologies reveals that our brains are domain-general when engaged in any significant cognitive challenge. That is, when stumped, most areas of the brain—not just isolated, specialized modules—are active. See Kotulak 1997.

    Further, it turns out that human brains are organized in exactly the same way as primate brains. That is, *every* module that has been identified in our brains has also been discerned in the brains of other ape species. This point is of tremendous significance because most nativism-based theories of learning and intelligence begin by positing the existence of modules (e.g., for language, for interpersonal skills) that are assumed to be unique to humans (see Donald 2001, esp. chap. 4, "The Consciousness Club").

7. Another manifestation of empiricism-based conceptions of teaching is the current topic of "best practices". This notion relies on an assumption of unambiguous measurability (i.e., one must be able to measure to compare one practice to another), which in turn is being used to support a renewed insistence on "scientific" (read: experimental design and statistical interpretation) research. For an extreme articulation of this movement, visit the U.S. government's website for its "No Child Left Behind" initiative on 2001 (http://www.nochildleftbehind.gov/). For critiques, see chapters 10–16.
8. Watson 1988/1924, p. 104.
9. Paulos 1988.
10. Locke 1690, Book 2, chapter 1.
11. Locke 1693.

Chapter 10 • *The Physical:* INTERSUBJECTIVITY V INTEROBJECTIVITY

1. Mayr 1994, p. 29.
2. See Dewey 1910.
3. I am aware of the redundancy here. See chapter 2.
4. Kuhn 1962.
5. Weaver 1948. The actual terms used by Weaver were *simple systems, disorganized complex systems*, and *organized complex systems*. I've opted for *simple, complicated*, and *complex* to reflect current usages within complexity science.
6. A core theme of theories rooted in the physical is the notion of evolution, from the Latin *evolvere*, "to roll out". Notably, Darwin avoided use of the word because, by the time he wrote, it had already been used in ways that carried a sense of progress toward perfection or a predetermined end (i.e., in senses consistent with a Platonic view of development). Darwin preferred the phrase "descent with modification" to foreground that, in his theory, evolution was about adequate responses to immediate conditions, as opposed to progress toward optimality (see note 10 of chap. 2).
7. See Wilson 1999.
8. Marx 1947/1844.
9. The phrase "opiate of the masses" is one translation of a phrase used by Marx in his essay "Toward the Critique of Hegel's *Philosophy of Law*", originally published in 1844. The phrase has also been translated as "opium of the people". See Padover 1974.
10. See Hiley, Bohman, & Shusterman 1991.
11. See Donald 2001, Norretranders 1998.
12. Rorty 1989, p. 5.

13. For further discussions of the notion of interobjectivity, see von Foerster 1995, Latour 1996, and Maturana 1987.
14. Berry 1977, p. 22. Emphasis in original.
15. This idea was developed by Edmund Husserl in the early 1900s. It was further developed in Merleau-Ponty 1962, and has since been taken up as a core principle in much of the cognitive sciences. See Lakoff & Johnson 1999.
16. See Norretranders 1998 for an overview of the past 50 years of research on this topic.
17. As developed in chapter 11, poststructuralism is an exception to this rule. The post- in this case is used to signal an elaboration, not a rejection of structuralist sensibilities.
18. For accessible introductions to postmodern theory, see Borgmann 1993 and Lyotard 1984.
19. Philosophically speaking, relativism refers to those trends that exaggerate the relative value of different views on knowledge—to the point of rejecting any means by which one might judge whether one claim might be "more true" than another. The tendency toward relativism is not specific to postmodern discourses. Nor is it a recent phenomenon. It seems that as long as there have been differences in opinion, there have been those who have argued that divergent opinions have equal merit.

Chapter 11 • *Intersubjectivity:* STRUCTURALISM V POSTSTRUCTURALISM

1. Berger & Luckman 1967, p. 15.
2. For a brief, nontechnical introduction to these geometries, see Mlodinow 2001.
3. Nicholas Bourbaki is not a person, but a pseudonym for a collective of mathematicians.
4. See Saussure 1959.
5. See Fang 1970.
6. See Glasersfeld 1995.
7. Significantly, there is only one recorded instance of Piaget's use of the word *constructivist*. See Davis & Sumara 2002.
8. The phrase "social constructivism" is a popular synonym for constructionism, particularly in the educational literature. I've opted not to use it because constant qualification would be required to keep it distinct from Piagetian-inspired discourses.
9. The first full English text of Vygotsky's work was Vygotsky 1962.
10. Kuhn 1962, Lakatos 1976, Popper 1963.
11. See, e.g., Foucault 1977, 1990.

12. See, e.g., Frye 1957.
13. Derrida 1980.
14. See Palmer 1969.
15. See, e.g., Lakoff & Johnson 1980, Lakoff & Núñez 2000, Johnson 1987, Rorty 1979.

Chapter 12 • *Structuralism:* TEACHING AS FACILITATING

1. Montesorri 1995, p. 7.
2. Among the records of the ERIC Clearinghouse on Information and Technology, an educational research database, through the 1970s the numbers of hits for *constructivist* or *constructivism* were in the single digits. By the early 1980s, the numbers had increased to two digits, then to three digits in the early 1990s. In 2000, the number passed 1,000.
3. See, e.g., Piaget 1954.
4. See Brooks 2002.
5. This point has been further underscored by sensory deprivation experiments. Without exception, humans who are cut off from continuous sensory feedback with the physical world eventually begin to experience hallucinations that become more and more extreme as minutes and hours pass. See Donald 2001, Hebb 1980.
6. See, e.g., Glaserfeld 1995.
7. See Lave & Wenger 1991. See also the Glossary.
8. See Engenström, Miettinen, & Raiija-Leena 1999. See also the Glossary.
9. Lave & Wenger 1991, p. 40.
10. See Gopnik, Meltzoff, & Kuhl 1999.

Chapter 13 • *Poststructuralism:* TEACHING AS EMPOWERING

1. Richard Shaull, in the "Foreword" to Freire 1971, p. 15.
2. Kuhn 1962.
3. Some references to this literature are in order here. See, e.g., Apple 1993, Britzman 1991, Ellsworth 1997, Grumet 1988, hooks 1996, Sumara & Davis 1999, Walkerdine 1988.
4. The phrase "making the familiar strange" is taken from Gordon 1972.
5. It is with some dismay that I acknowledge my own participation in the privileging of the knowledge of White males. The huge majority of thinkers represented in the bibliography fall into that category.
6. For a discussion of the notion of "hidden curriculum", see Anyon 1980.
7. See Postman & Weingartner 1969.

8. In Freire 1971, p. 54.

9. Although popular, the notion of "teaching as giving voice" is troublesome on several levels. For instance, it casts the learner as voiceless (without efficacy) and the teacher as imbued not just with cultural power, but with the power to mete out power. In general, among critical theorists, the dynamics of "voice" are understood as much more subtle and complex.

Chapter 14 • *Interobjectivity:* COMPLEXITY SCIENCE V ECOLOGY

1. Abram 1996, p. 22.

2. Maturana 1987.

3. Abram 1996, p. 90.

4. See Sapir 1949.

5. The influence of the biological is not just ignored within most intersubjectivist discourses, but explicitly rejected by some—particularly those that are oriented by desires to overcome societal prejudices that are based in race, gender, and sexuality. The reasons for this rejection are in some ways justified: For example, to undo systemic discriminations, one must render problematic the assumed-to-be-given (i.e., biological) bases of difference. As the same time, it has given rise to some serious problems especially in the medical sciences (see, e.g., Epstein 1995).

  The underlying problem here seems to be a metaphysics-based dichotomization of the physical (biological) and the mental (interpretive)— a separation that is rejected and reframed within complexity science and ecological discourses.

6. The suggestion that language began with gesture is not a recent one. Both Rousseau and Vico developed the idea centuries ago (see, e.g., Rousseau 1986/1750 and Vico 1961/1725).

7. Ong 1988.

8. Olson 1996.

9. The Book of Genesis 1:28.

10. Waldrop 1992.

11. See Johnson 2001.

12. See Capra 2002.

13. For discussions of these and other historical examples, see Capra 1996, Johnson 2001, Kelly 1994, and Waldrop 1992.

14. A bottom–up dynamic is a necessary, but not sufficient condition for a complex system. There must also be an emergent top–down quality. From the "bottom", the diverse agents that comprise a system provide it with alternatives that the emergent system can access. This pool of possibilities is acted on selectively by the distributed whole through different

sorts of feedback structures that emerge as part of the system (see Juarrero 1999, esp. chap. 9, "Constraints as Causes").

15. See Johnson 2001 for several examples. See Davis & Simmt 2003 for an example of such efforts within a classroom.

16. See, e.g., Capra 2002.

17. Varela, Thompson, & Rosch 1991, Varela 1999.

18. The phrase used by Varela is "structurally coupled". See the Glossary.

19. Adapted from Maturana & Varela 1987.

20. See Donald 2001.

21. See, e.g., Lakoff & Núñez 2000.

22. This phrase is used in Kauffman 1995a.

23. Lovelock had been hired by NASA for a project to study the existence of life on other planets. Early on he "proved" that Mars is lifeless, arguing that its atmospheric gases are in a predictable equilibrium. By contrast, Earth's atmosphere is a highly volatile mix—indicating that something must be at work to push and hold the balance out of chemical equilibrium. See Lovelock 1988.

24. See, e.g., Cohen & Stewart 1994.

25. See, e.g., Williams 1997.

26. Sustainability discourses, in general, are oriented by the desire to reduce humanity's impact on the natural world while maintaining current populations and lifestyles.

27. For more on deep ecology, see Berry 1990, Naess 1996.

28. See Rozsak, Gomes, & Kanner 1995.

29. See Warren 2000.

30. I borrow the phrase "biology of belief" from the subtitle of Newburg et al. 2001. The discussion of the physiological bases of mystical experiences is based mainly on their book.

31. Ibid., pp. 108, 130.

32. See Saver & Rabin 1997.

33. See Newburg et al. 2001, especially chapter 5, "Ritual".

34. I reported on some of the results of Greeley's 1987 survey at the start of chapter 4.

35. Lévy-Bruhl 1985/1922.

36. See Dennett 1991, Norretranders 1998.

37. See Donald 2001.

Chapter 15 • *Complexity Science:* TEACHING AS OCCASIONING

1. Stuart Kauffman, quoted in Ruthen 1993, p. 138.

2. See Kauffman 1995b.

3. See Calvin 1996.

4. See Norretranders 1998.

5. See Gopnick et al. 1999.

6. Donald 2001, pp. 205–206.

7. Harris 1998.

8. Unfortunately, the word *redundancy* is often associated with senses of excessive, superfluous, and even needless repetition. Such is not the sense intended here. Rather, redundancies—samenesses, commonalities, repetitions—among agents in a complex system are utterly necessary for their interactions. In contrast, redundancies in mechanical systems are usually more wasteful than useful.

9. For an elaborated description of this particular activity, see Kieren, Davis, & Mason 1996.

10. See Davis et al. 2000, especially chapter 2, "Learning and Teaching Structures".

11. Davis & Simmt 1993, Davis et al. 2000, Doll 1993, Fleener 2002.

12. Children, for example, play important roles in the evolution of language (see, e.g., Deacon 1997).

Chapter 16 • *Ecology:* TEACHING AS CONVERSING

1. Muir 1998/1911.

2. The word *right* is derived from the Latin *rectus*, "straight". In English, it is a word that is caught up in a web of associations that reaches across almost all aspects of human activity. See Appendix B.

3. Anthropomorphism continues to be prohibited by the American Psychological Association. See American Psychological Association 2001, Item 2.04 (pp. 38–39).

4. Varela 1999.

5. The sense of *mindful* intended here is often associated with the Buddhist notion of mindfulness awareness—a notion rooted in the principle of the virtuality of self. The term *participating* might also be associated with other non-Western worldviews, particularly those that are attentive to the interobjectivity of human observers and the observed natural world. See Varela et al. 1991. See also Heshusius 1994 for a discussion of the relevance of participatory epistemologies for educational issues.

6. Ashton-Warner 1963.

7. Noddings 1984.

8. van Manen 1991.

9. Bowers 2001.

10. Davis 1996.

11. See Donald 2001.
12. See Norretranders 1998.

Chapter 17 • *Reinventions of Teaching:* EXPANDING THE SPACE OF THE POSSIBLE

1. Pagels 1988.
2. In a book that I co-authored with Dennis Sumara and Rebecca Luce-Kapler (Davis et al. 2000), alternative framings and vocabularies for many aspects of teaching are developed.
3. This particular list can be extended to a considerable length. Other entries with some relevance to the current discussion include *abduct, adduce, conducive, conduct, conduit, duct, seduce, seductive, subdue, taut, team, tie, tow, transduce,* and *wanton.*
4. This list can also be readily extended: *apply, application, exploit, multiply, perplex, reply, replicate,* and *splay*—to mention a few.
5. See, e.g., Greenberg, Greenberg, Greenberg, Ransom, Sadofsky, & White 1992.
6. Davis et al. 2000, p. 3.

Appendix B • *A Brief Introduction to Fractals*

1. *A geometretos medeis eisito.*
2. See Stewart 1989.
3. For those interested in experimenting with different seeds and rules, I recommend visiting some of the many dynamic, interactive fractal websites. A Google search (at http://www.google.com) with the key terms *fractal, interactive,* and *tree* will generate a list that includes several possibilities.
4. This point is of particular relevance to the notion of interob-jectivity, developed in chapters 10 and 14. The notions of recursion and scale independence can be used to foreground the role of the observer in the phenomenon observed. What one sees when looking at a fractal is not the way it is in any enduring or totalized sense, but the way it is at a given moment and at a given scale.
5. See Mandelbrôt 1977, especially chapter 2, "How Long is the Coast of England?"
6. See Gleick 1987, Stewart 1989, Stewart 1998.
7. Mandelbrôt 1977.

REFERENCES

Abram, David. 1996. *The spell of the sensuous: perception and language in a more-than-human world*. New York: Pantheon.

American Psychological Association. 2001. *Publication manual of the American Psychological Association, fifth edition*. Washington, DC: American Psychological Association.

Anyon, Jean. 1980. Social class and the hidden curriculum of work. In *Journal of Education*, vol. 162, no. 1: 67–92.

Anyon, Jean. 1986. Social class and school knowledge. In *Curriculum Inquiry*, vol. 11, no. 1: 3–42.

Apple, Michael W. 1993. *Official knowledge: democratic education in a conservative age*. New York: Routledge.

Armstrong, Karen. 1994. *The history of God: the 4,000-year quest of Judaism, Christianity and Islam*. New York: Ballantine.

Armstrong. Karen. 2000. *The battle for God: a history of fundamentalism*. New York: Ballantine.

Ashton-Warner, Sylvia. 1963. *Teacher*. New York: Simon & Schuster.

Bacon, Francis. 1620. *Novum organum*.

Bacon, Francis. 1862. Proemium to *The Great Instauration*. Reproduced in *The works of Francis Bacon*. Edited by James Spedding, R.L. Ellis, & D.D. Heath. Boston: Houghton Mifflin. Originally published 1620.

Barrow, John D. 1993. *Pi in the sky: counting, thinking and being*. New York: Little, Brown & Company.

Bateson, Gregory. 1979. *Mind and nature: a necessary unity*. New York: E.P. Dutton.

Berger, Peter L., & Thomas Luckman. 1967. *The social construction of reality*. Harmondsworth, UK: Penguin.

Berman, Morris. 1984. *The reenchantment of the world*. Ithaca, NY: Cornell University Press.

Berry, Thomas. 1990. *The dream of the Earth*. San Francisco: Sierra Club Books.

Berry, Wendell. 1977. *The unsettling of America: culture and agriculture*. San Francisco: Sierra Club Books.

Borgmann, Albert. 1989. *Crossing the postmodern divide*. Chicago: University of Chicago Press.

Borwein, Jonathan. M., Peter B. Borwein, Roland Girgensohn, & Sheldon Parnes. 1996. Making sense of experimental mathematics. In *Mathematical Intelligencer*, vol. 18, no. 4: 12–18.

Bowers, C.A. 2001. *Educating for eco-justice and community*. Athens, GA: University of Georgia Press.

Britzman, Deborah P. 1991. *Practice makes practice: a critical study of learning to teach*. Albany, NY: State University of New York Press.

Brooks, Rodney. 2002. *Flesh and machines: how robots will change us*. New York: Pantheon Books.

Calvin, William H. 1996. *How brains think: evolving intelligence, then and now*. New York: Basic Books.

Campbell, Joseph. 1991. *The power of myth*. New York: Anchor.

Capra, Fritjof. 1996. *The web of life: a new scientific understanding of living systems*. New York: Anchor Books.

Capra, Fritjof. 2002. *The hidden connections: integrating the biological, cognitive, and social dimensions of life into a science of sustainability*. New York: Doubleday.

Cohen, Jack, & Ian Stewart. 1994. *The collapse of chaos: discovering simplicity in a complex world*. New York: Penguin.

Damasio, Antonio. 1994. *Descartes' error: emotion, reason, and the human brain*. New York: G.P. Putnam's Sons.

Davis, Brent. 1996. *Teaching mathematics: toward a sound alternative*. New York: Garland.

Davis, Brent, & Elaine Simmt. 2003. Understanding learning systems: mathematics education and complexity science. In *Journal for Research in Mathematics Education*, vol. 34, no. 2: 137–167.

Davis, Brent, & Dennis Sumara. 2000. Curriculum forms: on the assumed shapes of knowing and knowledge. In *Journal of Curriculum Studies*, vol. 32, no. 6: 821–845.

Davis, Brent, & Dennis Sumara. 2002. Constructivist discourses and the field of education: problems and possibilities. In *Educational Theory*, vol. 52, no. 4: 409–428.

Davis, Brent, Dennis Sumara, & Rebecca Luce-Kapler. 2000. *Engaging minds: learning and teaching in a complex world*. Mahwah. NJ: Lawrence Erlbaum.

Davis, Philip J., & Reuben Hersh. 1986. *Descartes' dream: the world according to mathematics*. New York: Harcourt.

Deacon, Terrance. 1997. *The symbolic species: the co-evolution of language and the human brain*. New York: W.W. Norton.

Dennett, Daniel C. 1991. *Consciousness explained*. New York: Little, Brown &

Company.

Dennett, Daniel C. 1995. *Darwin's dangerous idea: evolution and the meanings of life*. New York: Touchstone.

Derrida, Jacques. 1980. *Writing and difference*. Trans. Alan Bass. Chicago: University of Chicago Press.

Descartes, René. 1999. *Discourse on method and meditations on first philosophy, fourth edition*. Trans. Donald Cress. New York: Hackett. Original French versions published in 1637 and 1641.

Devlin, Keith. 1998. *Goodbye, Descartes: the end of logic and the search for a new cosmology of the mind*. New York: John Wiley & Sons.

Dewey, John. 1910. The influence of Darwin on philosophy. Chapter 1 of *The influence of Darwin on philosophy and other essay*. New York: Henry Holt: 1–19.

Doll, William, Jr. 1993. *A post-modern perspective on curriculum*. New York: Teachers College Press.

Donald, Merlin. 2001. *A mind so rare: the evolution of human consciousness*. New York: W.W. Norton.

Dyke, Charles. 1988. *The evolutionary dynamics of complex systems*. Oxford: Oxford University Press.

Ellsworth, Elizabeth. 1997. *Teaching positions: difference, pedagogy, and the power of address*. New York: Teachers College Press.

Engenström, Yrjv, Reijo Miettinen, & Punamäki Raiija-Leena, editors. 1999. *Perspectives on activity theory*. Cambridge, UK: Cambridge University Press.

Epstein, Julia. 1995. *Altered conditions: disease, medicine, and story-telling*. New York: Routledge.

Erdman, David V., editor. 1965. *The poetry and prose of William Blake*. Garden City, NY: Doubleday.

Fang, Joon. 1970. *Bourbaki: towards a philosophy of modern mathematics*. St. Catharines, ON: Paideia Press.

Fleener, M. Jayne. 2002. *Curriculum dynamics: recreating heart*. New York: Peter Lang.

Foucault, Michel. 1977. *Discipline and punish: the birth of the modern prison*. Trans. Alan Sheridan. New York: Pantheon.

Foucault, Michel. 1990. *The history of sexuality, an introduction*. Trans. Robert Hurley. New York: Vintage.

Freire, Paulo. 1971. *Pedagogy of the oppressed*. Trans. Myra Bergman Ramos. New York: Seaview.

Frye, Northrop. 1957. *Anatomy of criticism: four essays*. Princeton, NJ: Princeton University Press.

Gadamer, Hans-Georg. 1989. *Truth and method*. Trans. Joel Weinsheimer. New York: Continuum.

Galileo Galilei. 1623. *The Assayer*.

Gallup, George, Jr. 1993. *The Gallup Poll: public opinion 1993.* Wilmington, DE: Scholarly Resources.

Gauthier, Clerment, & Maurice Tardif. 1995. Pedagogy and the emergence of an academic order in the seventeenth century. In *JCT: Journal of Curriculum Studies*, vol. 11, no. 3: 7–11.

Gauthier, Clerment, & Maurice Tardif, editors. 1996. *La pédagogie: théories et pratiques de l'antiquité à nos jours.* Montréal: Gaëtan Morin.

Glasersfeld, Ernst von. 1995. *Radical constructivism: a way of knowing and doing.* London: Falmer.

Gleick, James. 1987. *Chaos: making a new science.* New York: Viking.

Gopnik, Alison, Andrew N. Meltzoff, & Patricia K. Kuhl. 1999. *The scientist in the crib: what early learning tells us about the mind.* New York: Perennial.

Gordon, William J.J. 1972. On being explicit about the creative process. In *Journal of Creative Behavior*, vol. 6: 295–300.

Gould, Stephen J. 2002. *The structure of evolutionary theory.* Cambridge, MA: The Belknap Press of the Harvard University Press.

Greeley, Andrew. 1987. Mysticism goes mainstream. In *American Health* 6: 47–49.

Greenberg, Daniel, Hanna Greenberg, Michael Greenberg, Laura Ransom, Mimsy Sadofsky, & Alan White. 1992. *The Sudbury Valley School experience.* Framingham, MA: Sudbury Valley School Press.

Grumet, Madeleine. 1988. *Bitter milk: women and teaching.* Amherst, MA: University of Massachusetts Press.

Harris, Judith Rich. 1998. *The nurture assumption: why children turn out the way they do.* New York: The Free Press.

Hebb, Donald O. 1980. *Essay on mind.* Hillsdale, NJ: Lawrence Erlbaum.

Heidegger, Martin. 1982. *The question concerning technology and other essays.* Trans. William Lovitt. New York: Harper Trade.

Herodotus. 1954. *The histories.* Trans. Aubrey de Sélincourt. Harmondsworth, UK: Penguin. Written c. 440 BCE.

Heshusius, Lous. 1994. Freeing ourselves from objectivity: managing subjectivity or turning toward a participatory mode of consciousness? In *Educational Researcher*, vol. 23, no. 3: 15–22.

Hilbert, David. 1988. *Foundations of geometry.* Trans. Leo Unger. Chicago: Open Court. Originially published 1899.

Hiley, David, James Bohman, & Richard Shusterman, editors. 1991. *The interpretive turn: philosophy, science, culture.* Ithaca, NY: Cornell University Press.

Hoffman, Donald D. 1998. *Visual intelligence: how we create what we see.* New York: W.W. Norton.

The Holy Bible.

hooks, bell. 1996. *Teaching to transgress: education and the practice of freedom.* New York: Routledge.

Howson, Geoffrey. 1982. *A history of mathematics education in England*. Cambridge, UK: Cambridge University Press,.

Johnson, Mark. 1987. *The body in the mind: the bodily basis of meaning, imagination, and reason*. Chicago: The University of Chicago Press.

Johnson, Mark H. 1997. *Developmental cognitive neuroscience: an introduction*. Oxford, UK: Blackwell.

Johnson, Steven. 2001. *Emergence: the connected lives of ants, brains, cities, and software*. New York: Scribner.

Juarrero, Alicia. 1999. *Dynamics in action: intentional behavior as a complex system*. Cambridge, MA: The MIT Press.

Kauffman, Stuart. 1995a. Order for free. In *The third culture: beyond the scientific revolution*. Edited by John Brockman. New York: Simon & Schuster: 333–343.

Kauffman, Stuart. 1995b. *At home in the universe: the search for laws of self-organization and complexity*. New York: Oxford University Press.

Kelly, Kevin. 1994. *Out of control: the new biology of machines, social systems, and the economic world*. Cambridge, MA: Perseus.

Kieren, Thomas E., Brent Davis, & Ralph Mason. 1996. Fraction flags: learning from children to help children learn. In *Mathematics Teaching in the Middle School*, vol. 2, no. 1: 14–19.

Kopp, Sheldon. 1974. *Even a stone can be a teacher: learning and growing from the experience of everyday life*. Los Angeles: Jeremy P. Tarchers.

Kotulak, Ronald. 1996. *Inside the brain: revolutionary discoveries of how the mind works*. New York: Andrews and McMeel.

Kuhn, Thomas. 1962. *The structure of scientific revolutions*. Chicago: University of Chicago Press.

Lakatos, Imre. 1976. *Proofs and refutations*. Cambridge, UK: Cambridge University Press.

Lakoff, George, & Mark Johnson. 1980. *Metaphors we live by*. Chicago: University of Chicago Press.

Lakoff, George, & Mark Johnson. 1999. *Philosophy in the flesh: the embodied mind and its challenge to Western thought*. New York: Basic Books.

Lakoff, George, & Rafael Núñez. 2000. *Where mathematics comes from: how the embodied mind brings mathematics into being*. New York: Basic Books.

Laplace, Pierre Simon de. 1951. *A philosophical essay on probabilities*. Trans. F.W. Truscott & F.L. Emory. New York: Dover. Original French version published 1814.

Latour, Bruno. 1996. On interobjectivity. In *Mind, Culture, and Activity*, vol. 3, no. 4: 228–245.

Lave, Jean, & Etienne Wenger. 1991. *Situated learning: legitimate peripheral participation*. Cambridge, UK: Cambridge University Press.

Lévy-Bruhl, Lucien. 1985. *How natives think*. Trans. Lilian A. Clare. Princeton,

NJ: Princeton University Press. Originally published 1922.

Locke, John. 1690. *Essay concerning human understanding.*

Locke, John. 1693. *Some thoughts concerning education.*

Lovelock, James. 1988. *The ages of Gaia: a biography of the living Earth.* New York: W.W. Norton.

Lyell, Charles. 1990. *Principles of geology.* Chicago: University of Chicago Press. Originally published 1830.

Lyotard. Jean-François. 1984. *The postmodern condition: a report on knowledge.* Minneapolis, MN: University of Minnesota.

Mandelbrôt, Benoit. 1977. *Fractal geometry of nature.* New York: W.H. Freeman.

Marx, Karl. 1947. Private property and communism. In *Essays by Karl Marx selected from the economic-philsophical manuscripts.* Trans. Ria Stone. New York: Martin Harvey. Originally published 1844.

Maturana, Humberto. 1987. Everything said is said by an observer. In *Gaia: a way of knowing.* Edited byWilliam Irwin Thompson. Hudson, NY: Lindisfarne Press: 65–82.

Maturana, Humberto, & Francisco Varela. 1987. *The tree of knowledge: the biological roots of human understanding.* Boston: Shambhala.

Mayr, Ernst. 1942/1982. *Systematics and the origin of species.* New York: Columbia University Press.

Mayr, Ernst. 1994. Population thinking and neuronal selection: metaphors or concepts? In *Selectionism and the brain.* Edited by Olaf Sporns & Giulo Tonini. New York: Academic Press: 27–39.

Merleau-Ponty, Maurice. 1962. *Phenomenology of perception.* London: Routledge and Kegan Paul.

Mlodinow, Leonard. 2001. *Euclid's window: the story of geometry from parallel lines to hyperspace.* New York: The Free Press.

Montesorri, Maria. 1995. *The absorbent mind.* New York: Henry Holt.

Muir, John. 1998. *My first summer in the Sierras.* New York: Houghton Mifflin. Originally published 1911.

Naess, Arne. 1996. *Ecology, community and lifestyle: outline of an ecosophy.* Trans. David Rothenberg. Cambridge, UK: Cambridge University Press.

Newburg, Andrew, Eugene d'Aquili, & Vince Rause. 2001. *Why God won't go away: brain science and the biology of belief.* New York: Ballantine.

Noddings, Nel. 1984. *Caring: a feminine approach to ethics and moral education.* Berkeley, CA: University of California Press.

Norretranders, Tør. 1998. *The user illusion: cutting consciousness down to size.* Trans. J. Sydenham. New York: Viking.

Olson, David R. 1996. *The world on paper: the conceptual and cognitive implications of writing and reading.* Cambridge, MA: Cambridge University Press.

Ong, Walter. 1988. *Orality and literacy: the technologizing of the word.* New York:

Routledge.

The Oxford English dictionary, new edition. 1991. Oxford, UK: Clarendon Press.

Padover, Saul K. *Karl Marx on religion*. New York: McGraw-Hill.

Pagels, Heinz. 1988. *The dreams of reason*. New York: Simon & Schuster.

Palmer, Richard E. 1969. *Hermeneutics: interpretation theory in Schleiermacher, Dilthey, Heidegger, and Gadamer*. Evanston, IL: Northwestern University Press.

Paulos, John Allen. 1988. *Innumeracy*. New York: Econo-Clad Books.

Piaget, Jean. 1954. *The construction of reality in the child*. New York: Basic Books.

Plato. 1955. *The republic*. Trans. Desmond Lee. New York: Viking. Original Greek version written c. 360 BCE.

Popper, Karl. 1963. *Conjectures and refutations*. London: Routledge & Kegan Paul.

Postman, Neil, & Charles Weingartner. 1969. *Teaching as a subversive activity*. New York: Delacorte.

Reddy, Michael. 1979. The conduit metaphor: a case of frame conflict in our language about language. In *Metaphor and thought, second edition*. Edited by Andrew Ortony. New York: Cambridge University Press.

Ridley, Mark. 1985. *The problems of evolution*. Oxford, UK: Oxford University Press.

Rorty, Richard. 1989. *Contingency, irony, and solidarity*. New York: Cambridge University Press.

Rousseau, Jean-Jacques. 1986. Essay on the origin of languages. In *Jean-Jacques Rousseau and Johann Gottfried Herder on the origin of language*. Edited and trans. by John H. Moran & Alexander Gode. Chicago: University of Chicago Press. Originally published 1750.

Rozsak, Theodore, Mary E. Gomes, & Allen E. Kanner, editors. 1995. *Ecopsychology: restoring the Earth: healing the mind*. San Francisco: Sierra Club Books.

Ruthen, Russell. 1993. Trends in nonlinear dynamics: adapting to complexity. In *Scientific American*, vol. 268 (January): 130-140.

Sapir, Edward. 1949. The status of linguistics as a science. In *Selected writings of Edward Sapir*. Edited by David G. Mandelbaum. Berkeley, CA: University of California Press.

Saussure, Ferdinand de. 1959. *Course in general linguistics*. Trans. W. Baskin. New York: Philosophy Library.

Saver, Jeffery L., & John Rabin. 1997. The neural substrates of religious experience. In *Journal of Neuropsychiatry and Clinical Neurosciences*, vol. 9: 498–510.

Sloek, Johannes. 1996. *Devotional language*. Trans. Henrik Mossin. New York: Walter De Gruyter.

Stewart, Ian. 1988. *Life's other secret: the new mathematics of the living world*. New York: Wiley.

Stewart, Ian. 1989. *Does God play dice?* Cambridge, MA: Blackwell.

Sumara, Dennis, & Brent Davis. 1999. Interrupting heteronormativity: toward a queer curriculum. In *Curriculum Inquiry*, vol. 29, no. 2: 191–208.

Thompson, William Irwin. 1989. *Imaginary landscapes: making worlds of myth and science.* New York: St. Martin's Press.

Underhill, Evelyn. 1990. *Mysticism.* New York: Doubleday. Originally published 1938.

van Manen, Max. 1991. *The tact of teaching: the meaning of pedagogical thoughtfulness.* London, ON: Althouse.

Varela, Francisco. 1999. *Ethical know-how: action, wisdom, and cognition.* Stanford, CA: Stanford University Press.

Varela, Francisco, Evan Thompson, & Eleanor Rosch. 1991. *The embodied mind: cognitive science and human experience.* Cambridge, MA: The MIT Press.

Vico, Giambattista. 1961. *The new science.* Trans. Thomas G. Bergin & Max H. Fisch. Garden City, NY: Doubleday. Originally written 1725.

von Foerster, Heinz. 1995. Metaphysics of an experimental epistemologist. In *Brain processes: theories and models.* Edited by Roberto Moreno-Diaz & José Mira-Mina. Cambridge, MA: The MIT Press.

Vygotsky, Lev S. 1962. *Thought and language.* Trans. Alex Kozulin. Cambridge, MA: The MIT Press.

Waldrop, M. Mitchell. 1992. *Complexity: the emerging science at the edge of order and chaos.* New York: Simon & Schuster.

Walkerdine, Valerie. 1988. *The mastery of reason: cognitive development and the production of rationality.* New York: Routledge.

Warren, Karen J. 2000. *Ecofeminist philosophy.* Rowman & Littlefield.

Watson, John B. 1988. *Behaviorism.* New York: Transaction Publications. Originally published 1924.

Watts, Alan W. 1957. *The way of Zen.* New York: Pantheon.

Weaver, Warren. 1948. Science and complexity. In *American Scientist* 36: 536–544.

Williams, Christopher. 1997. *Terminus brain: the environmental threats to human intelligence.* New York: Cassell.

Wilson, E.O. 1999. *Consilience: the unity of knowledge.* New York: Vintage.

Wolfram, Stephen. 2002. *A new kind of science.* Champaign, IL: Wolfram Media.

ACKNOWLEDGMENTS
& DEDICATION

In the fall term of the 2002–2003 academic year, along with Dennis Sumara and Elaine Simmt, I co-taught EDSE 608 ("Cognition and Curriculum") in the Department of Secondary Education at the University of Alberta. This course, originally developed by Tom Kieren a decade earlier, is a doctoral seminar structured around a review of recent philosophical, theoretical, and empirical research into cognition, all framed by the particular concerns of educators and educational researchers.

As co-teachers, Dennis, Elaine, and I decided before we began that our study would be partly structured around a collective project—something for which everyone involved would share responsibility. We weren't actually sure what that project might be, but we felt a useful exercise to assist the collective in sorting through the possibilities was to assemble an alphabet- ized glossary of key vocabulary as the course evolved.

Almost from the moment we began, it was clear that the structure of an alphabetized list of definitions wasn't going to work. The terms seemed to resist such an arrangement. Instead they kept clustering according to the eras in which they arose and the mindsets in which they're embedded.

In the processes of grouping terms and juxtaposing groups, we were occasioned to pay more attention to the deep similarities among divergent academic traditions. In other words, and somewhat ironically, the clustered glossary deflected our attentions away from definitions and toward the evo- lutions and co-evolutions of words and phrases—specifically toward those moments and movements in which shifts or breaks in opinion contributed to different ways of thinking about knowledge, learning, and teaching. In an effort to make sense of the branches of thought that had begun to appear, I proposed an earlier version of the genealogical tree that was to become the skeleton for this book.

I recount these details in an effort to better frame the contributions of the participants in that seminar and in a follow-up special topics course that I co-taught with Dennis in the winter 2003 term. The idea for this book emerged in an event of collective sense-making—in a manner that renders the notion of single authorship highly problematic. Thus, in addition to acknowledging the tremendous conceptual contributions of Dennis and Elaine, I would also like to recognize the roles played by Darcey Dachyshyn, Mildred Dacog, Lara Doan, Khadeeja Ibrahim-Didi, Eun-Jeong Kim, Mijung Kim, Helena Miranda, Elizabeth Mowat, Immaculate Namakusa, Francie Ratner, Darren Stanley, David Wagner, and Martha Zacharias. As well, colleagues Tom Kieren, Joyce Mgombelo, Gloria Filax, Linda Laidlaw, Rebecca Luce-Kapler, and Susan Walsh each contributed in important ways to the thinking represented in this writing.

This book was made possible through financial support provided by the Canada Research Chairs program and the Social Sciences and Humanities Research Council of Canada.

Other essential support, in forms that extended well beyond the conceptual, was generously provided by my partner, Dennis Sumara. I dedicate this book to him.

INDEX

instructing, 78; introducing, 59; liberating, 143; mastery, 57–59; mediating, 135; mentoring, 135; mindful participation, 176; minding, 178; ministering, 59; modeling, 135; nurturing, 54; occasioning, 170; orchestrating, 135; participating, 171; pastoring, 59; pedagogical thoughtfulness, 177; pedagogy, 143; remediating, 87; structuring, 170; 87; telling, 78; training, 59, 88; tuition, 58; tutelage, 84; tutoring, 54. *See also* teacher.
tekhne, 26
teleology, 18, 197
telling, teaching as, 78
theism, 45, 48, 64, 98, 197
Thompson, William Irwin, 220
Thorndike, Edward, 88
training, teaching as, 59, 88
transcendence, 151, 155, 158–159
tuition, teaching as, 58

tutelage, teaching as, 84
tutoring, teaching as, 54

Underhill, Evelyn, 41
unexamined life, 78

van Manen, Max, 177
Varela, Francisco, 153, 176
versus, etymology, 11
Vico, Giambattista, 116–117, 131
vocation, 59
voice, 143
Vygotsky, Lev S., 116, 121–122, 134–137; Piaget and, 122, 136; teaching and, 135–138

Watson, John B. 88–89
Weaver, Warren, 93–95, 104
Wenger, Etienne, 135–136
wisdom, 35, 156
writing, alphabetic, 148–149